THE SUPERSTAR PROSECUTORS

The Battle for the Streets

Ronald E Bowers

Former Senior Prosecutor
Los Angeles County District Attorney's Office

Some names and locations have been changed to protect the privacy of individuals connected with these stories. Certain events and statements have been inferred from the facts of these cases and public articles about these cases.

Ronald E. Bowers, Publisher
losangelestruecrime@aol.com

ISBN 978-1-7326655-0-7

First release March 2018

INTRODUCTION

Throughout history we have seen elite groups do incredible feats. Often these special groups are military in nature, such as Seal Team Six and the infamous Delta Force. Society has always created elite groups to do tasks that are essential for the well-being of the community. Military elite groups are defined as units that require a higher standard of competency for their personnel in comparison to regular units. That is why the elite units are often tasked with more difficult missions.

Eventually these elite units' accomplishments often give these groups a magical quality. Over time no one knows for certain how much is myth or reality. I remember hearing about the French Foreign Legion when I was growing up. I didn't know much about them, but I was always impressed by the operations they carried out abroad. The Legion was established in 1831 and was composed of soldiers from different nationalities. It was best known for its achievements in Algeria and other French Colony territories.

Although it is part of the French military, it doesn't swear allegiance to France but to the Foreign Legion itself (Honour and Fidelity). It is well known for its intense esprit de corps, which is achieved through the development of camaraderie. The legionnaires are loyal and they take pride in being soldiers in this elite unit. The French Foreign Legion consists of 8,900 men, and even to this day it remains one of those elite groups that are shrouded in mystery.

Most people associate this elite unit as being somehow connected to the military. Still, there are many elite groups in law enforcement. The most well-known group is the Special Weapons and Tactics Teams better known as SWAT. The Federal Bureau of Investigation has a Hostage Rescue Team, and the U.S.

Secret Service, a Counter Sniper Unit, both of which may not be as well-known as other special units.

As a matter of fact, many forms of government have carved out special groups to take on special operations. Even large companies have created special units with highly trained staff to take on the most difficult tasks in their respective fields.

The same is true about the District Attorney's Office. Anyone who remembers their Government classes in high school or college will remember that the DA's Office represents the public in the criminal courts. Basically, the prosecutor makes a determination as to what charges to file against someone who has been arrested by the police. The prosecutor then appears as the People's attorney from the arraignment to the trial and concluding with the sentencing.

Certain cases require special attention because of the nature of the crime or parties involved. In those situations, a special attorney is assigned to those cases to make sure the preparation and handling of the case is properly conducted.

In the larger DA's Offices, special units are created to handle these unique cases. In Los Angeles County, the DA's Office decided to have a special prosecution unit made up of the best and brightest attorneys to concentrate on those especially tough cases. Over the years this special unit went by various names. Originally it was the Organized Crime Section, which later split off to be the Special Trials Unit. Since Los Angeles was having so many publicity cases, it was decided to change the name to "**Major Crimes Division**."

Thus was created one of the most unique elite units that few know about. Some of the news media have become aware of the DA's Major Crimes Division when they were covering some of the high publicity cases in Los Angeles. However, the general public has no idea of the existence of this highly skilled elite DA's Division.

The Major Crimes Division does not seek recognition of its activities and prefers to operate below the radar. Notoriety is the last thing that the Division wants. However, it may be time to shine a bright light on one of those special treasures that you the public have inherited and are totally unaware of. The news media spends so much of the time telling you about how dysfunctional government is and how crime has become so rampant that it is unsafe to walk the streets of your community.

This book is meant to give you some hope that the world isn't falling apart. There are positive things that are going on around you. This elite group of prosecutors who make up the Major Crimes Division functions incredibly well. Also, these prosecutors are some of the most amazing individuals who you have never heard about. True, these attorneys can't walk on water, but they can perform many unbelievable feats in the courtroom.

This special group consists of eight to ten highly skilled prosecutors who are supervised by a head deputy. They were housed in the northeast portion of the DA's Office on the 17th Floor of the Criminal Courts Building. (Today they are located in the Hall of Justice Building)

The selection process of who was chosen to join Major Crimes Division was always a sensitive subject. Every attorney worth his or her salt would think that they should be included. Since there are only 10 positions in the Division, many of the 1000 attorneys in the LA DA's Office may be qualified but just don't make the cut.

When selecting new prosecutors, the administrators are looking for attorneys who have unique qualities such as:

Quick Learners- Need to be able to handle complex factual situations

Legal Smarts- Understand the case law & know how to use it

Disciplined- Need to prepare and organize a case on their own

Attitude- Need to project confidence and likeability

Tenacity- Need to be willing to persevere against all odds

Communicator- Need to be able to convey facts and the law to jurors (using visuals)

My book series, **<u>DA Delta Force</u>**, gives you the reader the rare opportunity to see how these elite prosecutors go about preparing and presenting their cases in court. You the reader will be fascinated by what remarkable jobs these prosecutors do.

For 40 years I worked in almost every aspect of the LA DA's Office. I remember when the Major Crimes Division was created. My assignment at the time was to create and operate a new Trial Support Division. In that capacity I worked closely with all the prosecutors in the Major Crimes Division. My job was to assist the prosecutors in the preparation of their cases as well as presenting their cases to the jury.

As a result, I became very familiar with their cases. These prosecutors were all highly skilled and can be described as attorneys who have strong-willed personalities. Some were willing to listen to new ideas, while others took longer to come around; however, eventually they all did. They were smart individuals who were self-confident in their ability to handle the most challenging cases. I have already written several books about several of these highly talented Major Crimes Deputies. Yet this book, ***The Superstar DA,*** will highlight three prosecutors. We will discuss several cases that they handled in order to illustrate what remarkable attorneys they were.

The first prosecutor we will consider is Darrell Mavis, who was elevated to Major Crimes partly due to his superb legal mind.

I have selected one of his trials to review. It is the case of ***People v. Michael Chia***, which is fascinating in two respects. The facts involve three DEA agents carrying out an undercover narcotics buy of a large amount of heroin. What makes this case unusual is the fact that the narcotics dealers were setting up the DEA agents for a major Rip-off. As it turned out, the dealers shot and killed two of the agents like in a turkey shoot. As bizarre as the facts were, what made the case such a challenge was that an appellate court reversed the conviction 15 years later after all the exhibits and evidence from the first trial had been destroyed.

Prosecutor Mavis took on the challenge and became creative in figuring out how to retry this case with all its obstacles. This book will give you insight as to how he attempted to reconstruct the crime scene without the original exhibits. Next, the prosecutor had to figure out a way to show the jury how this defendant was involved in the counter surveillance phase of the Rip-off.

After you the reader have become familiar with Prosecutor Mavis, we will move on to another case he handled. That case involved a brother hiring a hit man to kill his sister so he could inherit the family home. Prosecutor Mavis had to figure out how to prosecute both the brother and the hitman without having to give one of them a free pass to get them to testify to against the other. Prosecutor Mavis had little evidence for his side except for the hit man's druggie girlfriend. She could testify as to how this all ended up as a double homicide.

we review may be considered one of the most gruesome cases of
ers have rejected the idea of recounting this case, because it is
ill warn the reader that if you have a low threshold for gore and
ay want to skip our discussion of the ***People v Rodriquez and***
reason I have included this case is to show how Prosecutor
ole to keep the jurors focused on the evidence and not merely
in facts of the case.

ase involved a gangbanger shooting in an apartment house. It was
significance; however, when an officer stopped him months later,
ulled a gun on the officer. Needless to say, the incident escalated
tle between one police officer and two gangbangers. Prosecutor
is work cut out for him, and he was able to convict the defendants
es.

revealing fact about this typical Hardcore Gang case was what
e sentencing. The judge sentenced the defendant to life plus 25
or Camacho was seated at counsel table only a few feet away from
The prosecutor was filling out the sentencing information on the
defendant got up from his chair at counsel table. He turned toward
macho and with all the force he could muster he kickboxed the
ocking him out of his chair and onto the courtroom floor.

Prosecutor Camacho wasn't seriously injured, the defendant was
ed for assaulting a government official. The Defense's argument at
that Prosecutor Camacho was NOT acting as a government official
as doing was writing the information about the sentence on the DA's

unbelievable was all the hard work that Prosecutor Camacho did in
angbangers off the street and that he subsequently ended up being
m of this gangbanger. It was remarkable that Prosecutor Camacho the
back at work on another case. He wasn't deterred by being physically

case I have highlighted illustrates the astonishing tenacity Prosecutor
ssesses to see that justice is administered. Everyone remembers the
ublicity the Manson Family case generated over the years, especially

The big challenge that Prosecu corroborate the testimony of the girlf ultimately it was the cellphone calls du became the critical corroboration neede

We move on to another incredible p name was Jeff Ramseyer and he handle that stand out from the rest. The first o teenager who had been working as a Ramseyer had the awesome task of tryin testify to the gruesome killing of her boyf

What made this intensely problemati shot in the head but by the grace of prosecution's case that she be able to tes had done to her. Prosecutor Ramseyer s terrifying moments of her life. Throughou in the courtroom less than 20 feet away just

At the same time, Prosecutor Ramseyer who was emotionally infuriated in court sin death. Throughout the entire trial, Pros witnesses who needed to be handled in the m

In order to show another side of Pro infamous murder of the owner of the Silent M in which the DA's Office wanted to get mastermind. Prosecutor Ramseyer did a phen case against both. It required him using cellph between the two killers.

The last prosecutor we discuss is Michael C was able to succeed in achieving extraordin approach is more like a stealth bomber. He quie hell out of the Defense's case in the middle of tri limelight as he willingly takes on the most dema witness or evidence problems.

The first case all times. Publish too repulsive. I w mayhem, you m *Torres* case. Th Camacho was a repulsed by cert

The second a case of no rea the defendant p into a gun bat Camacho had h of all the charg

The most occurred at th years. Prosecu the defendant DA's file. The Prosecutor Ca prosecutor, kn

Although later prosecu that trial wa since all he w file.

What wa getting the another vict next day wa attacked.

The last Camacho p extensive

the plan that Charles Manson was trying to create a racial war. However, what was interesting was the lack of publicity when a defendant by the name of Tony Barron went around the community trying to find Blacks to kill. The lack of public interest may have been because the victims weren't celebrities.

The real reason this racially charged case of ***People v. Tony Barron*** didn't receive much notice was because Prosecutor Camacho built a solid case against the killer. As a result, Barron can no longer drive around the community looking for Blacks to kill. Prosecutor Camacho was willing to prosecute the defendant for a double homicide before three separate juries, only to see the case end up with a Hung Jury. Prosecutor Camacho is one of those rare human beings who is willing to stand up for what was right no matter the odds against him. He is the perfect example of what the word TRUE GRIT really means. John Wayne's character, U.S. Marshal Rooster Cogburn, would have a lot in common with Prosecutor Camacho.

This book only reviews the careers of three prosecutors who served as part of the unique DA's Major Crimes Division. These three are just a few of the unsung heroes who are meticulous and tenacious in doing their job, one which makes you the reader safer in your community. They all did a phenomenal job without fanfare or any recognition. By the time you finish this book, *The Superstar Prosecutors*, you will understand why the DA's Major Crimes Division is often called by many the DA Delta Force.

CONTENTS

WAR ON DRUGS

People v. Michael Chia

SUPERSTAR PROSECUTOR

Darrell Mavis

* * *

CHAPTER 1 LOOKING FOR A NEW CRUSADE

The year was 1987, and the Cold War was winding down. Echoing in every American's ears were the immortal words President Reagan said standing in front of the Brandenburg Gate: "Mr. Gorbachev, tear down this wall." No one knew what was around the corner in the '90s with the fall of Communism and the unraveling of the mighty Soviet Union. Without the Cold War, the country needed a new "Cause," something to battle against. The United States felt invincible.

The politicians decided that the new evil that the country would fight was the drug problem, hence the inception of the so-called War on Drugs. That was something that the nation could rally behind. The media had painted a picture that most of the narcotics traffic in the country was done by a few Drug Lords. The news media made it seem that if the government concentrated its resource on these few syndicates, the drug supply would virtually be eliminated.

The basic premise for combating the drug problem was later found to be grossly oversimplified. In hindsight, it became apparent that there weren't a limited number of drug organizations. It turned out that drug trafficking was made up of many small groups that were able to operate in the nation's underworld. With a country that prided itself on so many personal freedoms and which encouraged entrepreneurs, it was no easy task to know how to fight this new War.

The politicians thought that if they gave more money to the Drug Enforcement Administration (DEA) that it would be a step in the right direction. The DEA had been formed in 1975 by President Richard Nixon. Back then the federal government combined the Bureau of Narcotics and Dangerous Drugs (BNDD), the Office of Drug Abuse Law Enforcement (ODALE), plus part of the Bureau of Customs. The DEA became a law enforcement agency under the U.S. Department of Justice with the sole responsibility for coordinating and pursuing U.S. drug investigations both domestic and abroad.

The mandate went out that the DEA would be the lead group on the War on Drugs. The pressure was on the DEA agency to come up with a plan and then to implement that plan so there would be a serious dent in the flow of drugs into the country. Part of that plan was to concentrate on the bigger suppliers and dealers.

Any police officer knows that one can go into any metropolitan area on any night and nab dozens of street dealers. For years the concept was that the police would arrest street dealers and try to put pressure on them to reveal who were their drug suppliers. In theory, the police should be able to work their way up the narcotics chain to "Mr. Big." This was a great idea, and in some instances it did succeed in getting bigger fish in the pond. But it didn't take long before the larger drug suppliers figured out ways to immunize themselves from being fingered by those low-level drug dealers the police could easily arrest.

The War on Drugs had to adapt to the changes. The DEA couldn't waste its time and resources on the little guy but had to develop a strategy to get to the many suppliers at the highest levels. The DEA realized that one plan was to stop the drugs from ever arriving in the country. This strategy required a concerted effort on the various groups that had overseas connections. The USA border with Mexico had been identified as one of the main thoroughfares for drugs entering the country. This wasn't a great revelation since most arrests at that time involved people from south of the border. The DEA had carried out many successful operations in seizing contraband and money from the Mexican and Latin American cartels.

But the big nut to crack was finding a way to impact the supply of heroin from the Orient. DEA was trying to make inroads into Asian suppliers, especially from Thailand. This was difficult since most of the DEA agents were not Asian but largely from Hispanic backgrounds.

The DEA had only one agent of Thai background. His name was Paul Seema, and he was fluent in the native language of Thailand. There were many Asians who would talk a good line about supplying drugs, but in the end it was discovered that they didn't have the connections they claimed to have. The DEA task force was finding that it was hard to assess information. Some pseudo dealers said they could deliver large quantities, but it turned out to be merely wishful thinking on their part.

DEA agent
Paul Seema

The DEA Los Angeles Office recognized that it had to make inroads into the Asian suppliers of the bulk of the heroin coming into the country. They assigned 'Group 4' to work with the local law enforcement agencies, thus creating a Joint Task Force which included Los Angeles Police Department, Los Angeles County Sheriff's Department, and other local law enforcement agencies. The joint task force operated out of the Monterey Park Police Department station. The advantage of this location was that it was directly in the heart of the Asian population in Monterey Park, California. This community is directly east of the city of Los Angeles and was predominantly made up of Asian residents.

It was practically impossible to make inroads in dealing with Asian suppliers. The Asian drug suppliers didn't trust anyone who wasn't Asian. The big dealers wouldn't deal with new buyers. They had their own connections and didn't trust any non-Asian. However, DEA agent Paul Seema, being Asian, was able to develop a relationship with some of the Asian suppliers. He was able to build a rapport with a small-time Asian dealer, Wen Kow. Over several months agent Seema was able to conduct small narcotics transactions with Kow. It seemed that a trust had been established to the point that Kow was willing to negotiate a major narcotics deal. At the beginning of February, Kow agreed to sell a large quantity of heroin for $80,000.

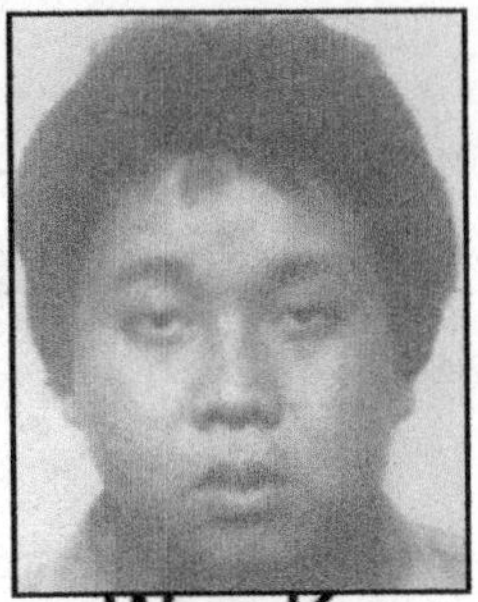

Wen Kow

CHAPTER 2 PREPARING FOR THE BIG BUY

This big buy was set for Friday, February 5, 1988, and everything was in place for this undercover buy. The DEA had brought in additional agents to assist in making sure that everything went according to plans. The Joint Task Force was going to provide assistance. The buy was for heroin, with the agents paying $80,000 to the Asian supplier. DEA had strict guidelines when agents were required to actually show the earnest money to the Asian supplier. The obvious problem in dealing in such large amounts of cash is that money can be misappropriated.

It could be released to the agents and end up in one of the agents' pockets. So DEA wanted to be sure that any money paid out was used for the purpose intended. Other problems can occur in that the agents can be ripped off in several ways, one being that the agents can be outsmarted and robbed of this large amount of cash. Or the agents can purchase the so-called drugs and later determine that the substance isn't narcotics at all but mere bunk.

The day of the big narcotics transaction, the agents had checked out $80,000 in cash and had it separated in denominations of $50 and $100 bills. It was kept in a carrying satchel so that it could be easily shown to the seller without having to hand it over physically to the seller.

The deal was set up with Wen Kow, who would be obtaining the narcotics from others who were higher up the ladder of Asian suppliers. In order to learn as much as they could about Wen Kow's background, they placed him under surveillance. The night before the big buy, the agents surveilled his apartment on Atlantic Blvd. in Monterey Park. An agent was placed in a parked vehicle across the street from Kow's apartment. She was in an undercover vehicle with dark tinted windows.

This agent observed two male Asians pull in and park in front of her car. The men exited and went to the rear of their vehicle. A Michael Chia placed the key in the lock and the trunk lid popped open. Then his head turned in both directions as he glanced up and down the street. Since it was late, there were no cars on the road. Across the street past the apartment building was a middle-aged couple walking a dog up the hilly street. Neighboring dogs barked out the usual serenade as the couple's dog paraded by.

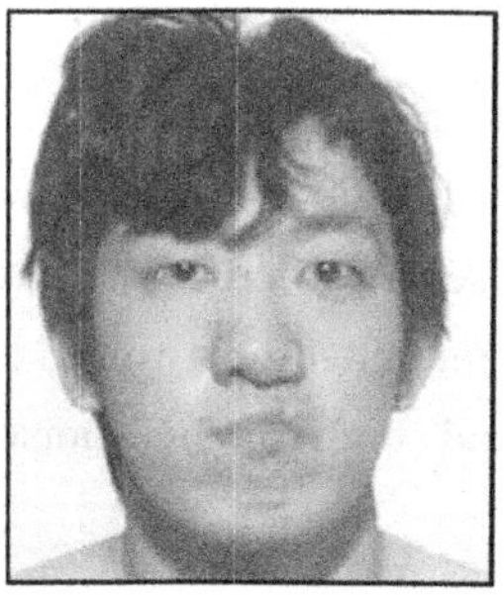

Michael Chia

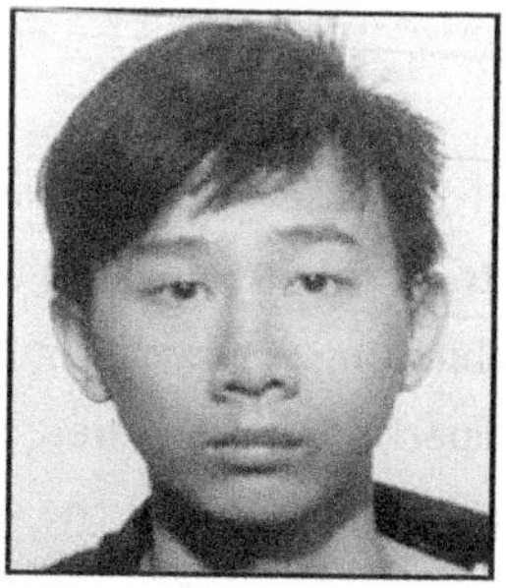

William Wang

The other male was William Wang, who reached into the trunk and grabbed the carpet covering the spare tire and lifted it up. With his other hand he picked up what appeared to be a handgun and brusquely insert it into his waistband.

Then he used his free hand to slam the trunk lid closed. Nervously, Wang turned his head from side to side and instantly scurried across the street toward a large apartment building. The other guy, Chia, remained next to the car. As Wang approached the apartment gate, there was a loud, high-pitched noise. He slowed his gait and turned to look back at the cars.

From the shrubbery near the gate he could hear the sound of crickets chirping (only male crickets can make the sound, which comes from wings that have ridges that they vibrate). When Wang recognized that the sound was from a cricket, he smiled to himself and felt an inner contentment. (In Chinese culture the chirping sound of a cricket is a good luck sign like a protective warning against potential danger.)

Wang disappeared into Kow's apartment and remained there for ten minutes. The other guy, Michael Chia, continued to pace back and forth next to the Mitsubishi. Then he crossed the street and went up to Kow's apartment. The surveilling agent was relieved that she wasn't spotted by the two males. The agent didn't know what to infer as to the taking of the gun out of the trunk. At least the DEA agents would be aware that some of the parties to the big heroin transaction would likely be armed.

Later, the surveilling agent saw William Wang and Michael Chia both leave Kow's apartment and return to the Mitsubishi and drive off. Shortly thereafter, another surveillance agent observed the two go into the trendy 8000 Nightclub and appear to socialize for the rest of the evening. As the hours grew later, Wang and Chia left the nightclub and drove over to a friend's apartment where they spent the night.

CHAPTER 3 WHERE TO MEET

It had been agreed that the parties to the big heroin deal were to meet at the Tiny Naylor's restaurant. This was a well-known restaurant chain founded by a gentleman who was anything but petite. Tiny Naylor was really 6' 4" tall and weighed over 320 pounds. His original restaurant was located on the corner of Sunset and La Brea Boulevards in Hollywood. The restaurant's claim to fame was that it was designed in the Googie architectural style (ultra-modern design) and was a —drive-in where the customers ordered and remained in their car while dining.

However, this narcotics deal had nothing to do with the food or service at this coffee shop/restaurant. The reason that the DEA agents decided to meet there was that it was a distinctive place easy to find and easy to get to. The Tiny Naylor's restaurant they were using was located in Monterey Park and didn't look anything like the Hollywood structure. This restaurant was in the shape of a Dutch Windmill with its fan blades meant to be twirling around and around. Originally the Van de Kamp Bakery restaurants chain had built the windmill-shaped building to project the image of wholesome, delicious foods. However, when the bakery chain went out of the restaurant business, the windmill buildings were converted into different forms of coffee shops like Tiny Naylor's.

The narcotics deal was scheduled to take place at 11:00 a.m. in the parking lot of the Tiny Naylor's restaurant in Monterey Park. Before that occurred, Michael Chia drove Wang for a second time to Kow's apartment. While the sellers were getting ready, the undercover DEA agents were scoping out the Tiny Naylor's parking lot. The DEA agents were deciding where to place the surveillance agents so they would have an unobstructed view of the narcotics transaction as it took place.

As the 11:00 a. m. moment was about to occur, all the surveillance agents were in place and they were using their handheld radios to communicate with each other. The first thing the agents observed was Michael Chia drive his car slowly through the restaurant's parking lot. As he pulled behind a food delivery truck, they lost sight of him. When his car reappeared, they could see Kow walking to the front of the restaurant. Apparently Chia had dropped off Kow, who was the contact person. Kow had agreed to deliver the narcotics after receiving the $80,000 in cash.

When the agents saw Kow, they knew the deal was on. The next key player was William Wang, who the agents had seen with Michael Chia at Kow's apartment the night before. They presumed Wang was armed since he had been seen carrying a .45 caliber handgun into Kow's apartment. Besides the weapon, the agents had no inside knowledge of Wang's role in the narcotics transaction. It was unclear as to what role Michael Chia would have with the deal. Up to this point, the agents knew that it was Chia's car that was used to deliver the handgun to Kow's apartment and that apparently he was the one who had driven Kow to the restaurant. There was another player in this drug deal, and that was Michael Sun. No one knew of his involvement except he was a companion and driver for William Wang.

CHAPTER 4 SHOW ME THE MONEY

M oney is the driving force in the narcotics business. Drug dealers by their very nature are conducting illegal business. Drug dealers by definition are criminals. And criminals by their nature aren't afraid to commit criminal acts such as stealing from one another. As a result, the drug business requires narcotics transactions to be conducted in cash. Obviously, narcotics transactions can't be conducted by using a credit card or writing a check. There is such a lack of trust in the narcotics business that the seller will not hand over the dope until he sees cold hard cash.

Everyone remembers the 1996 movie Jerry Maguire in which Tom Cruise played a slick sports agent and his client Rod Tidwell (Cuba Gooding, Jr.) continually demanded, ***Show me the money.***

Whenever there is large narcotic transaction it will involve a huge amount of cash, which sets the stage for a possible 'Rip-off'. This is especially true in the big drug deals since it is such a temptation to grab the drug money and run. The poor buyer who is ripped off doesn't have any real recourse. He can't go to the police and file a theft report. All buyers are keenly aware they can be easily robbed and all they have to protect them is their own self-help.

Self-help may come in the form of always being surrounded by your own well-armed bodyguards who are willing to use their weapons if anyone tries to fleece them. In this case, it was the DEA agents who were the target of the Rip-off. They were well armed just like the Asian parties who had their .45 semi-automatic and .38 revolvers ready to use.

On February 5th, the day of the transaction, there were two teams at work. One was the DEA Task Force that thought that they were outsmarting a drug supplier by buying from him. As soon as they got their hands on the heroin, they would arrest him and put him out of business. At the same time, these four young male Asians thought they were going to 'Rip off' some naïve drug buyers who had $80,000 in cash. They would end up with a huge amount of cash, and there was nothing that the buyer could do to these well-armed robbers.

Neither side knew what they were up against. The agents thought that they had the upper hand since they had three undercover agents who were well armed backed up by a surveillance team of over a dozen officers. The Asians had to think that they were well armed and had the advantage of surprise on their side. The worst that could happen was that they would have to shoot and kill three drug buyers. In all likelihood none of the buyers would survive, and no one would ever be able to identify them for stealing the $80,000.

Besides the money and the weapons, the narcotics suppliers and dealers were driving sports cars. The guys planning the Rip-off had two cars at their disposal. The one was a red 1987 Nissan 200SX, which was a stylish sports car in 1988. Michael Chia had a jazzy black Mitsubishi which had custom rims and was the type of car a preppy type would want to be seen in.

However, when it came to horsepower the DEA agents seemed to outclass the Asian drug dealers. The surveillance agents were staked out with a Thunderbird, a Firebird, and a Camaro. The undercover car was a white Volvo, which wouldn't be considered a 'sporty set of wheels' but would more likely be described as a family car. The reason for the 'plain Jane' Volvo was that it was meant not to appear too flashy. It was also believed that it would be a safe car in case they got into a chase situation. The surveillance agents' justification for all the fast sport cars was that they needed to be fast enough to catch up with the suspects. Often when they do surveillance, they drive on parallel streets in order not to be seen. This day would require all these cars to be tested to their limits as to how well they could perform in a serious high-speed chase situation.

CHAPTER 5 THE PERFECT CONTROL BUY

After Kow had been dropped off by Chia at Tiny Naylor's restaurant, the 'Rip-off' Conspiracy plan had been set into motion. The agents were confident that they would be able to make a controlled buy that would result in arrests or possibly lead to bigger suppliers in the near future.

DEA agents are trained to conduct control buys in an open setting where the undercover agents can be surveilled at all times. Every DEA agent wants to go home at the end of the day. All the agents recognized that there are risks involved in ever buy situation. But the idea is to minimize the risks to a manageable level and be vigilant at all times.

Over the years, the Monterey Park Police Department had encouraged the Narcotics Task Force to use the Atlantic Square Shopping Center and the Prado Shopping Center at the far southwest end of their city. It was an easy place to set up undercover buy operations. There were two restaurants on opposite ends of the shopping center that could be used for meeting places for undercover activities. Tiny Naylor's restaurant was a perfect place for a transaction since it had a huge parking lot with no obstructing buildings or landscaping.

These shopping centers were good venues for controlled buys. The initial purpose of the meet was for the parties to agree on all the terms. Kow met agents Seema and Jose Medina (pseudonym) outside and walked into the restaurant together to work out the final arrangements. Kow told the agents that the heroin was ready and that it was being held in a 'stash house' in Pasadena. There was additional small talk and finally Kow asked to see the money. The agents explained that they didn't have it on them but they had it in their car in the parking lot. Kow was a smart dealer in that he knew that anyone can talk about big money but having physical possession of it was another thing.

He wanted to be sure the buyers had the dinero. In this case it was especially important that the buyer have the cash since the entire purpose of it all was to 'rip off' the buyers. To prove to Kow that the undercover agents had the cash, they had to show him the actual money even though they didn't want him to get his hands on it. In the narcotics world this is called the "Flash." In other words, the money is flashed so the seller can see that it is real and it is all there.

The restaurant was a great place to meet but not the appropriate place to "Flash" the money. So the agents suggested that they step out to their car in the parking lot where they would show him the money. All three of them walked out of Tiny Naylor's and approached the Volvo with agent Montoya seated in the driver's seat.

George Montoya

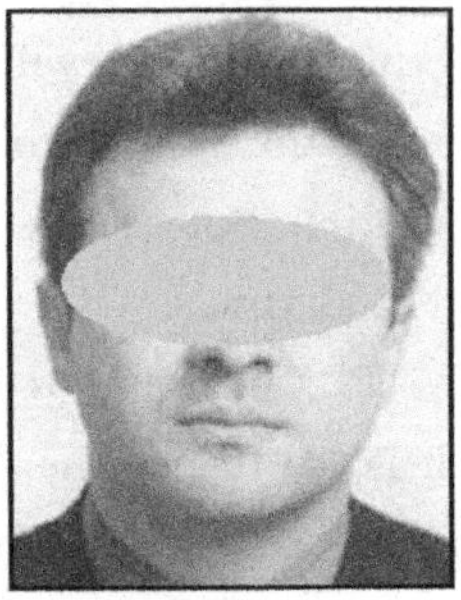

Jose Medina

Upon the arrival of the three next to the Volvo, agent Montoya got out of the car and moved into the backseat. Kow continued to ask to see the money and agent Montoya told him to get in the back seat on the other side. Montoya directed agent Medina to go to the trunk to get the money. Medina opened the trunk and removed a leather satchel and brought it around to Montoya and handed it to him in the backseat. The satchel contained the $80,000 in cash. Montoya opened the satchel so Kow could look inside it. As Montoya firmly held the satchel, Kow placed his hand inside and thumbed through the stack of bills. After a moment he seemed satisfied and said, "Okay, let's go to Pasadena."

Montoya moved the satchel of money to the other side and tucked it securely against the seat. At that point Agent Medina was the driver and started up the Volvo and pulled out of the parking space. They headed to the exit of the shopping center and waited for the traffic signal to give them a green light. When the light changed the Volvo pulled onto Atlantic Boulevard and headed toward Pasadena to pick up the heroin.

CHAPTER 6 LET'S PICK UP THE DOPE

When the agents and the dealer left the Tiny Naylor's parking lot, a whole set of actions occurred as the surveillance vehicles took up positions to follow the Volvo. As the undercover car pulled out going northbound on Atlantic Boulevard, Michael Chia, who was driving his Mitsubishi, went directly across in front of the undercover car and ended up going in the opposite direction. This meant that Chia was cut off from being in a position where he could catch up with the undercover Volvo.

At the same time, the other Asian dealers were driving a red Nissan 200 SZ parallel to the Volvo going up Atlantic Boulevard. The driver of the Nissan was Michael Sun and the passenger was William Wang. They were able to position their red Nissan behind the Volvo as they were proceeding up Atlantic Boulevard. They were able to do this without attracting the attention of the undercover agents in the Volvo.

Wang and Sun, in the red Nissan, were unaware that they were being followed by several DEA agent surveillance cars. At this point the DEA surveillance agents felt everything was safe since the undercover car had three DEA agents in it with Kow the lone dope dealer. The DEA surveillance cars had good sightings on the red Nissan and could see that there were only two occupants of that vehicle.

All these cars proceeded northbound through the city of Alhambra without attracting any attention. At the north end of Alhambra, Atlantic Boulevard turns into a smaller street by the name of Los Robles Avenue. At this point, they left Alhambra and began traveling through the City of San Marino. This city is one of the most affluent areas in Southern California. As they were proceeding north they were driving by larger homes that were well landscaped. This was an area where no one would expect drug transactions to take place.

Finally, there was a fork in the road; both choices led to the city of Pasadena. The road to the right proceeded by some old estates. The other street to the left became Marengo Avenue through a quiet upscale neighborhood. By this time it was mid-day. This seemed to be a peculiar route to travel to a dealer's stash pad. Jose Medina continued to drive the Volvo down this tree-lined street with picturesque houses that looked like something out of a Norman Rockwell painting. The DEA agents began to wonder where this stash pad could be located.

As the Volvo maneuvered up a slight incline, Kow abruptly said, "Pull over." Kow indicated they were getting near the place where he had to pick up the dope. At this point along the road, there were large homes set back from the curb covered with high trees and shrubs. This area didn't resemble any stash pad they had ever seen.

Medina, the driver of the Volvo, pulled close to the curb and slowly continued forward. Kow in a demanding voice stated, "That's far enough." Medina stopped the car as close to the curb as possible without hitting it. Kow abruptly opened the passenger-side rear door and stepped out. The agents remained in the car. All three of them leaned their heads down slightly to get a better look up the driveway of the house they had parked in front of.

Volvo parked next to curb

The agents were trying to figure out where all of this was going. From the appearance of the surrounding homes, this was a very well-heeled community. This was a surprising place for drug dealing to be conducted, but the agents thought this was a new approach since no one would suspect this part of town to be a haven for drug dealing. The agents didn't want to appear uncomfortable with the situation since they were trying to play the role of anxious drug buyers.

Kow turned his back to the agents, giving the appearance that he was starting to walk down this long driveway. Then, in a flash, Kow swung around facing the agents and pointed a gun at them as they remained in the car. Kow's facial features were stone-cold deadly. It was like in the movie ***Dr. Jekyll and Mr. Hyde***. While in the car Kow had been pleasant and almost flippant in his conversation, but when he spun around with the gun in his hand his demeanor turned sinister.

CHAPTER 7 IT'S A RIP-OFF

Kow shouted out, "Put your hands on your head." The agents seemed frozen in disbelief. This had to be some type of ploy the dealers were using to check them out. Since everyone was hesitant to comply with Kow's demand, he reiterated his command in a brasher shrill voice to put their hands on their head.

This change of events caught the agents off guard. The windows were down on the passenger side. Then Kow barked out the order to lock the doors of the car. This command seemed peculiar; however, Kow wanted to make sure the agents didn't try to escape. Then the moment of truth came as Kow yelled at them to hand over the satchel containing the $80,000. At that moment the three agents knew that they had gotten themselves in a real live Rip-off. Agent Medina, the driver, turned his head further to the right and he could see a red Nissan about 75 feet behind their car. That vehicle pulled over to the curb and stopped. He didn't know what to read into the arrival of the other car.

Out of the corner of his eye he could see one of the occupants from the red Nissan had exited and run up to join Kow. Later, that individual was identified as William Wang. He positioned himself near the front passenger door of the Volvo and pointed a gun at the two agents in the front seat. At that moment in time, the agents realized that they were sitting ducks. Kow and Wang had their guns trained on the undercover agents. Again Kow demanded George Montoya in the back seat to hand over the money.

There was a moment of deafening silence. Would the agents be willing to hand over the $80,000? The agents were seated in such a way that they couldn't get to their weapons, which were in their back waistbands. There was no way that the agents could draw their weapons without being shot. Kow and Wang were standing outside and had their guns pointed directly at the heads of George Montoya in the back seat and Paul Seema in the front passenger seat. The agent didn't have any alternative but to hand over the money.

Without any discussion, Montoya reluctantly handed them the satchel. This seemed to be the end of a Rip-off situation. The agents had been outsmarted, at least up to that moment. The agents knew that there were surveillance agents who would be on the tail of these robbers as soon as they got a block away.

This part of Pasadena was such a tranquil area with little traffic. The only sounds that could be heard were the faint sounds of a lawnmower and two dogs barking at each other. It was a typical day of nothingness, just the way the residents liked it. Then all this civility in the old money world of Pasadena abruptly changed.

Without any warning, Kow and Wang looked at each other and immediately started firing their guns at the agents inside the car. Paul Seema in the front passenger seat was shot in the head and chest and the impact made his body lean into the dashboard. At the same time George Montoya was likewise shot in the head and chest, and slowly his body fell on to the back seat. Jose Medina, the driver, realized that he would be next. He was furthest from both the gunmen. He hadn't actually locked his door as Kow had ordered.

He grabbed the door handle and leaned against the door. It flew open and he fell out onto the paved street. He didn't want to be shot like his fellow agents, so he half-crawled and stumbled away from the car. He didn't want to waste precious time looking back at the shooters. His eyes were intently focused on the driveway across the street hoping he could find some cover.

As he was racing away, he could hear more gunfire. With his right hand he grabbed his gun from his back waistband. As he ran toward the driveway, he could hear the bullets whizzing around him. Suddenly he felt an intense pain in his leg. When he put pressure on that foot, his leg felt like it was made of rubber as it buckled under his weight. He realized he had been hit in the leg.

Since he hadn't found cover, he knew he was vulnerable. The basic human instinct of Fight or Flight had kicked in and he could see that Flight was no longer an option. His last resort was to Fight. He automatically spun around, pointing his gun in the direction of the gunfire. To him it all looked like a blur. He could barely see two figures running toward the red car parked behind. He tried to take aim at the moving targets and began to fire his weapon. His main objective was to stop them from continuing around the Volvo to shoot him.

His firing back seemed to force the shooters to retreat. They jumped into the red Nissan, which was being driven by one of their companions.

CHAPTER 8 THE KILLERS ESCAPE

Minutes earlier when the Volvo had stopped at the curb, two of the surveillance cars which were following had no place to go but to drive past the Volvo hoping not to attract any attention.

As they were driving by, the surveillance agents were shocked to see the big guy, Kow, was standing on the passenger side with what looked like a gun in his hand pointing at the agents in the Volvo. The surveillance agents didn't want to be noticed in their accidental drive-by. However, as they continued to gaze at the men pointing the guns at the Volvo, it became clear to them what was going down.

One of the agents grabbed his handheld radio and shouted in the microphone, "It's a Rip." As soon as they found an area where he could make a U-turn he spun the car around to drive back up the hill. The other surveillance unit at the top of the hill on hearing "Rip-off" immediately put the car in reverse so he could return to the location of the Volvo.

There had been a total of 17 law enforcement cars in the vicinity of the Volvo. When they heard that it was a Rip-off, all of a sudden police and agents units came flying from all directions. Within seconds they had converged on the area of the shooting.

Whether Kow and Wang had come to grips with the hornets' nest about to befall them wasn't clear. At first they may have thought they had come up against a large drug dealer who had security and they were trying to protect themselves from being robbed. However, when police cars and helicopters got involved, the three Asian guys had to realize that they had miscalculated as to who they were up against.

Sun could be described as the 'Designated Driver.' When his two buddies jumped into his red Nissan, he knew that it was his job to get them out of the area as fast as possible. As he was attempting to pull away, he pressed 'the pedal to the metal' and his small Nissan sport car veered around the Volvo parked in front of him. As he was attempting to pass the Volvo, he came into contact with Agent Jose Medina, who had positioned himself behind a tall tree. Although this agent was injured in the leg, he was able to shoot accurately enough to strike the windshield of the red sports car as it passed by.

With the windshield shattering, the guys got a taste at what they had gotten themselves into. As Sun continued to drive up the incline, he came near Steve Geller (pseudonym), the supervising agent in charge of the operation, who was driving down the street. In that one split second both drivers had to decide what to do. Both were accelerating at a high rate of speed heading toward each other. The agent was determined to prevent the Nissan from getting away.

Michael Sun, who was driving the Nissan, was transfixed on what had just happened. He thought his colleagues had just shot some drug dealers and taken their money. Moments later his windshield was shot by someone who was armed. Now he was faced with a car heading directly toward him. At that moment in time he had to think something big had gone wrong with their simple plan to 'Rip Off' some drug buyers.

Could this have been an undercover set up? He didn't know the answer, but his immediate concern was to avoid a car from crashing directly into him. He turned the car to the side abruptly, and the agent's car hit the back section of the Nissan, spinning it around. Sun was able to regain control and keep the Nissan on the road and continued north. The chase slowed him down enough so he could see that there were several cars coming up very fast from behind.

Sun tried to accelerate in order to get away from the pursuers. He didn't know in what direction to go and didn't have any time to consider his options. He was in unfamiliar territory, but the initial urge was to go back in the direction he had come from. He knew the area around the cities of Alhambra and Monterey Park. When he came to the first street, which was Allendale Road, he made a right turn and sped as fast as he could without losing control. He couldn't seem to shake all the cars following him. He made more turns hoping the others would lose sight of him. Somehow he was back on Marengo the street where the Rip-off occurred. He didn't want to go back by the scene of the shooting so he made another turn to get over to another parallel street going south.

Agent Steve Geller could see they were momentarily back on Marengo. He realized that there were enough agents following the Nissan, so he headed back to the scene of the shooting of the undercover agents. The front end of his car had been damaged sufficiently to take him out of the pursuit of the Nissan.

Agent Geller drove the short distance down the street and came upon an eerie scene. The Volvo, the undercover car, was still parked next to the curb and there was no one standing around it; however, the driver's door was wide open. Because of the noise from the shooting and the squealing of tires, residents from nearby were appearing from their houses. Some were standing in their front yards. Some of them had a puzzled expression on their faces in disbelief. A few looked shocked, and one lady had her one hand over her mouth and the other pointing in the direction of the Volvo. The startled residents were unprepared as to what to do. No one had processed the situation in their mind as to what really had happened. They were frozen in a gawking gaze. So far no one had shifted their thinking to try to render aid to the injured agents.

All that Agent Geller could see was the Volvo abandoned. He abruptly stopped his vehicle and jumped out, sprinting over to the Volvo. His eyes came upon the most sickening sight that any DEA supervisor could ever come upon. There he saw two of his best agents lying motionless with blood seeping from their heads and chest. Initially, he was nearest to Agent Montoya, who was lying across the back seat. The shot agent didn't show any signs of breathing and no pulse could be felt. Agent Geller went around the car to the front seat and saw Agent Paul Seema's body leaning forward with his head resting on the dashboard. He seemed to be struggling to breathe.

Instantaneously, other law enforcement officers converged on the scene. Frantically, a call went out to summon medical help. Within moments the Pasadena paramedics arrived and the emphasis was on trying to save the lives of the two shot agents. The shooting had occurred almost in the shadow of the

Huntington Memorial Hospital, which is one of the finest hospitals in Southern California.

The million-dollar question was whether the agents could get to the hospital in time for the medical staff to perform some type of miracle in saving their lives. Within minutes the two agents were placed into an ambulance with agent Geller their supervisor, and they raced to the hospital. The ER team started to work on Agent Seema, since there was a faint pulse. Agent Montoya was not responding to any of the medical attention.

CHAPTER 9 THE SAN MARINO SHOOTOUT

In the meantime, the other agents who had started to follow the red Nissan heard the shocking radio communications about the critical condition of both agents Seema and Montoya. The realization was that it was imperative that they didn't lose the shooters in the Nissan. The pressure was on to apprehend the shooters.

The Nissan at first sped through the residential streets of Pasadena; however, within a few blocks they had crossed over into the city of San Marino. By that time they were driving at a high rate of speed down Old Mill Road.

Back in 1988, Law Enforcement wasn't as restrictive regarding high-speed pursuits. These days, the police are so afraid of being sued by innocent civilians who are injured as a result of a police pursuit, the policy of the police is to back off and let the criminal escape. In a litigious society, the criminal gets a pass when it comes to police pursuits. On this day in 1988, when the law enforcement personnel heard that two DEA agents had been shot, the attitude was more like 'Let's get those Bastards.'

But mere determination wasn't going to be enough to stop this red sports car as it sped through the tranquil streets of San Marino. This small affluent community is considered one of the cultural jewels of the west coast. Back in 1903 Henry E. Huntington, the famous railroad baron, built his large mansion on the site of one of the original Spanish ranchos. To show how steeped in culture he was, he created the Huntington Library, which houses spectacular botanical gardens and a world-renowned art collection and rare-book library. As a matter of fact, it possesses one of the Gutenberg Bibles.

It is highly unlikely that the three rip-off suspects, Sun, Wang, or Kow, were overly impressed by the fact that they were driving by where one of the original 49 copies of the Gutenberg Bible was located. With local police units joining the pursuit, the Firebird and Camaro had more horsepower on their side, as was shown by them gaining on the little red Nissan. Eventually, one of the agents got up alongside the suspects' vehicle and nudged the Nissan, causing it to veer against the curb.

Driver Sun in the Nissan made a desperate attempt to keep the car on the road without losing control. Sun's attention was directed to the agent's car banging against the driver's side of the car. Little did Sun realize that he was driving by the home of one of the most highly revered U.S. Army Generals, George S. Patton, Junior (better known as old Blood and Guts). This General was totally fearless in combat. However, the irony was that he didn't die in battle but died of injuries suffered in a minor traffic accident after the war.

Sun may not have been aware that another agent's vehicle had come up from behind. The agent from behind accelerated, and his Firebird went plowing into the rear of the Nissan. The jolt was so severe that the Nissan went airborne. The front end landed in the grassy parkway next to the curb. The impact was so great that it blew out one of the tires, causing the Nissan to become wedged on the high curb.

For an instant there was the sound of squealing of brakes as law enforcement vehicles totally surrounded the little red Nissan that wasn't going anywhere. It was a replay of the movie ***High Noon***. What was everyone going to do? The three suspects Kow, Wang, and Sun all had their trusty guns ready to use. The three of them had to feel like sitting ducks who were crammed into this little sports car with nowhere to go.

Of course, all the agents and officers knew that their colleagues had been shot by this group of desperados. When the cops exited their vehicles they had their guns drawn, ready to impose justice if necessary. Both sides had their guns in the ready position. Who would be the first to initiate a gun battle in which only one side could be victorious?

It wasn't long before the sound of a single gunshot could be heard. Then a roar of gunfire could be heard as both sides unleashed their firepower. The suspects did their best from the confines of the little Nissan. They were outgunned while being pinned in an indefensible position. The suspects were in dire need of a white flag, but no one had thought of bringing a white handkerchief along with them when they had dressed that morning.

One of the problems with shootouts is to know when to cease firing. Gun Battles aren't like prize fights where a referee counts to 10 and if the fighter on the canvass doesn't get up the fight is over. The law enforcement side had no sympathy for the suspects who had shot their colleagues. Eventually, when the little red Nissan was reduced to Swiss cheese, there was a recognition that the suspects weren't firing back any longer.

When the guns on both sides had grown silent, it was time to assess the situation. The agents approached the Nissan to check on the suspects. They found that Sun, the driver, appeared to be motionless. As agents looked in the backseat, they found Kow crunched over in a curled-up position. The agents' attention was directed to Sun, who was in front, and they started to pull his limp body out through the driver's door. When his body was checked for a pulse, none could be found. He was placed on the asphalt of the street until the paramedics came to render a final opinion.

The focus was then on Kow, who was in the backseat of the small two-door Nissan. The agents tried to pull him out, but he was too large to be immediately extracted from the car. They reached in to check his neck to determine if there was any pulse. Nothing could be felt so they moved on to Wang, who had been shot 12 times but still had the resolve to stay alive.

When the paramedics arrived, they were directed to Wang since he showed the most likelihood of surviving. Immediately he was placed on a stretcher and transported to Huntington Memorial Hospital. Ironically, he was taken into the same emergency room where the doctors were trying to save the lives of the two wounded DEA agents. After all the heroics had been done to save the lives of those shot, it was Wang who would be the lone survivor, while the two DEA agents would be transported to the morgue.

CHAPTER 10 INVESTIGATION AND PROSECUTION

Back at the location where the red Nissan had come to rest, law enforcement had a perplexing issue as to what agency was in charge. Originally the DEA was in charge; however, no one knew the scope of the situation. If all the suspects had been killed, then there would be no criminal charges. At the crime scene no one knew for certain whether a homicide investigation would be necessary. Or, if necessary, who would be in charge of such an investigation.

Since it involved the shooting of federal agents, it might require the FBI to conduct the investigation. On the other hand, since the shooting of the agents occurred in the City of Pasadena, their police department may be the proper agency to conduct the investigation. Since the shootout continued and was completed in the City of San Marino, there was the possibility that their police department might be called upon to oversee the investigation. Because the San Marino police department was considerably smaller than Andy Griffith's Mayberry police department, the Los Angeles County Sheriff's Department might be asked to step in to handle any homicide that occurred in the tiny city of San Marino.

From the very beginning, law enforcement administrators were perplexed as to who should be conducting the investigation. Next, the big question was what type of investigation should be conducted. The public doesn't care who conducts the investigation; however, in this case the defendants could be prosecuted by either the federal or state prosecutors. The U.S. Attorney could have jurisdiction since the victims were federal, DEA agents. At that time there was no provision for the Death Penalty in the federal courts that could be imposed on the killers; however, the State of California did have the Death Penalty. State prosecutors could seek the Death Penalty for anyone who killed a law enforcement officer whether state or federal. Even at the beginning, no one knew whether the U.S. Attorney's Office or the DA's Office should be involved.

Back at the San Marino crime scene, law enforcement jointly took charge of collecting evidence. When the agents were checking on the status of the suspects in the car, they came upon the $80,000 in cash next to Kow in the backseat. They also noticed three handguns located near each of the suspects.

While most of the attention was focused on the Pasadena and San Marino areas, there were other important events unfolding in Monterey Park where the drug deal meeting originally took place. The Narcotics Task Force had released to law enforcement information about Michael Chia and his Mitsubishi vehicle. Later in the afternoon, a deputy sheriff was on patrol when he noticed a Mitsubishi vehicle pull out of the Tiny Naylor's restaurant parking lot and proceed northbound on Atlantic Boulevard.

At first the deputy was in disbelief, so he followed the Mitsubishi to get a better look at it. After several blocks, the deputy became convinced that he had the correct Mitsubishi. He turned on his red lights and got the driver's attention as the car pulled over to the curb. When he contacted the driver, he determined he was Michael Chia and placed him under arrest for being a part of a conspiracy to rob the DEA agents.

After Wang's medical recovery from his 12 bullet wounds, it was decided that Wang, the only survivor of the shootout, and Michael Chia should be prosecuted for both agents' murders and conspiracy to kill the agents. After considerable legal debates it was decided that the matter should be handled in the state courts instead of the federal court systems. The task of prosecuting the case was given to the Los Angeles County District Attorney's Office. After a lengthy trial, both defendants Wang and Chia were convicted of the double murder of the two DEA agents as well as the conspiracy charge. Both defendants appealed their cases in the state appellate courts and all appeals were denied. Also, all of the federal appeals were rejected.

Everyone moved on with their lives. The memories of that fateful February 5, 1988, faded over time. The surviving agent and the other officers who were present were able to put this nightmare behind them. Everyone was able to find their own form of closure. Unfortunately, this was a tragic situation that touched many lives.

Many of the initial officers had feelings of guilt. Had they done enough to protect their colleagues? Could they have done more? Many members of the law enforcement family had second thoughts as to what more they could have done and the thoughts of the tragic day continued to be replayed in the minds of many of those who experienced this horrific event. Only time helps to erase the self-doubts and enables them to go on with their lives.

CHAPTER 11 WHAT HAPPENED TO CLOSURE?

One day 18 years later, the federal Ninth Circuit Court of Appeal decided to reverse the conviction of Michael Chia. The Ninth Circuit held that the trial court erred when it didn't permit Chia to introduce, during his trial, the co-defendant Wang's statements to the police. The Ninth Circuit's opinion *Chia v. Cambra* 360 F.3d 997 is as follows: *"Wang confirmed to local and federal authorities that Chia had nothing to do with the conspiracy. The trial court, however, excluded these statements from being heard by the jury. Federal law as determined by the Supreme Court is clear that due process requires that the "minimum essentials of a fair trial" include a "fair opportunity to defend against the State's accusations" and the right to be heard in [one's] defense. The trial court's decision to exclude reliable material evidence of Chia's innocence therefore constitutes an objectively unreasonable application of clearly established federal law. We reverse the district court's denial of Chia's petition for writ of habeas corpus and remand with instructions to grant the writ.*

There wasn't any new law that had been passed or case law that had come down specifying that such evidence was admissible. This was a legal issue that had been raised in other cases and had been rejected as being without merit. What was so surprising about this opinion was that it completely changed the Rules of Evidence regarding hearsay statements. The Ninth Circuit court was saying to the state courts that their Rules of Evidence that had been followed for over 50 years could not be used to prevent a defendant from using hearsay statements from another which may be helpful to the defendant.

Such a fundamental change in the Rules of Evidence would be better done by the appropriate bodies such as the legislature in conjunction with the state Supreme Court. The question became why would the federal Ninth Circuit Court of Appeal feel so compelled to change the Rules of Evidence in a habeas corpus hearing, 18 years after the trial. In order to find a (justifiable) reason why two judges of the Ninth Circuit would come to such a far-reaching conclusion, one needs to explore who were these two judges and what were their backgrounds.

The judge who wrote this opinion was D.W. Nelson, Senior Circuit Judge. I, your author, am well aware of Judge Nelson, whom I better knew as Professor Dottie Nelson. She taught several of my law school classes at USC Law School. I remember her well for her discussions about judges' accountability. In one of those classes, I remember her raising the issues of how accountable should judges be to the public.

She set up the discussion by comparing the federal system, in which judges were appointed to serve for life, and the state system, in which the judges are subject to reelection every six years. She pointed out the pitfalls of having judges run for reelection. Would those judges make their judicial decision based on how it would affect their chances of reelection? Would they look favorably to groups that potentially could contribute to their election campaign?

Professor Nelson compared the state system to the federal system, in which there are no elections in that the judge served for life. Although the federal system seems so superior and truly makes the judges totally independent, she pointed out that federal judges aren't accountable to the public. They could make bizarre rulings and even continue to serve when they are senile. There is no check and balance on federal judges except they can be impeached like the U.S. President, which seldom if ever happens.

At the end of the class Professor Nelson stated that both systems have their pitfalls, but that she favored the state system of requiring judges to go before the electorate every six years. She felt it was more democratic and eliminated the tyrannical effect of the federal system in which judges served for life

Most of my fellow law school colleagues liked Professor Nelson as an instructor because she would have us visit various parts of the justice system. She opened our eyes to the various state and federal courts, giving us a chance to ask questions to real judges and attorneys. On one occasion she had our class visit an autopsy in the basement of the Hall of Justice. My fellow students didn't soon forget the distinctive smell of the morgue. However, it took weeks before we could forget the high-pitched grinding sound from the coroner's bone-cutting saws. That sound prevented many of the students from having any desire to visit their friendly dentist for years.

Although the law students had a favorable impression of Professor Dottie Nelson, many of the students' common complaint about her teaching technique was that she was constantly trying to teach us how to act and think like a judge. She wasn't interested in us being attorneys but being judges. To all of us, this seemed peculiar because we needed to be attorneys first, long before any of us would be considering a judgeship.

Shortly after I graduated from law school, Dottie Nelson became dean of the law school in 1969. She was a mover and shaker, and it wasn't long before she convinced the alumni to contribute money for a new law school building. She served as the law school dean for ten years, and there was no doubt she was well respected. In 1979, President Jimmy Carter nominated her for a new position on the Ninth Circuit Court of Appeal. This was a surprising nomination since she had never served in the capacity as a judge in either the state or federal courts. Her only court experience was during the three years after she graduated from UCLA law school, while she was in private practice.

With this total lack of litigation experience, this pleasant law school dean, Dottie Nelson, was given the lofty position as a judge of the Ninth Circuit court of appeal. How was a career in academia going to qualify her to deal with appellate decisions? There are those who say she was bright and a quick learner who could think outside the box. That may be so, but she was a person who had no practical experience of prosecuting or defending those accused.

Whether her appointment was a mistake can be debated forever. However, she sat on the Ninth Circuit of Appeals for 15 years until 1995 when she was made a senior circuit judge. So when she became involved in the Chia case in 2000 she was acting as a senior circuit judge.

Your author can only think of what Dean Nelson taught him 50 years ago in law school. She stressed the pitfalls of federal judges who had lifetime tenure and were totally unaccountable to the public. That may explain why she was willing to reverse Chia's conviction 18 years after his trial, after all the court exhibits had been destroyed and it would be virtually impossible to retry Chia in a new trial.

CHAPTER 12 PRICE FOR HAVING LIFETIME JUDGES

he other judge who concurred with Judge Nelson in reversing the Chia case was Judge Alex Kozinski. He served on the Ninth Circuit for over 30 years and was the TChief Judge for the Ninth Circuit starting in 2007. Many would classify him as an enigmatic judge. Although he was appointed to the position by President Ronald Reagan, he certainly turned out to be less than what many would describe as a Law and Order judge. He was born and raised in Romania when it was a communist country.

Most judges stay out of the public view trying to remain neutral. However, Judge Kozinski seems to enjoy being a commentator and author of books criticizing the judicial system. In 2015 Judge Kozinski wrote a law review article titled Annual Review of the Criminal Procedure. He expressed his opinion that it was a myth that prosecutors play fair. He wrote:

The Supreme Court has told us in no uncertain terms that a prosecutor's duty is to do justice, not merely to obtain a conviction. It has also laid down some specific rules about how prosecutors, and the people who work for them, must behave—principal among them that the prosecution turn over to the defense exculpatory evidence in the possession of the prosecution and the police. There is reason to doubt that prosecutors comply with these obligations fully.

Judge Kozinski's scathing attack on prosecutors was further extended to the police as he wrote that it was a myth that Police are objective in their investigation as he stated the following:

In many ways, this is the bedrock assumption of our criminal justice process. Police also have a unique opportunity to manufacture or destroy evidence, influence witnesses, extract confessions and otherwise direct the investigation.

If one were to wonder about Judge Kozinski's objectivity, one only has to look at his jaundiced comments about prosecutors and police. There is no doubt that the criminal justice system can be improved, and it is fair to look at all aspects to see what needs improving. What is perplexing about Judge Kozinski's criticism is that he didn't mention one instance of how defendants and Defense attorneys abuse the criminal justice system. Strange how Judge Kozinski is willing to overlook the rampant abuse Defense attorneys commit in not complying with their obligation to turn over discovery to the prosecution.

What is interesting is that all attorneys such as your author are restricted from criticizing the courts. The California State Bar states the following:

An attorney's communications about the legal system should at all times reflect civility, professional integrity, personal dignity, and respect for the legal system.

For example, in communications about the legal system and with adversaries: *An attorney's conduct should be consistent with high respect and esteem for the civil and criminal justice system.*

What is interesting is that a Judge of the Ninth Circuit can boldly state that 'Prosecutors don't play fair'; however, prosecutors are ethically not permitted to criticize the criminal justice system such as saying 'Judges don't play fair.'

In other words, an attorney could not publicly state that a judge who maintains his personal porn library on the court computers was improper. As well as a number of law clerks who have made claims against that judge as to how he sexually harassed them when they were clerking for him. Even if that were true, any attorney who made such claims against a judge might be found by the State Bar to be in violation of the canon of ethics for being disrespectful of the judicial system.

(Fortunately while writing this book the 'Me Too Movement of 2017' erupted onto the world stage. All of a sudden Judge Kozinski's behavior was no longer tolerated. After the news media did numerous investigative articles about his bizarre and whacky conduct, he decided to resign as a senior judge of the Ninth Circuit Court of Appeal. If only he had resigned years ago we wouldn't be talking about this Chia case.)

This gives you the reader some insight on the background and thinking of the two judges who reversed Chia's conviction. As previously stated, Ninth Circuit judges serve for life and seldom if ever is a federal judge removed from office. In other words, Ninth Circuit judges can follow the law set down by previous court rulings, or they can make new law depending on their interpretation of what they believe to be fair. The American judicial system has been based on the concept of "Stare Decisis," which means the court looks to the past to decide the present case.

When the Ninth Circuit judges change the law, only the U.S. Supreme Court can try to rein them in. So it was understandable that Judges Nelson and Kozinski had the perfect opportunity to try to change the rules of evidence in the name of providing the defendant a fair trial. The Chia case provided them the opportunity to do a little Ninth Circuit justice. The Chia case had already gone up to the US Supreme Court and it had sent it back to the Ninth Circuit. The Ninth Circuit figured another way to reverse the Chia case which they did sending it back to the state court. The final opinion was written by D.W. Nelson and concurred with Alex Kozinski; however, Justice Brunetti provided a dissent to the opinion.

The Ninth Circuit is the largest circuit of all the federal appellate courts. It basically includes all the western states and is made up of 29 Active judges and 18 Senior judges. For years the Ninth Circuit has been a haven for liberal causes. Of all the Circuit courts in the country, the Ninth Circuit has gained the reputation for its extremely liberal-leaning rulings and opinions. Since they are judges appointed for a lifetime, many people believe that they have taken it upon themselves to legislate their liberal philosophy. Even though the courts are supposed to follow the law, some of the Ninth Circuit judges see their role as to make the law not just interpret it.

As a result, eight out of 10 cases from the Ninth Circuit are reviewed by the Supreme Court and ultimately overruled, according to a 2010 analysis published by the American Bar Association. The Ninth Circuit has the second-highest reversal rate of the 13 appellate courts.

CHAPTER 13 EIGHTEEN YEARS IS A LONG TIME

As we have seen, it was easy for Judges Nelson and Korzinski to reverse the Chia case. However, another question is, do the appellate judges consider the impact of their decision as to the retrial of the case? Most likely neither of the Ninth Circuit judges ever considered the impossible conditions that their reversal of a case 18 years after the original trial created. Some would say the emphasis should be on the defendant who has been unfairly convicted. If a defendant didn't receive a fair trial, the appellate courts should immediately rectify it.

Everyone would agree with the concept of 'fair trial,' but what does that really mean? Does it mean that a defendant should be given the right to present any and all evidence that would be helpful to his Defense? That would seem to be fair; however, the courts have created the Rules of Evidence, which limit what actual evidence can be heard by the jury. The reasoning has been that certain constitutional rights such as the Fifth Amendment Right Against Self Incrimination cannot be overlooked. In other words, a defendant can't force another person to testify in a trial if that person believes such testifying might incriminate him or her. That is even true if the defendant believes that person's testimony would exonerate the defendant.

Also, the courts have spent over a hundred years carving out what evidence can and cannot be heard by the jury. The courts have been most concerned that only reliable evidence be presented to the jury. That is why the hearsay of a co-defendant can't be used in court unless it falls within one of the carved-out exceptions to the Hearsay Rule.

Legal authorities can debate the merits of what evidence a defendant may present at trial. If the rule of law is to be changed, then it should be done in an orderly fashion. However, these two judges of the Ninth Circuit decided that they would rewrite the law in order to assure a defendant like Chia a so called 'fair trial.'

The crime occurred in 1988 and the trial was held in 1989. It wasn't until 2004 that the Ninth Circuit issued its ruling reversing the Chia case. This was 15 years after the original trial. Immediately after defendant Chia was convicted, he brought numerous appeals in both the state courts and the federal courts. All those appellate courts considered all the issues raised in Chia's appeals, and they were all found to be without merit. As a result, Chia's conviction was affirmed and he remained in prison.

After so many years, the Court Clerk has to clean out their storage facility and destroy the exhibits in all the cases that have passed their appeal time. However, the appellate courts permit habeas corpus proceeding to be brought after the appeal period has run. (Habeas Corpus is an old English legal concept ordering a prison official to bring a prisoner to court to determine if that prisoner is being lawfully detained). A defendant can bring a Habeas Corpus writ many years after the appellate period of his or her case has run. In Chia's case, he brought this Habeas Corpus many years after the court clerk had destroyed all the exhibits related to his case.

What is interesting about the Ninth Circuit reversal of the Chia case is the judges were saying that Chia had to be retried and this time he could have the jurors hear about his co-defendant's statements. What seemed to be completely ignored by the judges is the fact that all the exhibits had been destroyed. How could the prosecution retry the Chia case without the exhibits? Could these judges have realized that their reversal was basically an indirect way to have the charges dismissed against Chia and have him released from prison?

However, let's give the judges the benefit of the doubt in their quest for perfect justice.

A reasonable solution would be to require all appeals and writs of habeas corpus be decided within a five-year period from the time of conviction. For those who subscribe to the concept of perfect justice, the burden is on the defendant to bring and litigate all issues during this five-year period or otherwise they waive those issues from later habeas corpus writs. If the five-year limitation concept isn't acceptable, then all court clerks should be ordered to maintain all records and exhibits on a criminal case as long as the defendant is still in custody.

In order to convey how much time had gone by we will walk down 'memory lane' to illustrate that 15 years is REALLY A VERY LONG TIME. Look at all that happened during that time:

Shooting of the agents occurred on February 5, 1988

1988 Events

The Los Angeles Dodgers beat the Oakland A's in the World Series 4-1

In Super Bowl XXII the Red Skins vs. Denver Broncos Score 42-10

Michael Jackson's hit songs *The Way You Make Me Feel & Man in the Mirror*

TV NBC had these hits: *The Cosby Show; Cheers; The Golden Girls; Night Court*

Academy Awards went to *Rain Man*

Grammy Awards went to *Don't Worry, Be Happy*

Tony Awards Best Musical was *The Phantom of the Opera*

1989 Events

Berlin Wall was torn down

Tiananmen Square Stand Off occurred

Exxon Valdez tanker ran aground

US Troops invaded Panama

The Satanic Verses written by Salman Rushdie

A Brief History of Time by Stephen Hawking

Academy Awards went to *Driving Miss Daisy*

Record of the Year by Bette Midler *Wind beneath My Wings*

1990 Events

Hubble Space Telescope launched

East and West Germany reunited

GPS first sold for car navigation

1991 Events

Gulf War waged in Middle East against Iraq

Soviet Union Collapsed

World Wide Web publicly debuted

1992 Events

Los Angeles Riots occurred, causing 60 deaths

Bill Clinton beat President George H. W. Bush

1993 Events

Waco, Texas, Branch Davidians standoff 81 deaths

Truck Bomb exploded in World Trade Center parking lot

Clinton Military Policy "Don't ask, don't tell'

1994 Events

OJ Simpson trial

NAFTA went into effect

Northridge Earthquake in Los Angeles killed 72 people

1995 Events

Oklahoma City Bombing killed 168

Federal Budget Crisis shut down the government

1996 Events

Olympic Park bombing

TWA Flight exploded over Long Island killing 230

1997 Events

President Bill Clinton second inauguration

Global economic crisis

1998 Events

Paula Jones accused President of sexual harassment

Lewinsky Scandal

1999 Events

Impeachment of President Clinton but later acquitted in Senate

Columbine shooting killed 13 students

2000 Events

Preparation for Y2K only minor computer-related problems

Olympics in Sydney, Australia

USS Cole bombed in port of Aden, Yemen, killing 17 sailors

George W. Bush elected president

2001 Events

9/11/01 crashing into Twin Towers, Pentagon, and Shanksville, PA

Invasion of Afghanistan

Anthrax attacks killed five

2002 Events

Euro became official currency for most of Europe

Department of Homeland Security was created

World Series Anaheim Angels beat San Francisco Giants 4 to 3

2003 Events

Columbia Space Shuttle destroyed returning to earth, killing 7 crew members

US and other countries invaded Iraq

Sadam Hussein captured by US

Arnold Schwarzenegger was elected Governor of California

2004 Events

USC Trojans beat Michigan 28 to 14 in Rose Bowl

Lord of the Rings *The Return of the King* won Academy Award

Earthquake and tsunami occurred in the Pacific Ocean killing 266,000

Ninth Circuit reverses Chia case on March 4, 2004

2005 Events

North Korea announced that it has nuclear weapons

Prince Charles and Camilla Parker Bowles were married

John Roberts, Jr. became Chief Justice of US Supreme Court

Lance Armstrong retired after winning his 7th straight Tours de France

IRA issued order ending armed campaign against the British

Hurricane Katrina caused severe damage to the Gulf Coast killing 1836

Retrial of the Michael Chia case began in Los Angeles Superior Court

(You the reader might think that it was unnecessary to list so many events. However, the point is that it is hard to sense how much happens in the lives of witnesses and investigators over a period of 15 years)

CHAPTER 14
DIFFICULTY RETRYING A CASE 17 YEARS AFTER CRIME

The Michael Chia case arrived back in the Los Angeles Superior Court stating that the conviction had been reversed. As stated previously, the clerk's office made it clear that they had destroyed the court exhibits after the appeals were completed. Therefore the crucial exhibits used in the original trial were no longer available from the clerk's office. What that meant was that the Los Angeles District Attorney's Office had two choices: either say to the Ninth Circuit, "You win. We can't retry the case without the exhibits. Therefore the case is dismissed." Or in defiance of the Ninth Circuit say, "Bring it on. We will try it again no matter what the obstacles are."

The latter is easy to say but requires incredible resources and perseverance. First of all, the prosecution must contact all the agencies involved as well as all of their investigators. Most of them had retired. Those that could be found were asked if they had copies of any of the documents or photos that were used in the original case. Many of the retired investigators and agents went through their old files to see what they might have saved.

Where there is a strong will and determination, miracles can occur. Through some fate of God, one of the ol-time investigators was a "Pack Rat." He started spending time in his garage going through old boxes filled with cases from 15 to 20 years ago. When he came across something involving the shooting of the two DEA agents he set it aside. Within a month several of the old timers were able to reconstruct a part of the case from what had been found. Of course, the guns and the slugs and expended shell casings were gone, but there were some photos that could be used to substitute for the original items.

Needless to say, the DEA was livid with the reversal of the Michael Chia case. It was felt by many others in law enforcement that the Ninth Circuit was purposely saying that it was okay to kill officers who are merely doing their job. (Although the judges didn't mean to imply this, feelings regarding the reversal were incredibly intense) Since the DEA couldn't strike out and do anything about the Ninth Circuit's ruling, their wrath was directed to the DA's Office. It didn't take long before DA administrators recognized that they had a 'Hot Potato' on their hands.

The two big issues were, can the defendant be legally prosecuted after the ruling of the Ninth Circuit's opinion, and was there sufficient evidence still available after all these years to be able to convince a jury to convict?

It didn't take the DA administrators long to figure out that this was a case that would require extraordinary analysis at the highest level. In other words, it was quickly tossed into the lap of Major Crimes Division. The Head Deputy realized that the prosecutors assigned to this elite Division were all like thoroughbreds that were incredibly sharp and experienced. The question was, who would be best to handle such a controversial case? What was needed was a prosecutor who was meticulous and unwavering in his or her determination to see such a case through all the colossal challenges. On top of that, he or she needed to be a highly skilled communicator with the jurors. There was one other factor that would be crucial, and that was this prosecutor would have the most delicate task of dealing with law enforcement officials who had a feeling that the judicial system was out to get them.

Fortunately, Darrell Mavis had been assigned to Major Crimes Division and was highly regarded. He had proved himself in the branch and area part of the office and had received high marks for his legal knowledge and courtroom skills.

Darrell's academic achievements were impressive. Few attorneys can claim that they studied politics, philosophy, and economics at Oxford University. Then he went on to graduate from MIT, followed by graduating from Harvard Law School. However, Darrell doesn't find it necessary to remind those around him that he has credentials that any attorney or judge would envy. He doesn't project the typical arrogant attitude that many academic types possess. His approach when working with others is to ask questions and then sit back and listen to their answers. In other words, he is a great listener and seems to have a gift for communicating through listening and not boasting how great he is.

Darrell has made a point of learning from every case he ever tried. As a new prosecutor, he was always willing to try any type of case just to gain experience. He recognized what worked and what missed the mark. His experience has taught him that there is no substitute for thorough preparation. He understood the importance in developing a rapport with the assigned detectives since later on he would call upon them to do further investigation on their case. Also, Darrell wanted to have personal contact with the witnesses in his case in order to know what type of witness they would make when testifying.

Darrell recognized that prosecuting the big cases meant working late at night and on weekends so he could explore every contingency that would possibly arise during trial. Further, he wanted to anticipate what the Defense issues would be and wanted a strategy to combat such issues.

Also, this case needed a prosecutor who had great communication skills. In the courtroom, Darrell gives the appearance of being self-assured but not in the way of being shrill or being cocky. He speaks in measured tones and statements. Since he is a master of knowing the facts, he methodically introduces the evidence in a way that is efficient and effective. He understands that jurors are normal people who don't talk in legalese terms. He breaks the legal issues down into common words and phrases that the jurors are familiar with. He is smart enough to know the best way to keep the attention of the jurors is to incorporate visuals into his verbal presentation. His civility is appreciated by jurors in that he has learned that being polite and respectful to witnesses and even the Defense attorney can pay dividends with the jurors.

As to knowing the law, Darrell has gained the reputation as a 'Lawyer's Lawyer,' meaning others go to him for answers to legal questions. Even judges recognized that Darrell has an affinity for knowing the finer points of law. Many Defense attorneys find it difficult to out-argue Darrell on technical legal issues. Some judges and attorneys believe that Darrell has a sixth sense of knowing the obscure case law on some of the most esoteric legal issues.

When one first meets Darrell, one is pleasantly surprised that he seems to always have things under control. He never panics but projects complete confidence that he can handle whatever he is faced with. He is like a chess player whose mind is three steps ahead of the game. The head of Major Crimes Division understood the delicate balance the prosecutor in the Michael Chia case would be required to exercise. Darrell was the perfect attorney to reassure the DEA and all concerned in law enforcement that the case was in good hands by someone who was on their side.

CHAPTER 15 INTENSE PREPARATION

Darrell's first concern in preparing for the Chia case was what physical evidence still existed. Since the case had been tried almost 17 years earlier, the trial court clerk's office had destroyed all the exhibits that had been used in the original case. Darrell contacted the lead DEA agent to see if the DEA Office had kept any of the items after the case. Fortunately, the agency had in their archive files some of the reports that had been generated about the shooting. However, as to copies of the exhibits and photos, little if any had been retrieved.

It wasn't until Darrell sat down with several of the agents that he learned that some of the retired agents had been able to find a few of the old photos and documents involving the case. Darrell immediately made copies of the few items that had been found. When Darrell started reviewing the facts of the case, he came to the realization that what still existed were items that proved that two DEA agents were killed. He knew that the Defense would utilize what evidence he did have to prove that the defendant Chia or his Mitsubishi were nowhere near the shootings in Pasadena and San Marino.

As Darrell spent hours with the DEA agents reviewing all the facts, he noticed that he was getting a little confused as to what each party was involved in. Part of that was due to the fact that there were so many parties in the case. There were three DEA agents involved in the shooting, but there were two who were killed. Also, there were four suspects involved; however, two were killed and two survived, and they were the ones who were prosecuted.

To eliminate the confusion for him and to help potential jurors in the future, Darrell prepared a "Parties In Case" chart. He listed the DEA agents who were in the undercover car at the top of the chart. He indicated which ones were the two who had been killed. Under the agents' photos he had a large oval, and he had the photos of the four suspects placed inside. Then he indicated what had happened to each one of them. Two of them were killed in the shootout, and the other two were the defendant Chia and his witness Wang who had been convicted of these crimes. This graphic proved to be useful for Darrell as well as all the witnesses who would be testifying. Most of all, this would help the jurors to better understand everyone's role in the shootings.

The other confusing part of this case was the fact that there were numerous locations where various events occurred. It wasn't the typical case where the actual crime and arrest occurred at the same location. Darrell knew that the jurors could easily become confused with all the various locations that the DEA witnesses would be testifying to. The crime had happened 17 years earlier, so the Defense would object to any present map being used in court since it wouldn't accurately show the layout of the streets when the crime occurred. Darrell asked the retired detectives if they had an old map circa 1988 that could be used in preparing a court exhibit.

Thankfully, Darrell was in luck since one of the retired homicide detectives had an old map from that time period that he had used in another case. It had some old ink writing on the left-hand side. Darrell realized he could make it do. To prevent the Defense from objecting, he placed a photo of the Chia's car over the ink spots on the map. In order not to make it too obvious that he was covering something up, he placed additional photos of the relevant locations, starting with the Tiny Naylor's Windmill restaurant in Monterey Park and going all the way up the map to the location of the Rip-off on Marengo Avenue in Pasadena.

CHAPTER 16 SHOWING CHIA'S INVOLVEMENT

Darrell knew that he had to develop a way to show the jury exactly how much Michael Chia had been involved in this Rip-off. After listening to the DEA agents, he realized that Chia was instrumental in the 'Counter Surveillance' during the meeting at Tiny Naylor's restaurant. Darrell had to figure out some way to emphasize Chia's countersurveillance activities. Even though Chia didn't participate in the shootouts, he had definitely taken an active role in all the driving around in the Tiny Naylor's parking lot.

Darrell couldn't afford having any of the jurors not understand what Chia had been doing in the parking lot. Darrell wanted to convey this information to the jury in two ways. One was by using some type of visual that showed an aerial view of the Tiny Naylor's restaurant which was depicted in the shape of a circle with the surrounding shopping area with their accompanying parking lots. Darrell inserted a photo of the Tiny Naylor's restaurant with an arrow pointing to the actual building.

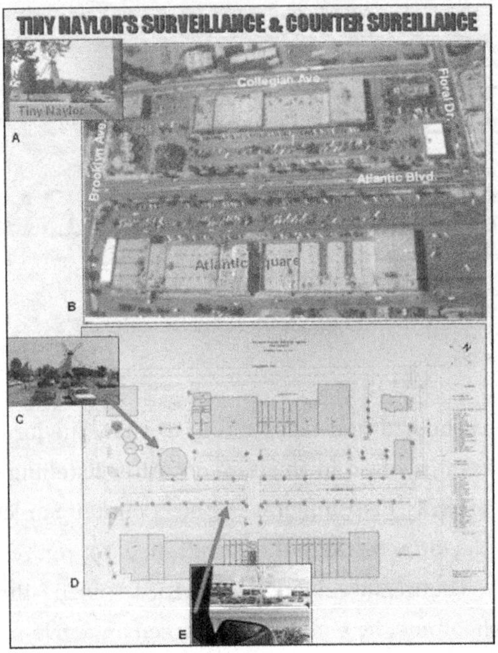

The other part of this visual display was a diagram of the same area without all the parked vehicles as seen in the aerial. In this way the jurors had two different perspectives of the same location. This type of diagram could be used during the DEA agents' testimony. The agents could mark on this exhibit to show where they had been located. Such a diagram could be used to show the movement of Chia when he was seen driving around in the Tiny Naylor's parking lot. Darrell made sure that the diagram included the Atlantic Square shopping center, which was across the street. That was where many of the surveillance agents were parked when they made their observations of Chia driving around the parking lot.

Darrell continued to prepare exhibits he would be using in the trial. He wanted somehow to show the jurors that the agents weren't merely testifying to their memory of what happened 17 years earlier. He asked the agents if any of them still had any photos of Chia in the parking lot. One of the agents remembered he had some old surveillance photos and he went through them to see if he had anything showing Chia.

Unfortunately, he couldn't find any photos of Chia, but he did have one of Chia's car parked in the parking lot. Although the photo couldn't be enhanced to show Chia in his car, at least it did show his car right where the agents had seen it.

Darrell was pleased with whatever the agents had. He would be able to use it as an exhibit proving to the jurors that Chia was in fact in the parking lot. The below photo was taken by one of the agents from his surveillance car looking at Chia's car parked across the street in the Tiny Naylor's parking lot.

Seldom does the prosecution have such compelling direct evidence that the defendant was present at the time of the crime. If the detectives hadn't found this photo, the Defense would have been able to argue that there wasn't any concrete evidence that Chia was in fact there. This one photo locked the Defense into having to explain why he was in the Tiny Naylor's parking lot at the crucial time.

Defendant Chia owned a brown Mitsubishi that had distinctive rims. There was a pink Chinese ornament hanging from his rearview mirror. Darrell wanted the jurors to be very familiar with this car. Most of the time the DEA agents in court would identify this car by the brown color and distinctive rims. The jurors had to understand why this car was recognizable, so Darrell used a photo display to show all the various angles of Chia's Mitsubishi. The center photo showed an oriental tassel hanging from the rearview mirror that several agents would refer to in their testimony.

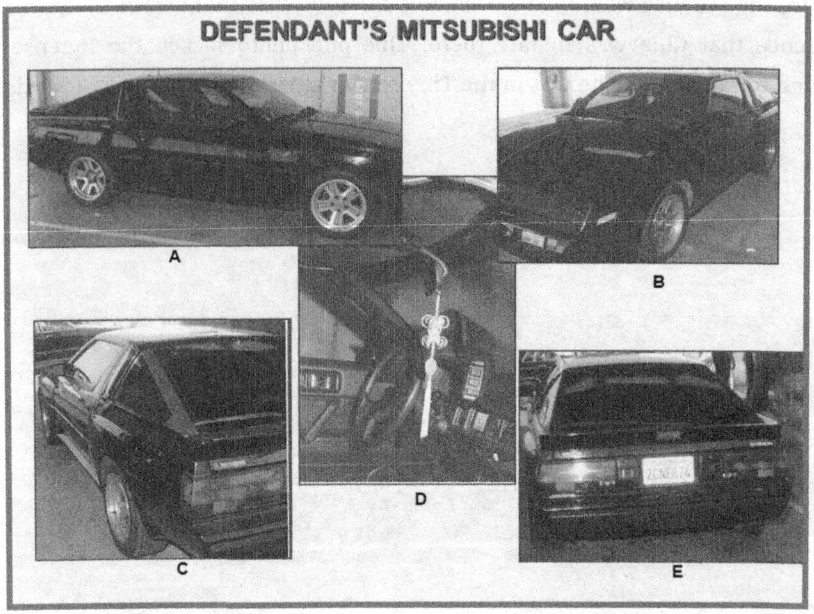

Darrell wanted each of the surveillance officers to explain to the jury what he or she saw. Since some of them were constantly moving around, their locations on the map were always changing. The more Darrell talked to the agents, the more he realized that the situation was dynamic and always changing with people coming and going. He didn't know how to convey all that crucial information to the jury.

Darrell soon realized that the best way to understand precisely how much Chia was involved was by creating a reenactment of Chia's activity that morning of the big buy. Darrell tried to figure out a way to use the limited number of photos to show the picture. However, it was the collection of statements of all the surveillance agents that painted the most accurate picture of Chia's role in the Rip-off scheme. The surveillance agents were in various locations, and they were reporting on a dynamic situation that was constantly changing as each subject moved about the parking lot.

Eventually Darrell recognized that a static diagram could not accurately paint the true picture of what happened. That was when Darrell came up with the idea of having a computer-generated image of the movement of the various subjects in the parking lot. Darrell came to me, your author, and asked me to construct a computer reenactment of the route of travel of each of the parties. I eventually was able to create a computer-generated reenactment which would permit the jurors to have a clearer picture of Chia's involvement.

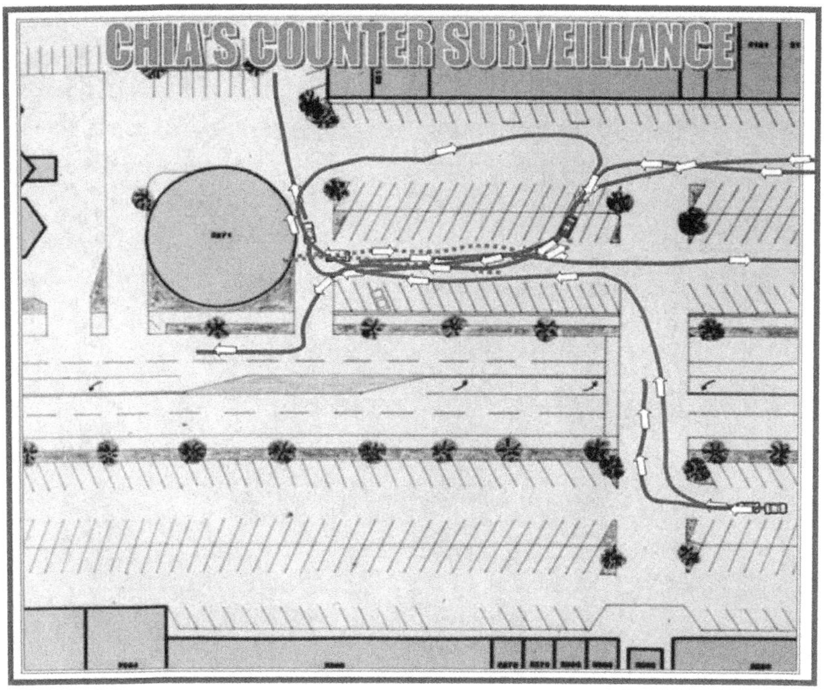

CHAPTER 17 OPENING STATEMENT

After an inordinate amount of legal motions, the retrial of the Chia case began. Darrell believed he was as prepared as he could possibly be with whatever he was able to scrape together in the way of physical evidence. Darrell may have been nervous with all the pressure that had been placed on his shoulders. However, when he walked into the courtroom he didn't exhibit any trepidation or sense of anxiety.

Darrell could best be described as a tall, impressive individual who requires the average-height person to tilt their head upwards in order to converse with him. He has a full head of hair and his angular face projects a congenial smile as he listens intently to others.

Darrell had put a great deal of thought into how to educate the jurors to the complex facts they had to know about if there was any chance of a conviction. The Opening Statement is the time when both sides can explain what the relevant facts of their case are. The prosecutor may refer to the Opening Statement to be like a roadmap that shows the jury where they are going and what they will see along the way. Darrell made sure that his Opening Statement laid a firm foundation for all the facts that the jurors needed to know and remember in order to convict Chia.

Darrell's approach could be described as restrained and relaxed. He speaks in common sense language without any of the usual lawyer talk. He isn't trying to impress the jurors as to how smart he is because he knows that isn't the issue. He is like a surgeon who knows through experience that it isn't the speed of the operation but the precise use of the right words that is the key. His delivery isn't loud, but measured, and he uses descriptive words to convey concisely the facts and law to the jurors.

Darrell used a PowerPoint slide show to convey the information he wanted the jurors to be familiar with. One of the first slides in his presentation was the previous graphic we discussed showing the Parties in Case.

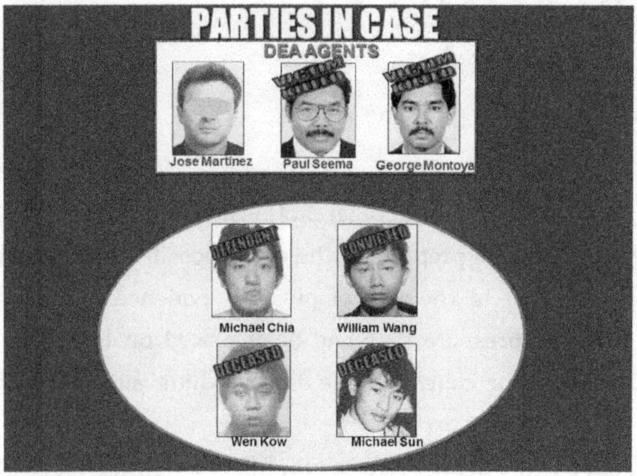

Likewise, Darrell wanted to have the jurors acclimated to the various locations, so he redid his map of the various locations and labeled it Locations of Events.

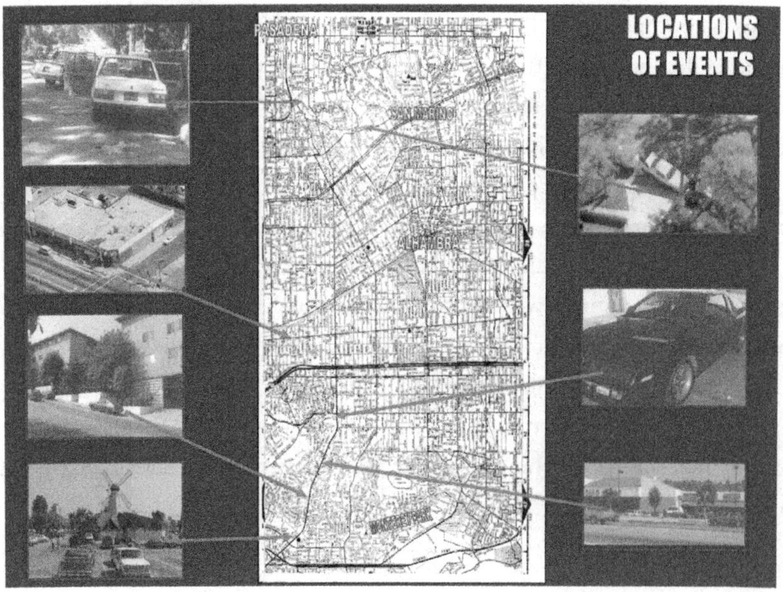

Darrell wanted to make sure that the jury understood that the night before the shooting Chia was associating with Wang and Kow. What was key evidence was the fact that two agents saw Chia park in front of Kow's apartment, get out with Wang, and open the trunk. Wang removed a .45 caliber semi-automatic and carried it up to Kow's apartment. The Defense wanted to attack this evidence, claiming that the agents couldn't see this happening. If it did happen, the agents still would be unable to determine the type of gun it truly was. Darrell combined several photos so the agents could use the visual below in his Opening Statement to show the jury what they saw the suspects do and what the suspects removed from the trunk and took up to Kow's apartment.

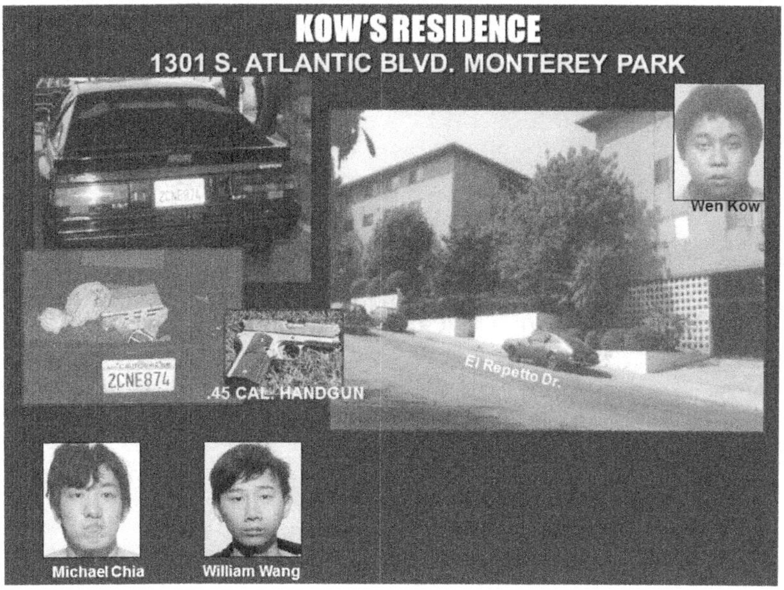

Darrell then wanted the jurors to see the one piece of physical evidence that showed Chia's car at the Tiny Naylor's parking lot moments before the meeting of the agents with Kow. This slide clearly showed Chia's brown Mitsubishi in the parking lot. Although the blow-up photo didn't show Chia seated in the car, at least it could be inferred that Chia was there at that critical time.

CHAPTER 18 DISCUSSION OF CRIME SCENES

Darrell moved onto the next topic, and that involved the crime scene on Marengo Avenue where the two DEA agents were shot. In order to orientate the jurors to the shooting location, Darrell used the below visual to help the jurors understand where the undercover car pulled over and stopped.

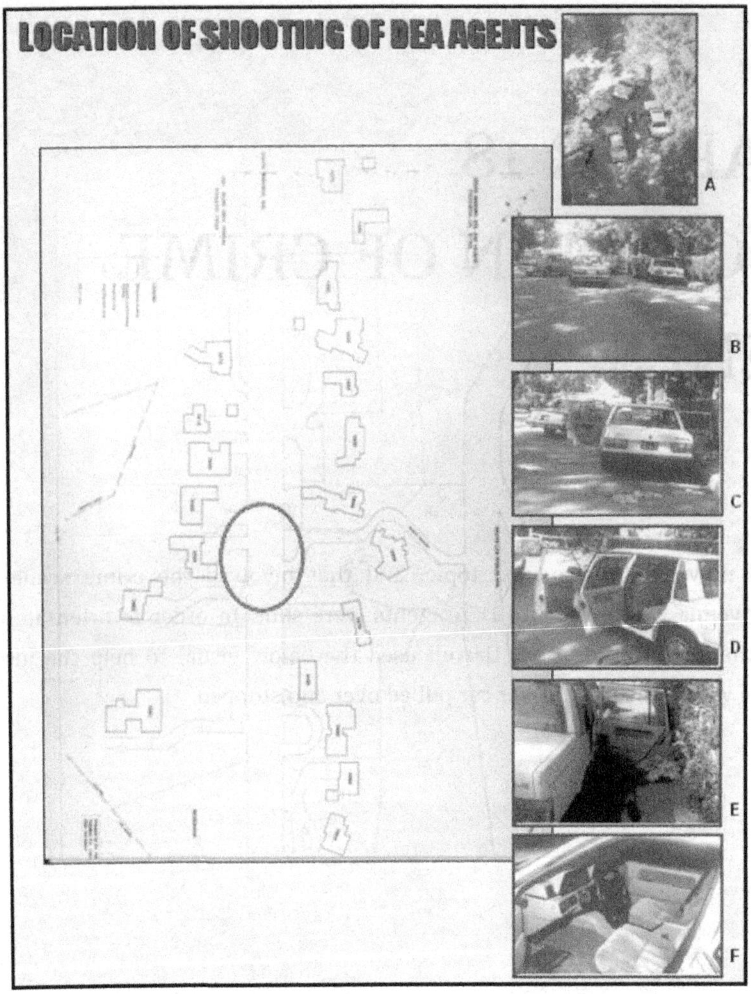

The diagram had been found in some of the old papers and had faded so much it was hard to see the locations of the various houses along the street. The photos of the undercover Volvo in which the agents were killed were displayed on the right-hand side.

Darrell used the next visual to show where everyone was located in the two cars. In the Volvo, Jose Medina was the driver with Paul Seema seated in the passenger front seat. In the rear left was the third agent, George Montoya, and in the right rear was the person who had set up the drug deal, Wen Kow.

A red Nissan was parked about 75 feet behind the undercover car. For the sake of illustration, it was placed closer to the undercover car so the jurors could see that Michael Sun was the driver and William Wang was the front passenger. It was Wang who ran up to Kow and helped him shoot the agents.

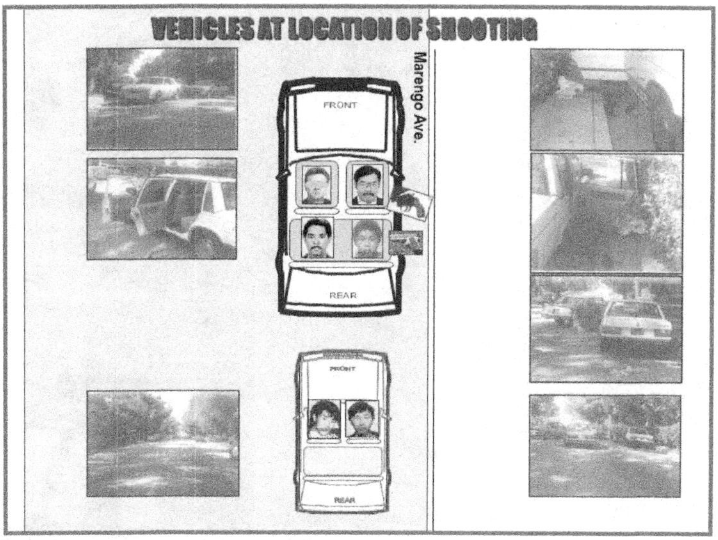

Again the final shootout scene was a two-edged sword for the prosecution. The Defense liked to make it appear that law enforcement overreacted when one of their own was killed. The Defense likes to dissect every action of the cops and tries to dwell on the conduct that might be considered excessive force. However, in the real world, law enforcement has to deal with life-and-death decisions when the adrenaline is flowing, and the officers have to make decisions without knowing all the facts.

Darrell knew that the Defense would dwell on the shootout and the fact that the cops fired some 200 rounds at the red Nissan. During the Opening Statement, Darrell explained that the agents would testify that the suspects were firing from the Nissan as they were racing through the streets of San Marino. Darrell prepared the below visual by using an aerial photo to show where the red Nissan finally came to rest. On the right side, Darrell had photos placed showing that the Rip-off money was found inside the back seat of the vehicle.

Up to this point, Darrell's Opening Statement was concentrated on the Rip-off and shootouts. Darrell now wanted to show the jurors how Michael Chia had been involved. He discussed how a deputy sheriff who had been patrolling in the East Los Angeles area had become involved. The deputy had heard a broadcast about some of the parties involved in the shootout. To see if he could be of help, he crossed into the City of Monterey Park. Ironically, around 12:45 p.m. near the Tiny Naylor's restaurant, the deputy saw a dark Mitsubishi. He couldn't believe what he had seen.

He started following the Mitsubishi, which contained three people, including Chia, who was the driver. The car continued to proceed northbound on Atlantic

Boulevard. He told the dispatcher that he was following the wanted car. The deputy didn't want to attract the attention of the occupants, so he didn't turn on his red lights or siren. As he followed the car, he could see the head of a young woman bobbing up and down. All of a sudden the Mitsubishi stopped and the driver, who was Chia, got out and started walking around in the middle of the street. As he stood there a dozen police units converged on the area. Law Enforcement didn't want anyone to get away. Chia and his two passengers were taken into custody without any incident on Atlantic Boulevard near Garvey Avenue.

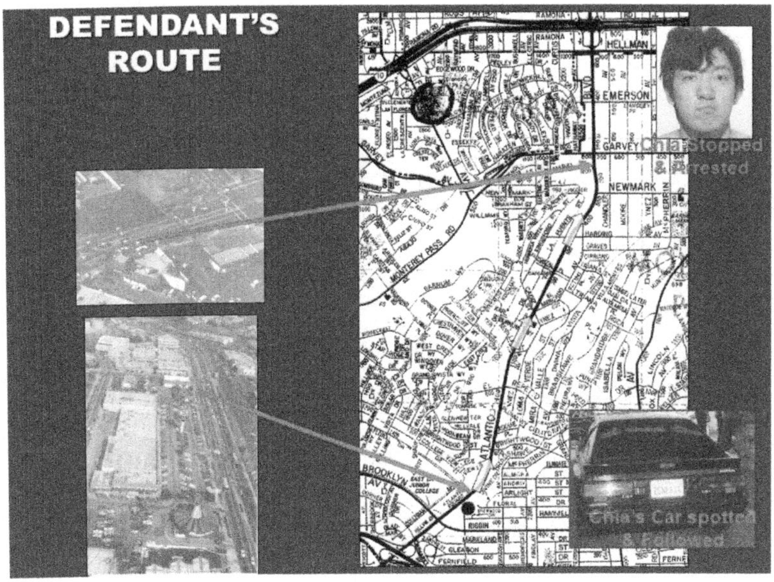

After connecting Chia's involvement into the countersurveillance activity, Darrell needed some way to summarize the case. He used what is called the Charges Against the Defendant visual to explain what the charges were and how they applied to defendant Michael Chia.

Darrell completed his Opening Statement and sat down. The Defense attorney started attacking the prosecution's case. He told the jury that the Defense would show that the only reason Chia was present in the Tiny Naylor's parking lot was to persuade his friend Wang out of being involved in the Rip-off.

CHAPTER 19 TIME FOR TRIAL

Trial time can be a nerve-racking experience for prosecutors since there are so many false starts on the big cases. You might have a firm date by which the judge has ordered everyone to be ready. But in the real world, Murphy's Law will find some cause for a delay. It may be that the Defense attorney is tied up in another trial or the judge's courtroom is engaged in trial of another case that lasted longer than expected. When the prosecutor agrees to a trial date, he or she has to have all the witnesses lined up to testify.

Witnesses can be upset when they have made plans to come to court and learn that the matter has to be continued and they have to set aside another date in the future to come to court and testify. A witness becomes upset for the disruption he or she has to endure. As a result, the witnesses tend to take it out on the prosecutor who continues to subpoena them to come to court. Prosecutors have to possess unique diplomatic skills to convince the unhappy witnesses to continue to cooperate.

With all this confusion and hassle one would think that Darrell would be frazzled by all the stress that comes along with the actual start of the trial. However, he projects complete calm, and all the chaos going on around him roles off him like water off a duck's back.

When Darrell enters the courtroom his customary attire is a three-button dark-blue suit that gives him a formal appearance. He often wears a red power tie during the Argument to the jury. Some say he resembles the famous attorney of bygone years, Clarence Darrow, who was considered one of the Great American Lawyers. Clarence Darrow was described as a sophisticated country lawyer, which isn't a bad description of Darrell Mavis.

Others claim Darrell is more like William Jennings Bryan, who was considered one of the great American orators of all time. If there is ever a modern-day 'Scopes Monkey Trial,' Darrell could be either the new Clarence Darrow or even the new William Jennings Bryan.

When Darrell encounters serious obstacles in his path, he only gives a pleasant smile and merely says we will somehow work it out. He doesn't let the little things distract him but maintains his focus on what ultimately needs to be done.

In the Chia case, Darrell had figured out what he needed to do to convince the jury that Chia was materially involved with the Rip-off of the two DEA agents. He came up with the idea of doing a reenactment that could be shown to the jury and authenticated by each of the surveillance agents who would be testifying.

What this reenactment showed was the defendant coming into the Tiny Naylor's parking lot four times and waiting in his car for considerable time and then leaving. On another occasion, he walked over to his friends Wang and Sun and talked to them and then went into the restaurant by himself. After being inside for several minutes, he came out, got in his car, and drove over to where Kow was standing and had a conversation with him. By looking at the reenactment, anyone could see how much Chia was involved in the 'counter-surveillance' part of the Rip-off.

This reenactment consisted of a 20-slide PowerPoint presentation with a title page describing the activity with the date and time. The next slide was a Legend explaining that the solid color lines represented certain cars and the hash lines represented the paths walked by suspects Kow, Chia, and Wang.

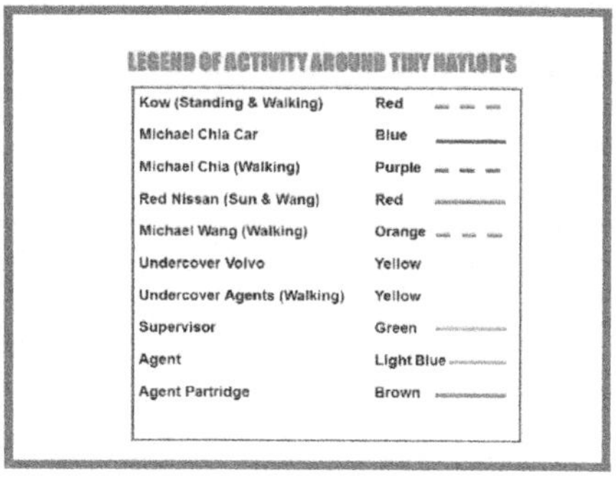

The first diagram represents how Chia originally drove into the parking lot and parked in one of the parking spaces. He remained there for several minutes, after which he drove off.

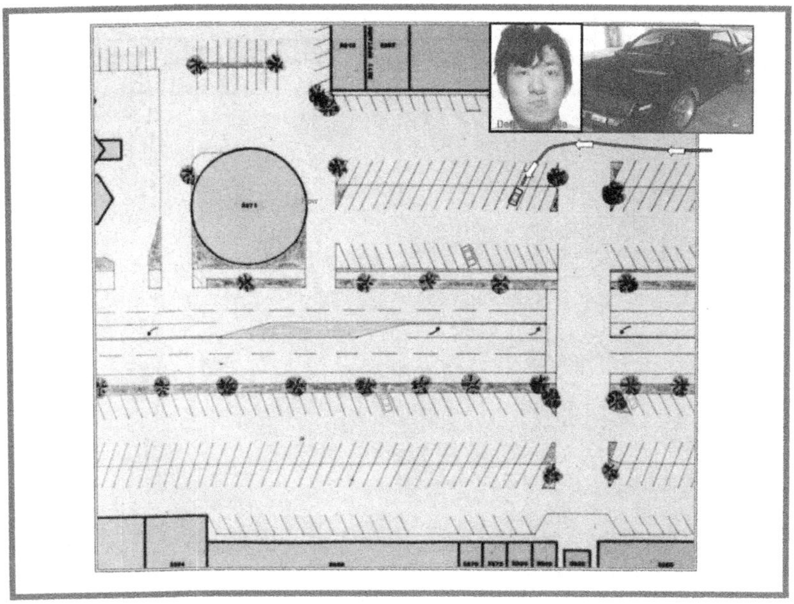

The second diagram showed the path Chia drove his car down to the entrance to the Tiny Naylor's restaurant.

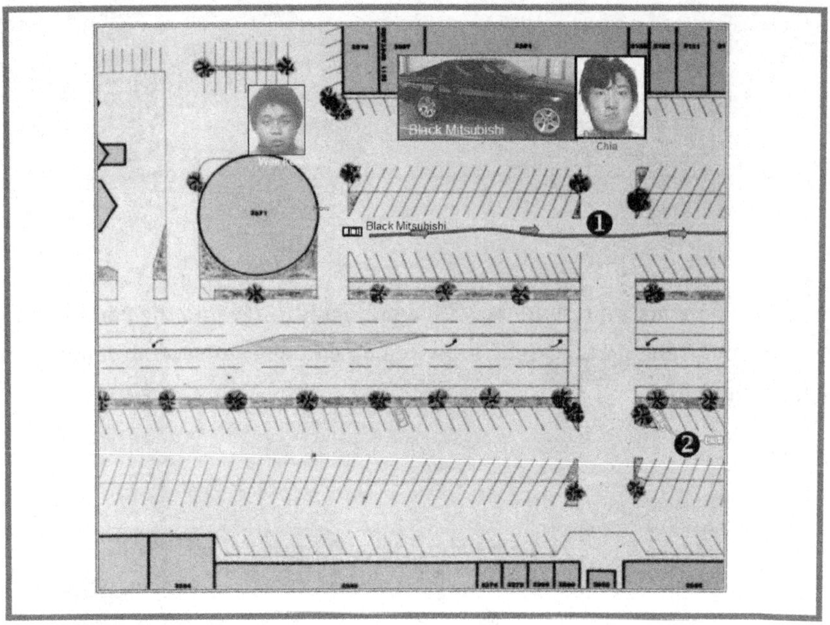

The third diagram illustrated how Chia had contact with Wang and later drove out of the parking lot as the two agents and Kow were inside the restaurant.

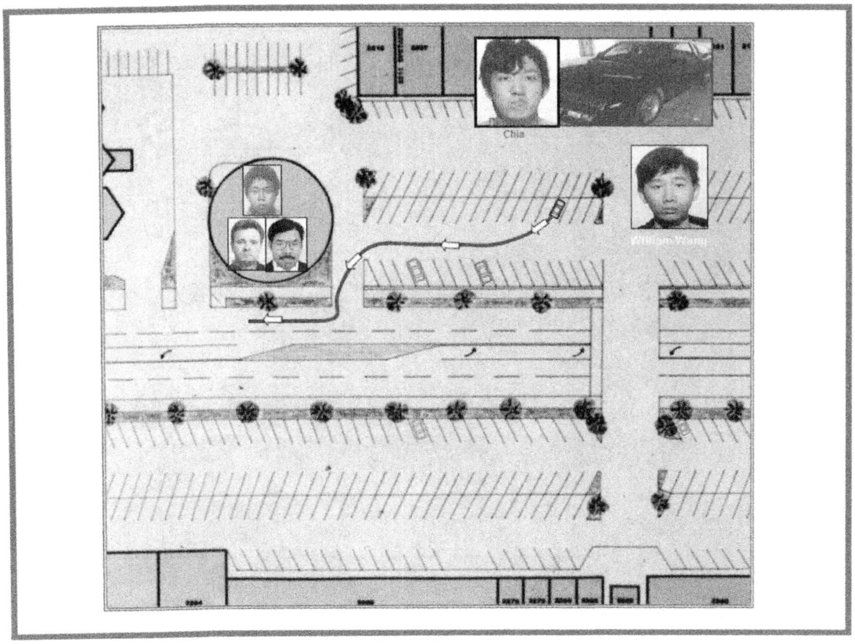

The fourth diagram showed Chia driving back into the parking lot and parking in the same location as before and just sitting in his vehicle as the two agents and Kow exited the restaurant.

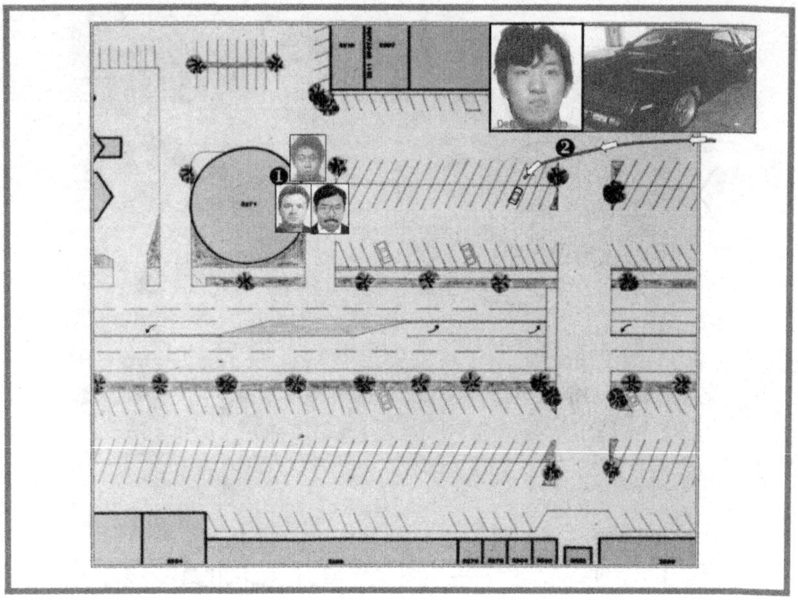

The following diagram showed the flashing of the money inside the Volvo.

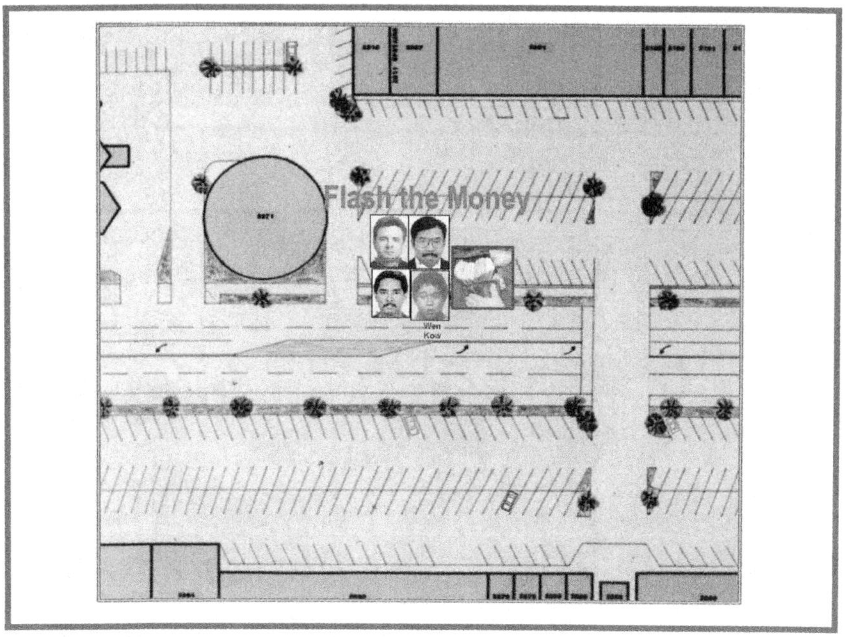

The following diagram showed Chia return to park again where he had parked before.

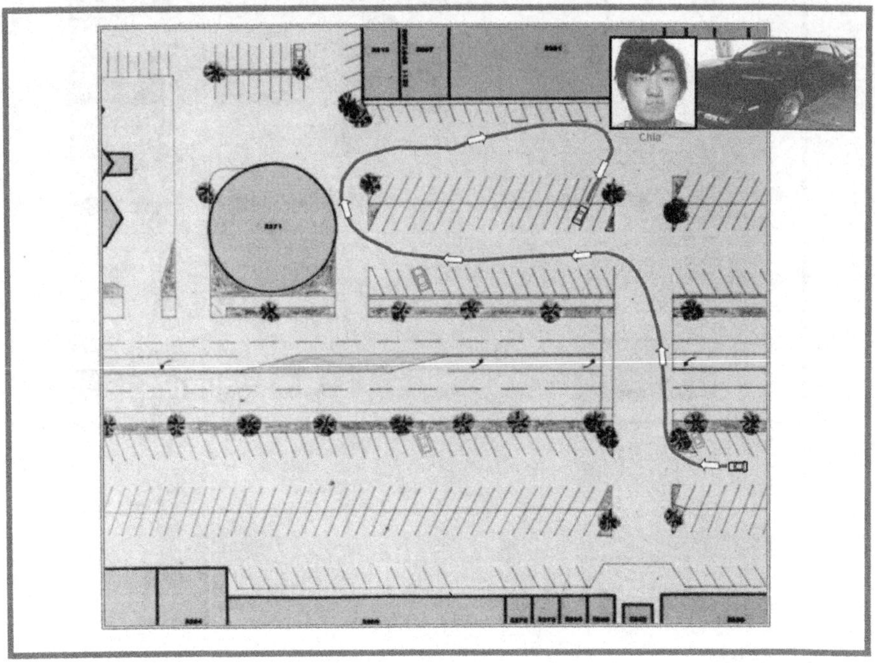

The final diagram of the reenactment showed Chia driving through the parking lot of the shopping center across the street and leaving by making a left turn as the agents' Volvo turned northbound on Atlantic Boulevard. As a result, Chia couldn't have followed the car going to the Rip-off in Pasadena.

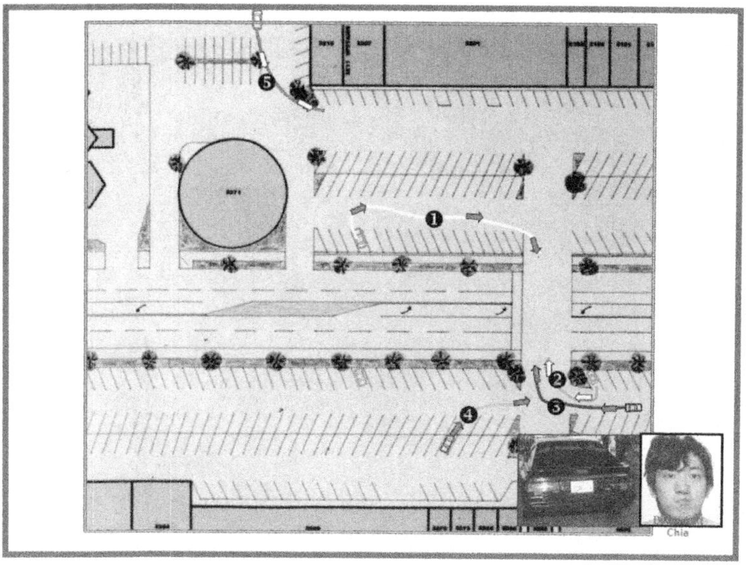

Darrell played this series of slides for each of the surveillance officers so they could authenticate that the actions of Chia in the slideshow were accurate.

During the trial, Darrell had to present all the necessary evidence to prove the Rip-off and the ultimate shootout. However, the crucial

evidence that Darrell wanted the jurors to remember was how involved Chia was in his driving around in the Tiny Naylor's restaurant parking lot.

CHAPTER 20 THE DEFENSE STRATEGY

There was a great deal of trial strategy that went into deciding how best to present the case to the jury. The defendant had not taken the witness stand in his first trial. It was unknown if he would take the witness stand in his second trial. The prosecution usually likes to cross-examine the defendant in the case if he or she decides to testify. Most defendants are not very convincing when they testify. As a rule Defense attorneys try not to have their defendants testify.

The Defense looks for ways to use other witnesses to tell the defendant's side of the case. Such witnesses could be friends or relatives of the defendant. In some cases it can be officers or detectives who the defendant had talked to. If those people can tell the defendant's story to the jury, then the defendant isn't subjected to cross-examination.

In this retrial, the Defense attorney had hoped to present the defendant's version of the facts by using certain prior inconsistent statements that the defendant had made to the investigators. However, the law states that the Defense can't introduce the defendant's prior statements without the defendant first testifying.

On the other hand, the prosecution can introduce the defendant's prior statements even though they would be Hearsay since they come within the Hearsay Exception as they are statements made against penal interest. Even though the defendant made some self-serving statements, Darrell wanted to introduce the inconsistent statements to show that Chia was in fact present in the Tiny Naylor's parking lot.

But Darrell's dilemma was that if he introduced Chia's statements, that would mean that the defendant wouldn't need to take the witnesses stand. So Darrell made the strategic decision not to use the statements, in hopes this would force the defendant to take the witness stand to explain his story as to his involvement, in which case he would then be subject to cross-examination.

To illustrate the DA's dilemma, Darrell had prepared the below chart which he was going to use in his final Argument to the jury. The chart showed what Chia had told the police originally and in the second column showed what he had told the police later. All the inconsistent statements made Chia look like a liar.

Darrell's strategy seemed to be working, and he was putting pressure on the Defense attorney to force his client Chia to testify. It appeared that the prosecution had boxed the Defense into a corner. But to Darrell's and everyone else's surprise, the Defense took a different approach. The Defense decided not to call Chia as a witness but to call the co-defendant William Wang. In that way, the Defense could get the defendant's story before the jury without Chia testifying. This would prevent the prosecution from getting all the inconsistent statements before the jury which would put the defendant in a bad light. As a result, Darrell decided to forgo the use of the above chart, which would never be seen by the jury during the Argument.

The calling of Wang by the Defense changed the dynamics of the case. The prosecution was placed at a disadvantage. At this point, Darrell would have to carefully cross-examine Wang so as to discredit his testimony. This would be difficult to do since he had had years to prepare for his testimony. At the first trial, Wang was convicted of killing the two DEA agents and had been sentenced to Life in Prison without the possibility of parole. Wang had nothing to lose in trying to help his friend. Even the threat of perjury wasn't a deterrent to a person in his situation.

When Wang testified he minimized Chia's involvement. He claimed that Chia was only trying to prevent any harm to come to him, Wang. He claimed that Chia was not part of the conspiracy plan and wasn't going to share in the proceeds of the robbery.

Then it was Darrell's turn to cross-examine Wang. Darrell asked Wang some pointed questions which caused him some difficulty in answering. When Darrell asked what the intention of the conspiracy was, both Darrell and everyone in the courtroom were surprised at Wang's answer. Wang admitted that it had been decided that he and Kow would kill the so-called "drug buyers" after they had robbed them of the $80,000. This seemed to be a callous approach that wasn't going to make Wang a sympathetic witness for the Defense in the eyes of the jury.

CHAPTER 21 A 'GOT YOU MOMENT'

Darrell walked Wang through Chia's movements in the Tiny Naylor's parking lot. Wang continued to say that Chia wasn't involved in the meeting in the parking lot. When Wang was pressed, he denied that Chia's car was parked in the restaurant parking lot. As a matter of fact, Wang testified that he and Sun weren't parked in the red Nissan which was backed up to Atlantic Boulevard. After Wang had adamantly committed himself to this story, Darrell asked the judge if he could approach the witness to show him a photo exhibit. The judge granted permission and Darrell reached down to the counsel table and casually picked up the photo of Chia's car parked in the Tiny Naylor's parking lot. Darrell walked by the jury box and stood near the witness stand. He placed the photo exhibit directly in front of Wang and asked him to look at it.

Up to this point, Wang must have been pleased in that his testimony was helping his old friend Chia. A surprised look came over his face. Within an instant, a slight smile came across Wang's face, and then there was a long pause. Darrell tried hard not to show any expression on his face. This was one of those 'Got You' moments where you don't want the jurors to see glee on your face.

Wang looked at the surveillance photo that showed that Chia's Mitsubishi was parked only several cars over from the red Nissan which Wang and Sun were using. Wang had to admit that he didn't know about the existence of this surveillance photo before testifying. With this one photo, Darrell had seriously impeached Wang's credibility. The photo proved that Chia was more involved than Wang was trying to convince the jury.

Wang continued to testify that the conspiracy plan was constantly changing. He testified that when he was aware of the three parties in the undercover car, he tried to contact Kow, who had already gone into the Tiny Naylor's restaurant to discuss the details of the deal with the so-called buyers. Wang testified that he went to a payphone to call Kow on his pager. Darrell pressed Wang on that point, in that Kow had seen the undercover agents drive up. Kow would have been able to see that there were three people in the car. There was no reason for Wang to warn Kow that there were three buyers since he had already seen the three.

At that point Wang's composure seemed to crumble. His answers seemed more guarded, and he was having difficulty keeping the facts straight. The Defense's claim that Chia wasn't present and had nothing to do with the Rip-off wasn't supported by the evidence.

The Defense continued to call additional witnesses to support the Defense position that Chia wasn't part of the conspiracy. The Defense decided to call the occupants in Chia's car when the deputy Sheriff pulled him over and arrested him. The female who was in Chia's car when it was stopped testified that Chia had called her at 11:45 a.m. She had told him that she needed a ride to the Pasadena courthouse to pay for a traffic ticket. Chia agreed to help her out and it was decided to pick her up at Jimmy Sun's apartment in Alhambra in order to drive her to court. When Chia arrived to pick her up it was agreed to take Jimmy Sun to work at an auto supply store south of the Tiny Naylor's restaurant.

She testified that Chia initially drove by the Tiny Naylor's restaurant so Jimmy Sun could get to work on time. After dropping off Jimmy Sun, she testified that Chia continued to driver her and a male friend northbound on Atlantic Boulevard. That was when a deputy sheriff started following them. She became frightened after Chia had stopped and a swarm of police cars surrounded them.

Her testimony was supposed to show that Chia couldn't be involved in this big conspiracy if he was merely transporting her to the Pasadena courthouse to pay a traffic ticket. However, her testimony ended up helping the prosecution since her times seemed to be off. She was adamant that Chia called the apartment at 11:45 a.m. and spoke to her about her need for a ride. In fact, there were many people who placed Chia driving around Tiny Naylor's parking lot up to 12:15 p.m. If such call were made, it would have to have occurred sometime after 12:15 p.m. or much later.

The Defense had done a masterful job of getting Chia's version of the facts in front of the jury without having the defendant to testify. The big question was whether the jury was going to put much credence in the testimony of the Defense witnesses such as Wang and the woman in Chia's car. The Defense originally tried to make it appear that Chia was not in the Tiny Naylor's parking lot. However, when the photo showed his car was present then they modified their Defense that he might have been there but he didn't do anything to further the Conspiracy.

CHAPTER 22 TIME FOR ARGUMENT

Based on Darrell's past academic achievements at Oxford, MIT, and Harvard, one would think that when it was time for Argument Darrell would appear to be cerebral. How could he relate to jurors who never experienced his Ivy League world? Through years of trial and error, Darrell had learned there are effective ways of arguing a case to the jury.

Attorneys by their very nature like to express themselves in a vocal manner. There is nothing wrong with speaking up and wanting to be heard. However, many attorneys don't know when to stop talking. Some critics claim that attorneys act like they are being paid by the word. Others claim that attorneys like to overanalyze things and are constantly trying to define things in legalese. Some say that some attorneys seem to be trying to impress their clients or in some cases the news media.

Sometimes the attorney misses the point that the Argument needs to be directed to the 12 jurors. Many male attorneys like to use their deep baritone voices to mesmerize the jurors. Even women attorneys will try to speak louder than the other attorney. It seems to be a contest as to who is the loudest. The infamous saying is that the 'loudest barrels are often the empty ones.'

Darrell certainly has learned that the decibel level and the verbosity of an Argument doesn't cut it with jurors. He takes a more relaxed approach as though he were talking to a neighbor over the backyard fence. He looks them in the eye and uses commonsense words to explain the evidence. He maintains affability and doesn't resort to name calling.

If he doesn't do dramatics and use catchy phrases, how does he maintain the jurors' interest? Darrell recognizes that communicating with a jury requires a two-pronged approach. Merely standing up in front of 12 jurors spewing one word after another can only work for a short time. However, all humans (even jurors) have short interest spans. In order to maintain the jurors' interest, the attorney needs something to catch their attention. That is when Darrell uses his visual aids to get the juror to focus on the point he is explaining. By meshing the sense of hearing with the sense of sight, the jurors' brain takes notice.

As stated earlier, Darrell had used a PowerPoint slide show as part of his Opening Statement. Likewise, he uses much of his earlier slides as part of his Argument. The main difference is that during his Opening Statement he was only telling the jurors what evidence he planned to present in court. However, in his Argument he flashes on the screen what he showed them in the Opening, and then he reviews what witnesses he used to prove that particular fact.

In part, Darrell's PowerPoint slide show is just solidifying in the jurors' minds that he did what he said he would do. However, there were several new slides that Darrell had inserted. One involved countering the Defense's claim that the occupants of the Red Nissan were unarmed and the cops had used unnecessary force against them. Darrell wanted the jurors to understand that allegation was untrue. It showed that there were three firearms in the red Nissan along with the three occupants.

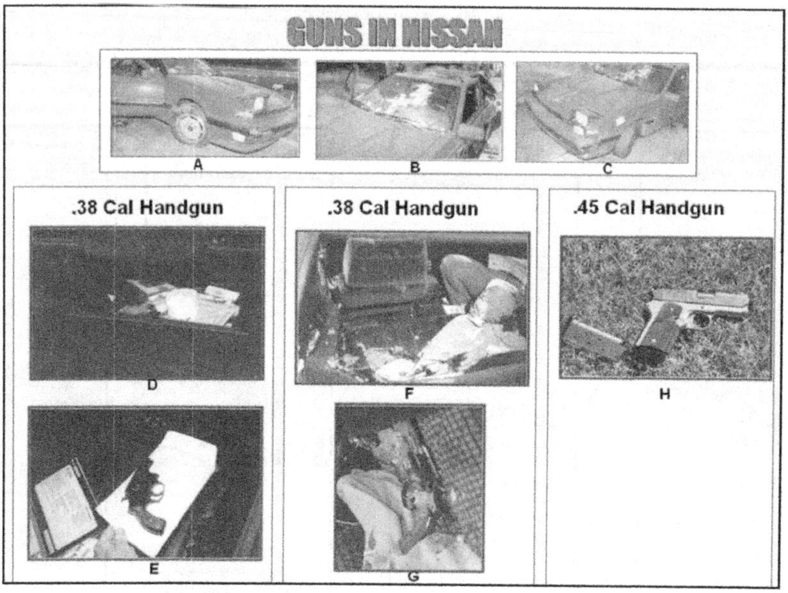

Two of the firearms in the car were .38 caliber handguns. One gun was found in the glove compartment and the other was found in the backseat. One of the .38 revolvers had been fired. Also found on the grass next to one of the dead suspects was a .45 semi-automatic.

Darrell recognized how important the .45 handgun was. It was the key gun that had a nexus to Chia. Darrell used the visual below to show the connection of the .45 to defendant Chia.

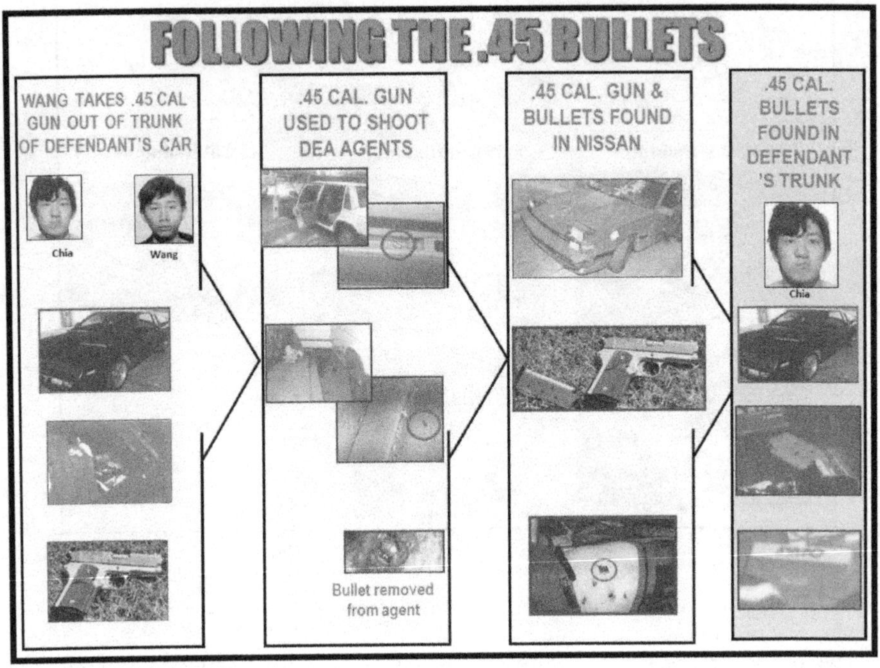

In the left arrow box, Darrell showed that Chia had opened his trunk and stood there as Wang took out a .45 semi-automatic and later carried it up to Kow's apartment. Darrell discussed the testimony of the female agent who said that she definitely could make out the firearm taken from Chia's car to be a .45 semi-automatic.

The next column on the visual showed that .45 caliber shell casings were found in the Volvo after the shooting and there was also a .45 slug removed from DEA agent George Montoya. The third column shows a .45 caliber semi-automatic which was found next to the Nissan as well as several live .45 caliber bullets.

Finally, the last column provided the corroboration that .45 caliber ammunition was found in Chia's trunk. By using this one visual, Darrel was proving to the jurors that Chia was a part of the conspiracy to Rip Off the agents.

The below visual was used by Darrell to show that the trunk of Chia's Mitsubishi contained so much incriminating evidence. Besides the .45 ammunition, there were three handcuffs and three ski masks in Chia's car

Darrell argued Chia was a participant in the Rip-off conspiracy. He may not have been as involved as Kow the so-called 'point person.' Darrell argued that the facts showed that Chia was the one who supplied the .45 semi-automatic that was used to pull off the robbery and shoot one of the victims. Then Darrell went to great lengths to make sure that all the jurors understood that Chia was definitely conducting countersurveillance in the parking lot. Darrell played the PowerPoint labeled "Chia's Counter Surveillance" so the jurors could see that Chia continued to drive his car around the Tiny Naylor's parking lot.

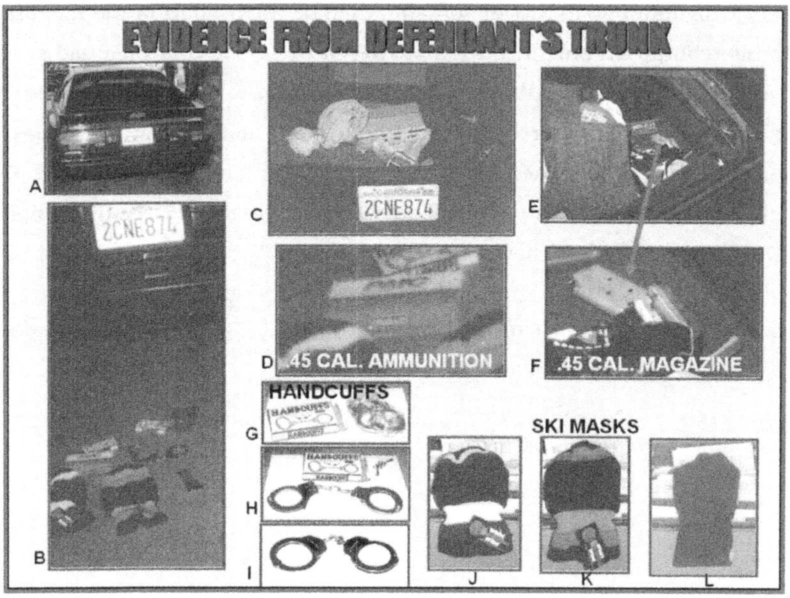

This prepared slide show didn't show Chia trying to reach his friend Wang in order to dissuade him from getting involved in the shootout. Chia was not following his friend Wang when he moved about the parking lot. Darrell argued that Chia's activity was more consistent with an active member of the conspiracy trying to make sure that the "drug buyers" were alone and that this was not in fact an undercover buy situation.

After Darrell had finished his Argument, the Defense attorney stood up and walked over to the jury box and addressed the jurors. He argued that Chia was merely trying to talk his friend Wang out of getting involved in the Rip-off. The attorney emphasized what a deep friendship Chia and Wang had. He explained how Chia wanted to make sure that his friend didn't get into something over his head.

The Defense attorney then made a transition in his Argument. He stressed the fact that no witness could place Chia anywhere near the Rip-off or the shootout. In fact the agents when they were testifying admitted that the last time they saw Chia was when he was crossing Atlantic Boulevard. The Defense reasoning was that since he didn't go to the Rip-off site, then he wasn't part of the Rip-off.

In his rebuttal argument, Darrell answered by saying that Chia had positioned himself at the signal on Atlantic Boulevard in such a way that he couldn't turn right and follow the undercover car without being noticed by the parties in the Volvo. That is why he turned left and never was able to be a part of the Rip-off. Darrell suggested that Chia possibly had spotted both agent Steve Geller and agent Leo Duff (pseudonym) as they started to follow the Volvo as it proceeded north on Atlantic Boulevard. Chia might have realized that things had gone bad and that he needed to situate himself with friends that could provide him with an alibi if the Rip-off didn't go well.

CHAPTER 23 IT'S FINALLY OVER DELIBERATION

After the Argument, both sides rested and the jury began its deliberation. The jury later during the deliberation had a question for the judge. They wanted some clarification as to the definition of Aiding and Abetting. The judge re-explained that if the defendant doesn't participate in the actual crime such as in this case the robbery or the murder, he can still be guilty of those crimes if he did anything in furthering those crimes to occur.

The jury continued to deliberate and on the third day they sent word that they had reached a verdict. The courtroom filled with spectators. Darrell had made a promise to agent Montoya's father that he would call him so he could be present for the reading of the verdict. The problem was that he lived some 20 miles away, which could take considerable time with LA freeway traffic. Darrell had quickly called Mr. Montoya, who said he was on his way to court. Then Darrell tried to diplomatically stall the reading of the verdict so the elderly Mr. Montoya would have sufficient time to be present.

Darrell was trying to make himself appear to be busy to further delay the verdict. However, he could see that the courtroom clerk was growing impatient after an hour delay. The pressure was on him to get things moving. He told the court personnel that he was going to walk out into the hallway to see if Mr. Montoya had arrived. Darrell strolled down to the elevators to look for any sign of him.

Darrell turned around to return to the courtroom feeling regret that he hadn't been able to keep his word to the victim's father. As he took one step down the hall he heard the elevator doors open. He stopped in his tracks and spun around to look at the elevator door. A broad smile came over his face as he saw the elderly Mr. Montoya shuffling out of the elevator.

Darrell had to wonder why he was trying to keep his word since the verdict could be a not guilty, which would be devastating for the Montoya family. Darrell greeted Mr. Montoya and told his law clerk to walk Mr. Montoya to the courtroom at the end of the hall. Darrell returned, in a half jog, trotted back to the courtroom. When he entered he hurriedly told the clerk everyone was present and as he took his seat at counsel table.

The Ninth Circuit Court of Appeal had certainly made it almost impossible to re-try the case for the prosecution. Darrell had done the best job possible with the limited amount of evidence that was still available. It was grueling sitting and waiting for the clerk to read the verdicts. If the verdicts didn't go well for the prosecution there would be many disappointed people.

The wait was soon over and the word "GUILTY" filled the courtroom. The jury found the defendant Chia guilty of First Degree Murder for the death of agents Paul Seema and George Montoya as well as Attempted Murder of Jose Medina. There were many emotions in the courtroom at that moment. Mr. Montoya put his head down, which seemed to show the relief he felt in hearing that the defendant hadn't gotten away with the death of his son, George Montoya.

When the Ninth Circuit Court of Appeal reversed Chia's case it reopened many deep wounds. Now it would take some additional time for the wounds to heal and for everyone to get on with their lives. This time the victims' relatives and all the old DEA agents were more skeptical in thinking of final closure. Was it possible that the Ninth Circuit Court of Appeal would try again to find a way to reverse this case?

CHAPTER 24 SOMETHINGS NEVER SEEM TO END

Not long after the ink was dry on the new conviction, Chia's attorney again filed an appeal. The basis for the appeal was that there was insufficient evidence to support the jury's finding that he aided and abetted the robbery, murders, and attempted murder. In particular, Chia claimed that the evidence didn't show that he acted with the intent to encourage or facilitate the crimes. The state appellate court reviewed all the evidence and said that there was more than enough evidence.

The second issue on appeal centered on the fact that the trial court had permitted the prosecutor to use a PowerPoint presentation at trial. The appellate court ruled that they had viewed the presentation and found nothing objectionable about it because all it did was illustrate the testimony of the DEA agents who were present at the scene. The relevance of the diagram as an aid to understanding the agents' testimony was great, whereas its prejudice, if any, was minimal at most and its admission was certainly not an abuse of discretion.

The state court of appeal made its ruling in 2007. It is unclear if and when the Ninth Circuit of Appeal will hear the case possibly on another Writ of Habeas Corpus. Will there be other judges looking for Perfect Justice? Will they again reverse Michael Chia's conviction on additional grounds? Or will the appellate courts allow the DEA agents and their families to have final closure?

Life moved on for everyone, especially the prosecutor Darrell Mavis, who had a very distinguished legal career as a prosecutor. I, the author, would like to take some credit for Darrell's success. My role was that I was in charge of the DA attorney hiring. Years earlier I decided to send someone to conduct interviews at Harvard Law School. I was greatly surprised when Darrell agreed to join the District Attorney's Office. He could have gone with any prestigious law firm and made a ton of money.

When we hired Darrell as a new deputy district attorney I could tell he was highly motivated. He was eager to gain as much experience in the shortest amount of time. In 1992 he immediately started trying DUI cases for the DA's Office. He continued to try any and all types of cases until 1998 when he moved over to the US Department of Justice for a short period between1998 to 2000. Upon his return to the Los Angeles DA's Office, he was soon transferred to the prestigious Major Crimes Division where he was given the toughest cases to try. There he remained until 2006 when he received an appointment to be a Superior Court judge.

He has been recognized for his keen legal mind and has been a member of the visiting Faculty for the Harvard Law School Trial Advocacy Workshop as well as an adjunct Professor of Law at Southwestern Law School. He was also the Chair of the State Bar's Criminal Law Section Executive Committee for a number of years.

The LADA's Office is pleased that he has become a distinguished juris on the Superior Court bench. However, the DA's Office will always regret losing him as a prosecutor because without a doubt Darrell Mavis will forever be considered a **SUPERSTAR PROSECUTOR.**

THE BROTHER SISTER BOND IS FOREVER??

People v. Gallegos and Cepeda

SUPERSTAR PROSECUTOR

Darrell Mavis

CHAPTER 25 BROTHER CHARLES AND SISTER CARMEN

This next case is an example of how certain cases can be impossible to understand. The Gallegos case involved an extraordinary convoluted set of facts. The DA's Office recognized the intricacy of the case and immediately transferred the case to the Major Crimes Division. The DA administrators realized that this case required a highly skilled prosecutor who could figure out how to explain the facts and the law to a jury. This is another homicide case which was assigned to prosecutor Darrell Mavis because of his unique ability to take a complex set of facts and somehow convert it into simple commonsense terms which jurors could understand.

The Gallegos case was added to this book for the purpose of illustrating how certain attorneys have a knack of being effective communicators. You, the reader, have already seen in the prior Chia case how Darrell was able to use visuals to present the facts to jurors. In the Gallegos case Darrell developed the below visual chart in order to put the facts in perspective and show how everything fits together. You will see that without reviewing this visual it is next to impossible to keep straight the facts as to who did what to whom and when. Also, the relationship between the parties is essential to understand in order to know what really happened.

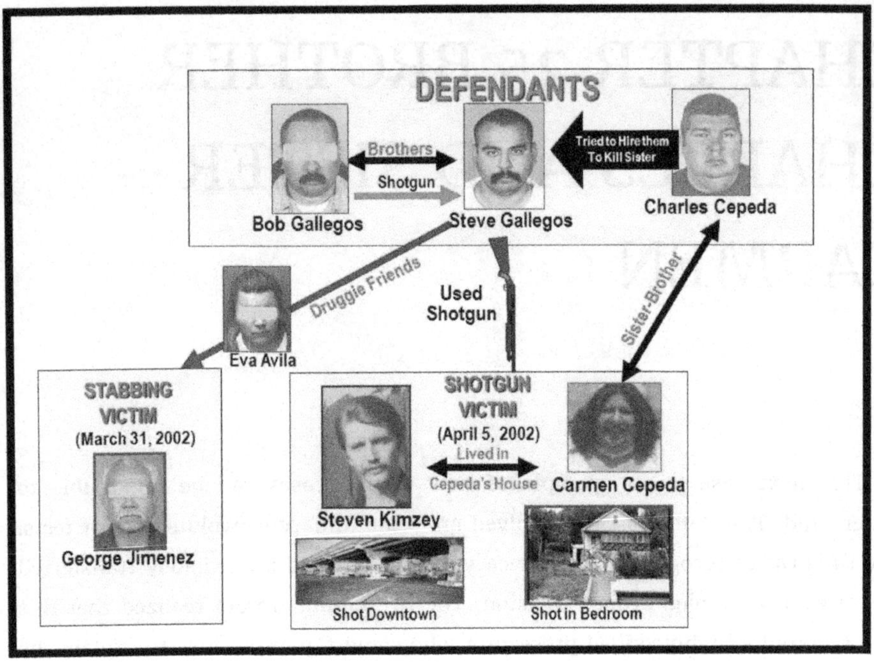

Make sure you have reviewed the above chart and are familiar with the information on it before you start reading the facts of this Gallegos case, which is spelled out on the next few pages. You may want to refer back to this chart throughout our discussion.

This story involves the unique bond between a brother, Charles, and his sister, Carmen. Many of us grew up with siblings and are familiar with the special relationship that is formed during childhood. We all remember famous brother-and-sister stars from the movies, such as Warren Beatty and Shirley MacLaine, as well as Peter Fonda and Jane Fonda. More recent examples are John and Joan

Cusack, and of course no Christmas would be complete without hearing the seasonal songs sung by Karen Carpenter with her brother Richard.

Our fondness for brother-sister duos has been etched in our literature with Hansel and Gretel, and of course we all grew up reading ***To Kill a Mocking Bird***, with the character Scout Finch learning about life with her brother Jem. On the comedy side we have brother Bert and sister Lisa Simpson, who seem to find a crazy way to survive their dysfunctional family life.

There are few bonds stronger than that of a brother and sister. The Cepeda brother and sister were no different in that they were inseparable as children. They lived their life in a cozy bantam-size white house in the Silver Lake district near to downtown Los Angeles. Later, their parents divorced and their mother, Mrs. Cepeda, continued to reside in the house.

In order to earn extra money, mother Cepeda decided to become a guardian for a man by the name of Steven Kimzey who had a mental disability. Earlier in his life his frontal lobe was removed. In the 1930s and '40s frontal lobotomy surgery was thought to be a way to control seizures. The procedure was performed by inserting a scalpel-like tool through the temple on the side of the head and cutting or scraping away the nerve connections to the prefrontal cortex. One of the more well-known patients who underwent this operation was Rosemary Kennedy, sister of President John F. Kennedy. Unfortunately, the lobotomy procedure left her incapacitated for the rest of her life.

Although Mr. Kimzey's removal of his frontal lobe was not the result of a lobotomy, he still suffered the same fate in that he couldn't care for himself. This is where Mrs. Cepeda helped by making sure he had a place to stay and sufficient food to eat. At night he would sleep on the couch after everyone else had gone to bed.

After completing her schooling, Carmen Cepeda moved out of the family home. When she got married she and her husband resided in Long Beach. Carmen could be described as having an assertive personality. She exhibited some of the traits of the famous character from George Bizet's opera CARMEN. That Carmen was a fiery gypsy character who worked in a tobacco factory in Seville, Spain. She seduced a naïve soldier named Don Jose, who abandons his childhood sweetheart for the seductive Carmen. The couple's love continued until Carmen became attracted to a handsome matador. Don Jose reacts by falling into a jealous rage which results in him killing Carmen, the love of his life.

Everyone can agree that the Carmen in the opera didn't have a happy ending to her life. Her life ended in tragedy, in that someone who had loved her ended up killing her. One wonders whether the name 'Carmen' is jinxed.

Our Carmen in our case is definitely a strong-willed individual with a fiery personality. She wasn't hesitant in speaking up and never seemed to have any difficulty telling others where to go and what to do. Carmen and her brother Charles may have been close as children, but as they passed on into adulthood they went their separate ways.

CHAPTER 26 SISTER MOVES BACK HOME

Charles, the brother of Carmen, went into the military service and strayed away from living a responsible life. Charles had a propensity of doing the wrong thing and getting himself into trouble. After making numerous bad decisions and associating with too many bad dudes, his family considered him the 'Black Sheep' of the family. As a result, he was no longer welcomed in the family home.

Since he didn't seem to be able to hold down a permanent job and was always in need of money, he ended up staying with friends. His life evolved into sleeping on their couches and often setting up his residence in a utility closet.

Some people were intimated by Charles since he was very large in stature, weighing 350 pounds. But in reality he wasn't such a brute. Charles may have projected the image of a dim-witted person, but in fact it was just that he did stupid things. Granted, he wasn't the brightest star in the sky, but his biggest drawback was that he lacked motivation and discipline.

Carmen's marriage failed and the Cepeda family's world changed. Carmen's husband came to the realization that he couldn't live with such a strong personality any longer and bailed out of the marriage. This caught Carmen off guard and she was faced with the fact she couldn't afford to live on her own. The most logical solution was for her to persuade her mother to let her move back into the family home. Her mother was getting older and starting to exhibit symptoms of Alzheimer's disease. Carmen's return home was definitely a godsend for her mother.

When Carmen moved back into the house, she wholeheartedly started fixing things up and adding her personal touch to the redecorating of the kitchen. During her marriage she never had a house of her own which she could fix up to her liking. At this point in her life she wanted the opportunity to have a place to call 'her home.'

At the same time her brother, Charles, was becoming envious of his sister's good fortune of living in the family home. He started thinking about how he had to live his life out of boxes he stored in his friends' houses. Why should his pushy sister get to use the family house when he deserved it just as much as she did?

The truth was that the title of the house was in the name of their mother. As time went on, the mother's Alzheimer's disease became more severe. She barely recognized her children, and she didn't know what was going on around her. Charles obsessed over the fact that he was getting the short end of the stick. He resented his sister and let it be known how unfair he had been treated and that something should be done about it.

As every parent knows who has had two or more children, there is always the concern not to show favoritism to one of the children thereby slighting the others. At least parents try not to show any form of one-sidedness. However, every child is keenly aware of their standing with their parents. It is often the perception the child encounters that determines who the favorite child is. The problem is that each child places different values on the parents' actions of giving or doing some benefit for one child and thereby excluding the other child.

In this situation, Charles suspected that Carmen had manipulated their mother into giving the house to his sister upon the mother's death. Although he didn't know for a fact that Carmen had pursued their mother to leave the house to her alone, Charles just wanted to get his fair share, which he believed was half ownership in the house. On several occasions there were family discussions about writing up a will or setting up a trust to divide the property equally between both children. However, there was always some excuse as to why it never got done.

CHAPTER 27 NEED TO FIND A HIT MAN

Charles over a period of time became obsessed with the notion that his sister was making sure that he was cut out of their mother's will. He believed that his only option was to find a way to get his "mean old sister' out of the house. There didn't seem to be any way to force his sister to move out of the house. The mother's health had deteriorated, and Charles became more desperate and could think of only one option. He believed that his sister had to be taken care of. If the only option was killing Carmen, then the next question was how it should be done and by whom.

For Charles it wasn't a difficult decision since he didn't like his sister especially because she looked down on him through the years for being such a loser. What mainly concerned Charles was how to kill his sister and get away with it. He didn't want his sister to be laughing in her grave if he got caught for her murder. Finally it dawned on him that it would be best if he could get someone else to do the actual killing. In that way he could set up a perfect alibi that he was nowhere near where his sister was killed.

As he tried to find a 'Hit man,' he quickly learned that it wasn't easy to locate a 'hired gun.' You can't look under 'H' in the Yellow Pages for 'HIT MAN' to find a reliable, responsible, and reasonable killer. He thought of all the 'questionable' people he knew and he didn't feel comfortable asking any of them to kill his sister. Then he thought about his old friend Steve Gallegos, who had been into gangs during his youth. His old buddy Steve always seemed to have guns around when he needed them. Could he trust Steve Gallegos to kill his sister without getting caught?

In order to see if Steve Gallegos would be interested, Charles set up a meeting with him. When they met, Charles floated the idea of somehow he wanted his sister to disappear. It didn't take Steve a long time to figure out what Charles wanted. Steve seemed to be amenable to the idea. However, Steve wanted to know what he would gain by doing this hit for a friend. Charles knew that the house was worth several hundred thousand dollars. Charles was willing to share a large portion of the profit from selling the house. Charles wasn't greedy and he was willing to give his longtime friend Steven Gallegos whatever he wanted.

Steve would best be described as a short man who made up for his shortness by his willingness to use force. He was not adverse to threatening people. When Steve pulled out a gun he suddenly appeared 10 feet tall in the eyes of the victim he was threatening.

Steve agreed to help out his friend Charles by taking care of his sister, Carmen. However, he needed to obtain a gun that wouldn't be traceable back to him. Steve was no dummy, in that he knew that handguns leave evidence behind in the form of bullets and shell casings that can be traced back to a particular gun that is recovered.

Steve had the brilliant idea that if he used a shotgun that fired buckshot there would be no traceable evidence left at the crime scene. That was when he focused on obtaining a shotgun to commit the killing. Steve knew that his brother George was in possession of a shotgun which he could borrow to shoot Carmen.

Steve and Charles thought about the situation as to how to carry out the shooting to deflect any suspicion that anyone would think that Charles was involved. The best way to do that was to make the killing look like a burglar broke into the house and there was a confrontation in which the burglar shot and killed Carmen. In that scenario, no one would think of Charles as a suspect since he had no reason to break into the house.

CHAPTER 28 TONIGHT IS THE NIGHT

It was Friday, April 5, 2002, and it was the big day to get rid of Carmen. Steve had been able to borrow a shotgun from one of his brothers. Charles drove his car to pick up Steve and they proceeded to the family house on Glendale Avenue where Charles and his sister had grown up. They parked a short distance away and waited impatiently in the car. The plan was not to be seen by any of the neighbors.

It had just turned 10:00 p.m. and no one was out walking about. The only sounds that could be heard were the barking of two dogs down the street. This was a blue-collar working-class area where everyone was in bed at this hour. Everyone was tired from a long, hard week of work. The Cepeda house was situated on top of a knoll. There were many steps to climb in order to reach the front door. This was the type of house young Halloween trick or treaters would avoid because of its lengthy set of stairs.

They waited in the car to review their plan and reflect on what they were about to do. Then it was time for both of them to exit the car and take on the task before them. Charles was the leader of the pack, with Steve following behind carrying the shotgun. Steve tried to conceal the shotgun by the side of his right leg.

About halfway up the stairs, Charles, with his 350-pound frame, needed to rest in order to catch his breath. Steve was starting to feel the weight of the heavy shotgun and began to wonder why he didn't decide to use a lightweight 'Saturday

Night Special.' Even as Charles became winded from the lengthy stairs, he never had second thoughts about killing his sister.

Cepeda House
Glendale Blvd.

Finally, they reached the top and walked to the front door. Steve looked at Charles and said, "Are you ready?" Charles, who was out of breath, sort of nodded indicating 'Game On' showing that he was ready for the murder plan to be carried out. Charles grabbed the door handle and found the door to be firmly locked. Since he had grown up here, he knew the old front door could be easily forced open. With a hard push from his shoulder, the wooden door jamb broke loose and they went flying into the living room.

Cepeda House
Front Door

Since it was dark inside, they waited for their eyes to adjust to the darkness. They seemed frozen in place while quietly turning their heads side to side assessing the situation. Charles was out of breath and tried hard to conceal his heavy breathing. Charles knew that there should be three people in the house, and he couldn't afford to wait long in fear someone might unexpectedly wake up.

Charles knew that his sister's bedroom was the one nearest the front door. He motioned to Steve to follow him to the door of Carmen's bedroom. Steve went in first with the shotgun in his hand and Charles followed right behind.

This is a diagram of their house.

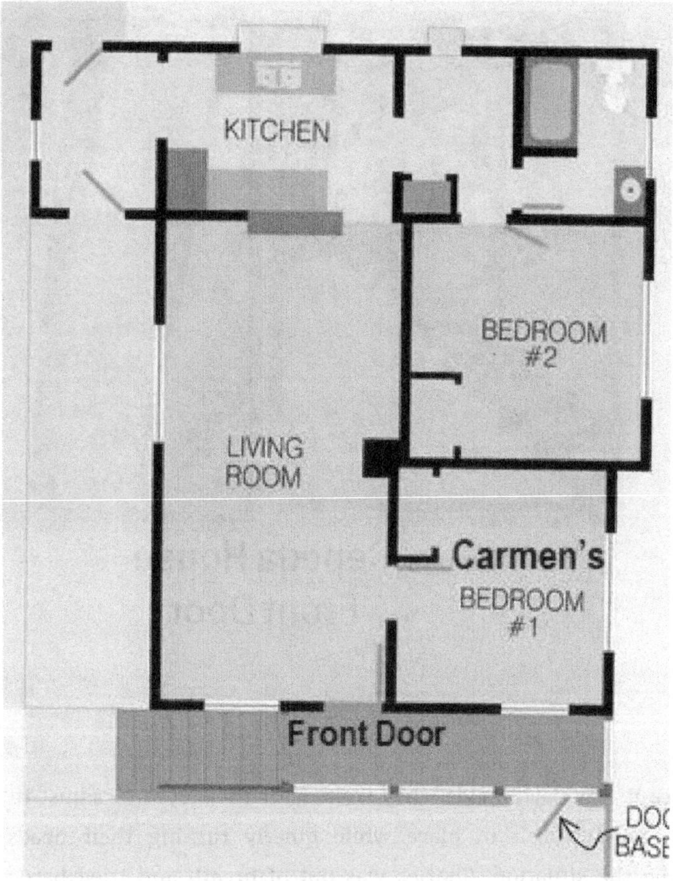

Diagram of House

CHAPTER 29 INSIDE CARMEN'S BEDROOM

As they entered the small bedroom they could make out a large lump covered by a bedspread. No one was moving and there was dead silence. Steve whispered, "Is that her?" Charles, looking directly at the bed, nodded in the affirmative. In one swift motion, Steve raised the shotgun up to his shoulder and pointed the gun at the large lump on the bed.

Carmen's Bedroom

At that moment he pulled the trigger and there was a thunderous blast that cut through the stillness of the night. Without any delay from the first blast was a second blast that reverberated through this small bedroom. Steve asked Charles if he had killed Carmen. They pulled back the bedspread to see if there was any life left in the body. Since it was pitch black, it was hard to see. Charles could faintly make out the figure of his sister, Carmen, who had been under the bedspread. Her body seemed to be moving. Was that movement just part of the death rattle, or could she have survived the blasts?

Steve motioned to Charles to move back. Steve raised the shotgun up again to his shoulder and aimed at the middle of Carmen's body. This was no easy feat for Steve since the room was so small and the shotgun was so long. Steve wanted to stand back just in case Carmen was merely injured and would try to grab the shotgun. He leaned far back to the side of the bed and pulled the trigger again and again. Each time Carmen's body rocked from side to side. Steve was satisfied that she was dead.

Even cold-blooded killers don't always know when enough is enough. Steve had lost count how many times he had shot at Carmen. By this time Steve and Charles almost became snickering. Charles' hatred for his sister seethed to the surface. They hatched the idea to shoot Carmen in the "ass." Charles was so ecstatic that he had triumphed over his nasty sister who had ignored him all these years. So for their coup de grace they stuck the barrel of the shotgun between her legs. This was the most indignant thing the two of them could think of doing. Then with great pleasure they emptied the shotgun up her "ass."

The shotgun went silent when they ran out of ammunition. Their euphoria was hard to describe. Charles was happy to have revenge over his sister. Steve on the other hand felt he had won the mega lottery with the promised proceeds from the sale of the house.

Expended Shotgun Shell Casings

After all this shooting, Carmen's bedroom was littered with expended shotgun shells. Some were red and some were green, all in the festive colors of Christmas. No one was thinking of picking up the empty shells. By this time their main concern was getting out of the house without being seen. But first they wanted to mess up the house to make it appear that a burglar had broken in and taken some property.

Their dilemma was whether to do a half-ass job so they could expedite their exit, or take their time messing up the house in hopes that the police didn't respond too quickly. They had to consider whether the noise from the shotgun blasts would have awakened neighbors who then would have called the police. Or would that shotgun racket have awakened the others inside the house? Charles knew that his mother was in the back bedroom, and he wondered whether all the uproar would have caused her to wake up to check on things. Steve and Charles quietly exited Carmen's bedroom.

CHAPTER 30 WHAT DO WE DO WITH THIS GUY?

As they turned around and retreated into the living room, they encountered Steven Kimzey, who was standing rubbing he eyes. He seemed dazed as to what had just happened. Charles knew that Kimzey had mental issues, so Charles wasn't too concerned. Steve on the other hand was surprised to find this person standing and looking at them just as they came out of Carmen's bedroom.

Steve's natural reaction was to lift up the shot gun and point it at Kimzey. Even with Kimzey's mental disability he recognized the seriousness of having a shotgun pointed at him. Kimzey was sufficiently frightened and meekly cowered next to the wall. As slender and submissive as Kimzey was, he definitely didn't pose any immediate threat to Steve and Charles.

For years Kimzey had lived in the bedroom where Carmen had just been killed. However, when Carmen moved back into the house with her mother, she took over Kimzey's old bedroom. That resulted in Kimzey having to sleep on the couch in the living room. Although it wasn't the most convenient arrangement for him, he willingly adapted to it since it was some place he could rely on. At night he took his shoes off and curled up on the couch with his clothes on.

After encountering Kimzey, the next person to appear was Mrs. Cepeda, the mother. She came from her back bedroom and started asking what was going on. Charles reassured his mother that everything was all right and for her to return to bed. The whole scene was sort of surreal. They had just shot and killed Carmen, and the mother with her Alzheimers was totally oblivious that her son had just assisted in killing her daughter.

Charles wasn't concerned about his mother fingering him, since she didn't have any memory of what was going on around her. Yet, the situation with Kimzey was quite different. Even though Kimzey was missing part of his frontal lobe, he still would be able to tell the police that it was Steve and Charles who came out of Carmen's room after all the noise. The guys realized that they needed to make a decision as to what to do with Kimzey. Steve had used up all the ammunition that they had brought with them inside the house.

As to Kimzey, he didn't know that the shotgun wasn't loaded, so he seemed to be sufficiently frightened of the shotgun. With every passing moment, Steve was becoming fearful that the police would have been notified and would be responding to the house. Both Steve and Charles knew that if they didn't quickly make an escape down the long set of stairs to the street they could soon be stranded inside the house when the authorities arrived.

As time was running out, Steve pointed the shotgun at Kimzey's head and ordered him to come with him as he approached the front door. When Kimzey walked by Carmen's bedroom, he tried to glance inside to see what had happened to her. Since it was too dark, he couldn't observe Carmen's dead body lying on her bed.

Kimzey then grasped that Steve was having him walk outside the house. Kimzey hesitated and tried to explain that he didn't have any shoes on and that he wanted to put them on. Steve curtly told him to keep walking in his socks as he walked out through the front door. Kimzey started the long descent down the stairs. Because of the stark darkness, Kimzey was moving slowly down the stairs without his shoes on.

The three of them deliberately snaked their way down the stairway. Since it was dark out, Kimzey cautiously took one step at a time trying not to stumble. Steve followed behind him, pointing the shotgun at Kimzey's back, and Charles was dragging up the rear. After descending the stairs they reached the wrought iron gates next to the street.

This was the moment of truth. What should the guys do with Kimzey? They could let him go in hopes that he wouldn't say anything to implicate either of them in the killing. Charles was well aware of Kimzey's reasoning process and the difficulty he had figuring out things like what day of the week it was. However, Steve had no interaction with Kimzey so he couldn't evaluate how serious a threat he posed for them.

Steve was a streetwise person and he didn't want to take any chances of getting caught. On his own Steve, made the executive decision to order Kimzey to get into the car so they could get him and themselves away from the crime scene. As Kimzey entered the car, Steve came to the realization that he couldn't easily point a long barrel shotgun at a person seated next to him in the car.

What surprised Steve was how docile Kimzey was, so he dropped the long shotgun on the floor of the car. Steve recognized that stern words could be just as frightening as the shotgun. Within seconds, Charles and Steve were pulling away from the curb. Kimzey was entirely cooperative and not posing any type of problem for the two of them. They kept driving toward the downtown area. They didn't know where to go, but they were smart enough to distance themselves from the crime scene. They continued driving, and Kimzey tried in his childish way to joke with the guys. They had to decide on what to do with Kimzey. Could they trust him to remain quiet as to their involvement? Charles didn't have any dislike for Kimzey, and had had enough killing for one day. Steve was more concerned and didn't want to take a chance that Kimzey would remain silent.

Charles' Vehicle

The three of them continued to drive eastbound on Sunset Boulevard in the direction of downtown Los Angeles. When they drove by the entrance to Dodger Stadium, the guys couldn't help but make a sarcastic comment about the team's chances during the coming season. Both Steve and Charles were ardent Dodger fans, but they hadn't seen a World Series since 1988. They were hoping this new season would put an end to the 15-year drought of a World Series. Within minutes the guys were downtown next to Olvera Street, the original roots of the city of Los Angeles when it was merely a Spanish barrio.

Steve's mind wasn't mulling over stopping to buy some tasty tacos every tourist has to try at the Olvera Street taco stands. He turned his thoughts to more practical things like how to get rid of Kimzey. The immediate problem was how to reload the shotgun without spooking Kimzey. The next question was where to carry out the killing of Kimzey. His concern was that if he used the shotgun the police might make a connection between both homicides. He decided that the further they took Kimzey away from the Silver Lake area the less likelihood the two killings would be linked together.

By then they had traveled a safe distance away. Steve and Charles were looking for a remote spot where there would be no witnesses. At this late hour the streets were devoid of any traffic.

CHAPTER 31 THE PERFECT PLACE TO KILL

When they turned north on Spring Street, they were passing through a homeless encampment under the connecting bridges of the Interstate 5 Freeway. This section runs along the Los Angeles River, which isn't anything more than a giant flood control channel consisting of concrete walls extending all the way to the sea. The bridges were like ribbons of concrete which the homeless use as roofs over their heads to protect them from the elements.

A homeless encampment wouldn't be complete without graffiti covering every surface. To some this may seem to be an eyesore, while others classify the graffiti as a perfect example of the freedom of expression. Most urbanites have a way of blocking out all the graffiti on the walls. This is an area of the city where most people ignore and stay away from. As the temperature rises, the stench can be overpowering from the homeless urinating and defecating all over the place. But at 2:00 a.m. the smell was tolerable since there was an evening breeze swirling through the underside of the North Spring Street Bridge.

Charles slowly pulled the car up directly under the bridge as the men surveyed the area. Not seeing any people wandering around, they told Kimzey to get out. He reluctantly opened the door and stepped out. He didn't know what was going to happen next. Should he run for his life or just stand there until told what to do? Since he didn't have any shoes on, he was reluctant to run through the area since there was broken glass. The headlights reflected the light from the smashed empty wine bottles. The next several seconds were going to be the pivotal point in everyone's lives.

Kimzey stood next to the car trying to be as obedient as a person could be who was missing part of his frontal lobe. He looked back at the guys seated in the car. His expression was more like a deer looking at the glare of headlights. Due to the lighting conditions, Kimzey couldn't see Steve pick up the shotgun from the floor of the car and point it at him.

Then Steve steadied his hand on the car's window edge in order to take better aim at Kimzey. Without a word being spoken, Steve gently pulled the trigger and the roar of the shotgun was deafening. Charles was shocked as to what Steve had just done. Steve also seemed to be startled, not so much by the noise but by the fact how the shotgun blast melted away the right side of Kimzey's face. Just like with the shooting of Carmen, Steve didn't know if he had killed Kimzey, who seemed to stagger backwards. Steve let loose with another blast. This one caused Kimzey to fall to the ground as lifeless as one can be.

Few people, besides professional hit men, have personal knowledge as to shooting people at such close range. What one may not comprehend is that when you blow a person's brains out it can be very messy. The entire right side of Charles' car was covered with brain and bone matter. Then Steve and Charles exited the car to assess the situation. They were shocked at the grotesque mess that had been created.

Their eyes surveyed all the blood and gore. However, their noses inhaled the stench of the burnt flesh from the shotgun blast. A panicked look came over their faces as to what to do next. If the police caught them in the car as it now looked, the two of them could end up fried in the electric chair if the state was still using it. Where does one go at 2:00 in the morning to clean the blood and brains off the outside of your car without attracting attention?

Charles wanted to tell Steve that it was a dumb idea to shoot someone with a shotgun so close to the car. But Charles could only think how thankful he was for Steve being willing to do the dirty work of killing his sister. He regretted that Kimzey had to be killed since Charles sorted liked the guy.

CHAPTER 32 TIME TO CLEAN UP

Charles knew that if they wanted to get away with a double murder, he had to clean up his car pronto. Charles thought of a friend he had in the city of Montebello by the name of Joe Alvarez (pseudonym). Charles occasionally stayed at his place when he needed a place to crash. Charles kept some of his clothes and personal belongings in one of Alvarez' closets. His friend Alvarez wasn't the judgmental type who would ask questions. Charles was confident that he could use Alvarez's place to wash his car off during the early morning hours.

Charles drove over to Alvarez' place in Montebello and he had to wake him up. Alvarez wasn't happy being disturbed by Charles at this early morning hour. When Charles asked if they could wash the car, Alvarez wondered why at that hour. He went out and looked at Charles' car and noticed what appeared to be red spots like blood all over the right side of the car.

Alvarez didn't want to get involved so he didn't ask any more questions. He turned around and matter of factually told Charles that the soap was in the cupboard and the bucket was in the backyard next to the hose. Charles and Steve picked up the items they needed and quietly washed down the filthy car in the dark of the night.

When Charles and Steve were finished with washing the car, they came inside with the shotgun and Charles put it in the closet with his personal belongings. He told Alvarez that he would come by and pick up the shotgun a little later in the day. Alvarez didn't ask any questions about the shotgun but was anxious for Charles to pick it up as soon as possible.

After the early morning car washing, Charles and Steve drove over to Steve's little house off of the Interstate 5 Freeway. Charles wanted to prepare himself for what was going to occur next. As the day progressed he knew that the authorities would learn of his sister's death and an investigation would occur.

Charles was no dummy. He knew that he would have to appear surprised when he was notified of his sister's death. Many family members knew how much he disliked his sister, so he couldn't appear to be crushed by the news of her death. But on the other hand he wanted to appear concerned and anxious in helping the police catch the person who killed her.

The police did contact him and he tried to appear surprised and willing to help. The police asked him about his whereabouts that evening and he stated that he had spent the entire evening with his good friend Steve Gallegos. This seemed to provide him with a solid alibi placing him some distance away from the house where Carmen had been killed.

Over the next several days, Charles played his role to a Tee. He appeared to be concerned about the death of his sister without overplaying his love for her. Since they had to do an autopsy on Carmen's body, the funeral had to be delayed until the police investigation was completed. At that point her body was turned over to the Forest Lawn Mortuary. Ten days would pass before the funeral could be held. Of course, everyone would be able to remember the funeral date since was on April 15th, which is a date that is indelibly etched in every American's mind as Tax Day. As the old saying goes, there are only two certainties in life and those are death and taxes. Well, April 15th had taken on a new meaning for Carmen's family and friends.

CHAPTER 33 WAKES AND FUNERALS CAN BE BORING

"The Wake" for the family and friends was set for the night before the funeral at the Forest Lawn Memorial Park and Mortuary in Glendale. The most recent internment of Michael Jackson had transformed this quiet resting place for celebrities into a new form of Disneyland. Fans from all over the world flocked to Forest Lawn to pay homage to their hero and mentor.

This large turnout of fans may have caused other celebrities to turn over in their graves since their grave sites were receiving little notice any longer. Seldom do visitors search out the headstones of the bygone stars such as Clark Gable, Jimmy Stewart, Humphrey Bogart, and Spencer Tracy.

Although this memorial park is home for the rich and famous, it only seemed appropriate as the final resting place for Carmen. Her brother Charles was nervous about going to the Mortuary. He didn't know if he could play the role of the grieving brother who had been estranged from his sister and regretted not making amends to her before her tragic death. Charles wasn't looking forward to having to face all his relatives. Charles knew that he had to be there or otherwise he would become a natural suspect in his sister's death.

Charles needed all the emotional support he could get. He felt close to Steve since they had pulled off a double homicide without getting caught. Steve and his girlfriend, Eva Avila, agreed to drive Charles to Forest Lawn and wait outside to pick him up after the Wake was over. Steve and Charles had worked out a little charade in which Steve would call Charles 20 minutes after he entered the funeral home. Charles would answer his cellphone in front of everybody and claim that an emergency had come up and he had to leave. The result of this little farce was that Charles would be able to be very visible at the beginning of the Wake but would be able to leave before everyone came up to offer their condolences to him.

Steve recognized the importance of making sure this sham actually worked. He and his girlfriend waited in his car in the Forest Lawn parking lot. They kept checking their watches to see if it had been long enough to make the phone call to Charles. Finally at 7:20 p.m. Steve used his cellphone to call Charles' cellphone. He let it ring a dozen times and no one answered. Steve thought that maybe it was too early for Charles to answer and he had purposely ignored it. Then at 7:39 p.m. Steve made the call again and he waited for Charles but still there was no one who answered.

Steve began to wonder what could have gone wrong with their ingenious plan. Steve's girlfriend, Eva Avila, was becoming anxious just sitting around in a car in a mortuary parking lot. Hours earlier she had been released from a Drug Rehabilitation facility where she was trying to kick her drug habit. She was ready to have some fun since she hadn't had any excitement while being closed up in the live-in facility.

It was getting later and later and Steve could feel the displeasure of his girlfriend while he felt like a failure in supporting his old friend Charles. Now it was 8:12 p.m. and he pounded in the number for Charles cellphone and again no success. Steve was perplexed as to how such a simple plan could go cockeyed. Steve was getting highly agitated with Charles not answering his phone. As displeased as Eva was with the lack of communication, she tried to calm Steve by suggesting that maybe the minister was talking at the Wake and Charles couldn't pull out his cellphone to answer it.

Unknown to Steve and Eva, Charles was inside wondering what went wrong with his friends who had promised to call him to get him out of this highly uncomfortable situation. Charles was experiencing a slow "melt down" as more and more family relatives and friends came by to speak to him. Why didn't his buddy Steve call him? He had thought he could rely on him and he felt deeply betrayed by him. Sometime after 8:30 p.m. Charles reached into his pocket to pretend that he was checking his phone for messages when he noticed that he had forgotten to 'turn on' his phone to receive calls. He immediately switched the phone to "on" and placed the phone back into his pocket.

Then at 8:51 p.m. Steve made another call to Charles' phone. Much to Steve's surprise, Charles answered. Charles said that he was unable to talk and he would call Steve back in a couple of minutes, which he did. They had learned one of the fundamental rules of electronic devices and that is that "Murphy's Law" (if anything can go wrong it will go wrong) always somehow occurs. In this case it was a mere turning on one's cellphone, but it was enough to disrupt their well-made plan.

Although the Wake didn't go well for the guys, things should improve for the funeral set for the next day. By that time Charles and Steve were seasoned masters as to how to set up calls. Number one: both parties must have their cellphone in the 'ON' position. During the funeral everyone knew what to do. Steve and Eva drove Charles to Forest Lawn and dropped him off for his sister's funeral. This time everything went flawlessly. At 12:52 p.m. Steve made the call and Charles took out his cellphone and started talking to Steve. Charles played the part that he had an urgent situation that he had to take care of. Charles excused himself and was able to leave without causing any suspicion. This time when he got into the car he was so pleased that he wanted to High Five everyone.

Charles began thinking of what a great team he and Steve made. They had been able to pull off a double murder and get away with it. It was just a matter of time that his mother would die and he would inherit the family home. That fact alone would make him a very rich man in his view of the world. Things couldn't be better. Charles didn't have to be subjected to his demeaning sister who always made him feel unwanted and treated him like a total failure.

CHAPTER 34 ONE WEEK EARLIER

As to Steve and his girlfriend Eva things were going well. Still, a little over a week before the murders, Steve and Eva were involved in a serious altercation. At that time Steve and Eva were living high. At least in the sense they were using drugs to get as high as they could and staying high as long as they could. Drug use has some downsides to it. One is that people under the influence can act strange and do peculiar things. It all started out pleasant enough as a group of druggies decided to smoke some crack.

It took place on March 31, 2002, when four people got into George Jimenez's van and started to smoke some crack. For some there isn't anything more relaxing than sharing someone else's dope and mellowing out with friends.

Euphoria is a wonderful place to visit with friends. Steve and Eva seemed to be bombed on the crack. George was feeling fine but not as high as the others. For some unknown reason, Steve grabbed a knife and started threatening George. He started accusing George of making advances toward Eva. As a result there was a heated argument and George felt offended and told Steve to knock it off. This provoked Steve to stab George numerous times.

The happy mood shifted to antagonism. Steve and Eva took over the situation as George lay on the floor of the van screaming in agony. Steve started driving the van around town, not knowing what to do. There wasn't any method to their lunacy. Eventually they went through George's pockets and took anything of value.

After getting next to nothing of value they looked for a place to stop the van. Finally they pulled to the curb and stopped. They slid open the side door, pulled his body out of the van, and dumped him in an alley. The knife wounds were deep, causing extensive bleeding, and within minutes George would bleed out and end up at the morgue.

As George lay in the alleyway about to expire, a Good Samaritan came by and noticed the trail of blood and contacted authorities. George was rushed to the hospital, where a team of surgical doctors were able to stop the internal bleeding, thereby saving his life.

At about the same time the medical staff was conducting surgery to save George's life, Steve and Eva were furthering their crime spree by looking for people to rob. They desperately needed money to finance their drug addiction. It was the morning of April first, and for many people it is the day to play practical jokes on each other and later embarrass them by shouting out the words 'April Fool.' This strange custom can be traced back in history to Geoffrey Chaucer's story in ***The Canterbury Tales*** in 1392.

However, this April first in 2002, a Karine Martin was walking down the street in broad daylight. Steve was continuing to drive the van with Eva on the passenger side. He spotted this woman walking alone on the sidewalk. He pulled up behind the woman and stopped. He exited and approached her from behind, grabbing her purse. At first Karine didn't know if this was just practical jokers or if it was for real. It didn't take long before Steve convinced her that he meant business. The whole robbery took less than a minute.

Steve was able to pull the purse away from the victim. He ran back to the van, getting in and speeding away. They both took turns looking through the purse to see if there was anything of value. Finding very little worth taking, they threw the purse and its contents in the back of the van. This robbery was a disappointment for all concerned. Eventually Steve and Eva were so tired that they dumped the van and walked over to Steve's little house where they crash from the lack of sleep.

By the time Eva woke up the next day, her mother had sensed that Eva was strung out on drugs. Her mother convinced her to commit herself to a drug rehab program. She turned herself in and moved into the facility, where she couldn't leave. She missed hanging out with Steve and would constantly call him up from the facility. One of the evenings after the double murder, Steve talked to Eva by phone. He mentioned that he and Charles had taken care of a little problem. He indicated that they both were going to come into a large amount of money.

Eva finally moved out of the live-in program and immediately hooked up with Steve again. This all occurred on the day of the Wake in which Steve and Eva drove Charles to Forest Lawn. Eva knew Steve was bad for her but she loved being around him. He seemed so much alive and every moment was exciting because there was no predicting what he would do next. Eva was far more impressed with Steve's spontaneous life style than with Steve the person.

CHAPTER 35 GOOD DETECTIVE WORK

The police at the LAPD Northeast Division had their hands full with this double murder and the attempted murder of George Jimenez that had occurred a week earlier. There was no way that the detectives would be able to connect these separate crimes. But sometimes cases are solved in the most mysterious ways. In the stabbing case of George Jimenez, the detectives were able to start to connect the dots. The Jimenez case involved a couple of crack-heads, which the detectives subsequently used to help solve the homicide cases.

When George Jimenez was taken to the hospital, it wasn't long before the police were called to take a report. He told the officers that his van had been stolen. The police listed it as a stolen van, putting out its description in an All-Points Bulletin in which officers were instructed to look for the van. Ironically, the van was found the next day parked in the same area where it had been taken but one block over.

Initially the detectives didn't know how serious George's injuries might ultimately be. In order to cover themselves if this turned into a homicide, the detectives ordered that the van be checked for latent prints. The CSI team was told that it was an Attempted Murder situation. They were directed to do a thorough check for prints.

After an exhaustive examination of the van, the CSI team was able to lift several latent prints, which they ran through the database. After several cross runs, there was a match to a Steve Gallegos and to an Eva Avila. The next step was to obtain prior booking photos of those two and place them in separate photo line-ups. Next the detectives took their photo line-ups and showed them to George Jimenez.

George pointed to Steve's photo and said that's the guy who stabbed me. Then when the photo line-up of the females was shown to George he studied it and looked at all the females. He kept coming back to Eve's photo and said that's the woman who was there. The detectives felt a degree of satisfaction in that they were able to solve a stabbing among a group of crack heads. That was not as rewarding as solving a homicide of an innocent bystander.

After the LAPD detectives obtained the identification of the suspects, the detectives commenced their search to track down both Steve and Eva. Between the two of them, Eva was the easiest to find even though she had relocated to New Mexico. The detectives made arrangements to talk to Eva to see if she was involved in the stabbing or was present during the attack.

When the detectives sat down to talk to Eva, they in their wildest dreams never could have imagined what they would soon learn. Eva freely discussed how the stabbing of George occurred. She remembered that her boyfriend, Steve, did stab George several times but she made it sound like it was more of a self-defense situation. The police didn't know who to believe since all of the parties were high on the crack.

Eva was intensely infuriated at Steve for getting her mixed up in a criminal investigation. All of a sudden she started talking about how Steve had bragged to her about killing two other people. This piqued the detectives' interest so they asked her for more details. She may have thought that the police didn't believe her, so she continued to give the detectives more information so they could verify her story.

She related that Steve Gallegos told her how he and a guy by the name of Charles Cepeda had crept into a small house with a shotgun. He told her that he emptied the shotgun in the female victim's 'ass.' Her boyfriend was very calm in telling her how he and Charles took Mr. Kimzey to an area under a bridge where they used the shotgun to blow part of this victim's head off. Steve was very matter of fact in explaining what he did to the victims. Eva made it sound as though Steve was proud that he was able to pull off a double murder without getting caught. He boasted how smart he was and how dumb the cops were.

These detectives were aware of these two homicides and went back to the detective's bureau to figure out what to do next. All they had was a vindictive female who wanted to get even with an old boyfriend who had gotten her in trouble with law enforcement. Most of what Eva was saying was hearsay since she wasn't personally present at either crime scenes.

The question was whether there was a way to corroborate what Eva was telling the police. The detectives tried to check out some of Eva's story and they went so far as to talk to Steve. He was so certain that he was smarter than everyone else that he had no problem talking to the detectives. When he was asked about his whereabouts on the night of the murders he laid out where he was and who he was with.

When the detectives asked if Charles Cepeda was with him, he adamantly denied that. This seemed strange to the detectives since when they had talked to Charles, he had claimed that he was with Steve Gallegos at a completely different location at the time the murders occurred.

When the detectives were investigating the death of Carmen Cepeda, they had heard from friends and relatives that there was some speculation that Charles Cepeda might have been involved in some way in the killing of his sister. Even though the detectives had some slight suspicion about Charles's involvement, they had not uncovered any solid evidence connecting him to the killing. Now, with the additional statements made by Eva, did the detectives have enough to go to the DA's Office for a criminal filing for murder on either Steve or Charles?

The detectives took all their police reports to the downtown DA's Office for a filing. A filing deputy for the Complaint Division of the DA's Office reviewed the reports. Without a doubt this set of facts of the two homicides was more than challenging. After lengthy discussions the DA's Office agreed to file criminal charges if Eva was willing to testify in court against Steve and Charles. Eva was in custody and she expressed through her attorney that she would be willing to turn state's evidence if she could get a deal as to her involvement in the attack and robbery of George Jimenez and the purse-snatch situation.

These types of situations can easily backfire on the prosecution. The problem was whether there was enough corroboration to support what Eva was willing to testify to. The DA's Office would be under a time deadline for filing charges against Steve and Charles. If no charges were filed, the two suspects would be released and most likely they would disappear into the hinterlands of Mexico.

In this case, the DA's Office was willing to file charges on the promise that the detectives would continue to uncover the necessary corroboration for trial. These are the situations where the prosecutor and the police have to trust each other. Since the DA's Office was sticking out its neck in filing this case, it was decided to transfer this case to the DA's Major Crimes Division. There, a prosecutor who had the time could make sure that the detectives followed up on their agreement to search for any corroborating evidence.

CHAPTER 36 CORROBORATION WAS CRUCIAL TO CASE

M ajor Crimes Division needed to assign a prosecutor who was highly respected by law enforcement and had an eagle eye as to the law on what constituted corroboration. The administrators recognized that prosecutor Darrell Mavis would be the perfect attorney for the job. You the reader are already familiar with Darrell Mavis's qualifications. As you may remember, he was a graduate from Harvard Law School and in his spare time as a prosecutor continued to teach at a local law school. He was very methodical in preparing his cases, but most of all he had a unique way of communicating with jurors. In this new case he would have to convince the jurors that they could totally rely on the testimony of Eva since everything she said was corroborated by independent evidence.

The DA's Office immediately permitted Eva to plead guilty to the charge of assault with a Deadly Weapon on George Jimenez. The plea bargain agreement was that she had to testify truthfully against her boyfriend, Steve Gallegos, and his friend Charles Cepeda. If she did as she promised she would receive a shorter time in state prison. This was a difficult arrangement since she and Steve had been very close and she still had emotional feelings for him.

However, she found herself in a problematic situation. She had completely confessed to being involved in the stabbing of George Jimenez. So pragmatically there was no way she wouldn't be found guilty of that crime. That meant she would be sentenced to a much longer time in state prison. In other words she had 'No Good Options,' so the idea of testifying against her ex-boyfriend was a better option than spending a good part of her life in prison.

Once the prosecution had obtained a complete statement from Eva as to everything she knew, the next step was to find the evidence that could corroborate her testimony. This was where the prosecution needed to have a legal-beagle type who understood all the nuances of the Law of Corroboration. Darrell Mavis was the right prosecutor for the job since his keen mind could navigate all the rules and exceptions to the Law of Corroboration.

Below is the jury instruction that is used to explain the Law of Corroboration to the jurors at the end of the case.

CORROBORATION OF ACCOMPLICE

- **To corroborate the testimony of an accomplice there must be evidence of some act or fact related to the crime by itself and without any aid, interpretation or direction from the testimony of the accomplice, which tends to connect the defendant to the crime.**
- **However, it is not necessary every element of the crime or every fact testified to by the accomplice be corroborated.**

CORROBORATION TEST

- **You must first assume the testimony of the accomplice has been removed from the case.**
- **You must then determine whether there is any remaining evidence which tends to connect the defendant with the crime.**
- **If there is, the ACCOMPLICE IS CORROBORATED.**

Darrell understood that the detectives had a vague understanding of what was meant by the legal term "corroboration." He explained to them that he needed evidence that connected Steve and Charles to the crimes which was independent from what Eva had told them. However, Darrell stressed to the detectives that they didn't need to obtain corroborative evidence on every fact that Eva told them.

Darrell gave the detectives an example of the type of corroborative evidence he needed for court. He explained that Eva made the statement that the guys told her that when they shot Kimzey downtown with a shotgun at close range, their car was covered with blood and human tissue. As a result they had to find a place to wash the car at 2:00 a.m. Eva related that they drove to a guy's place named Joe in Montebello for the purpose of washing the car.

Darrell explained to the detectives that they needed to track down this 'Joe.' If Joe could verify that Steve and Charles came by to wash blood and human tissue off of their car, that information would be corroborating evidence. In fact, the detectives tracked down Joe Alvarez in Montebello, who related that he permitted Steve and Charles to wash their car at 2:00 p.m. He was able to add more corroboration when he explained that the guys had a shotgun which they asked to leave at his house.

Another example of corroboration that the prosecutor mentioned to the detectives was to obtain the cellphone records for both Steve and Charles. If those phone records showed that calls were made from Steve's phone to Charles' phone at the precise time told by Eva, that would qualify as corroboration.

Darrell explained to the detectives that they themselves could supply evidence of corroboration. One example was they could verify that both red and green shotgun shell casings had been used by the shooter. Also, they could confirm the layout of the house where Carmen's bedroom was located. This information could dovetail exactly with what Eva had told to the detectives.

Other corroboration would come from the Coroner, who would verify Eva's statement that Carmen was shot up the 'ass' with a shotgun. Then Darrell asked the detectives to find Carmen's relatives, who could verify how much Charles resented his sister and felt he had been unfairly treated by her. After several interviews of family members, the detectives were able to find people who could provide that form of corroboration.

CHAPTER 37 NEED VISUALS TO ORIENTATE THE JURY

Darrell knew that the facts and charges of this case required the heavy use of visual aids to orient the jurors to all the details. Darrell wanted to use a visual that would graphically show the jurors who was involved. It had to confirm that there was a separate attempted murder charge which involved only Steve. The connection to the victim George Jimenez was Eva. Darrell wanted to place this crime to the left since chronologically it happened earlier on March 31, 2002. The main crime was the double murder involving Carmen Cepeda and Steve Kimzey, which occurred on April 5, 2002.

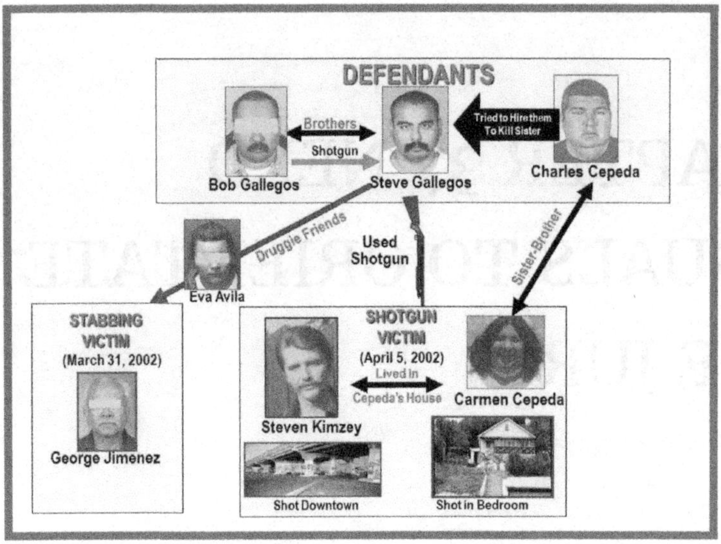

You saw this above chart earlier in order for you, the reader, to better understand the facts of this confusing case. Darrell had this visual prepared so he could use it in his Opening Statement. The purpose of this chart was to show the jurors who were the players in the case and what was their relationship to each other. The jurors needed to have firmly implanted in their minds the significance of the relationship between Charles Cepada and his sister Carmen Cepada.

After Darrell had used this graphic in his Opening Statement, he used it again during the trial by showing it to witnesses like Eva who could identify the various parties and explain their role in the crimes. After several of the witnesses had referred to this chart, Darrell decided to ask the court to mark and receive the chart as evidence. At that point Steve Gallegos' attorney objected to the chart being received as evidence.

The judge asked what the basis for the objection was. The Defense attorney waited a moment and gawked at the chart. Then he blurted out that the chart showed 'clip art' of a shotgun and there was no evidence that any shotgun was ever recovered. Darrell responded that the coroner had said that the female victim had been shot by a shotgun. Therefore we can infer as a fact that a shotgun was used even though it was never recovered.

The judge seemed to be leaning toward admitting the chart as evidence when Steve's Defense attorney made another objection. He pointed to the words "Used a Shotgun" which were on the chart under a photo of his client. He claimed that the words were unfair since the shotgun was pointed at the victim. Darrell responded that there was testimony that it was Steve who was accused of using the shotgun.

The judge listened to the Defenses' objection and instructed Darrell to remove the clip art of the shotgun and the words about the shotgun if he wanted that chart to be accepted as an exhibit. Darrell was in the middle of the trial and didn't have time to reprint the chart. Many attorneys would have given up on the chart. However, not Darrell; he understood how important this chart would be during the jury deliberations.

During the next court recess, Darrell opened his brief case and pulled out a pack of "Post-its" and tore one off. He quickly walked over to his chart and stuck the yellow 'Post-it' over the clip-art shotgun and the words "Used a Shotgun." After the recess, Darrell stood up and addressed the judge, saying that he wanted the chart received in evidence now since he had covered up the 'objectionable language.' The judge glanced over to the chart next to the blackboard. He could see the colorful yellow "Post-it" in the center of the chart. A halfhearted smile came over the judge's face as he looked directly at Darrell and stated, "The chart will now be received into evidence." That meant that the jurors would have this chart in the jury room which they could refer to in order to keep straight who all the parties were.

Another problem that Darrell had when he was creating this Parties Chart, was finding recent photos of the two victims. The detectives were only able to come up with Carmen's wedding photo. Darrell knew that the Defense would strenuously object to Carmen's wedding photo being shown to the jury. So the photo of Carmen had to be carefully cropped so the jury wouldn't be able to see that it was a wedding-day photo of Carmen.

The other challenge was finding a recent photo of Steve Kimzey. After his auto accident he became withdrawn and avoided having his photo taken. Finally the detectives were able to track down family members who submitted several family photos that may have been taken ten years before his death. Again Darrell had to do some cropping to get some type of likeness of Steven Kimzey. After cutting out other family members, Darrell had a photo that would be acceptable.

Darrell knew that jurors needed to see images of the people who would be testifying. He knew it was important to have the jurors think of the victims as human beings just like themselves. Words and names can't evoke the necessary feeling that a prosecutor needs the jurors to feel in order to connect with the victims. Photos of the victims humanize them and the jurors can better feel what that victim went through.

Next Darrell wanted the jurors to understand where each event occurred. The below map incorporated several photos to show who lived where and how close they live to each other.

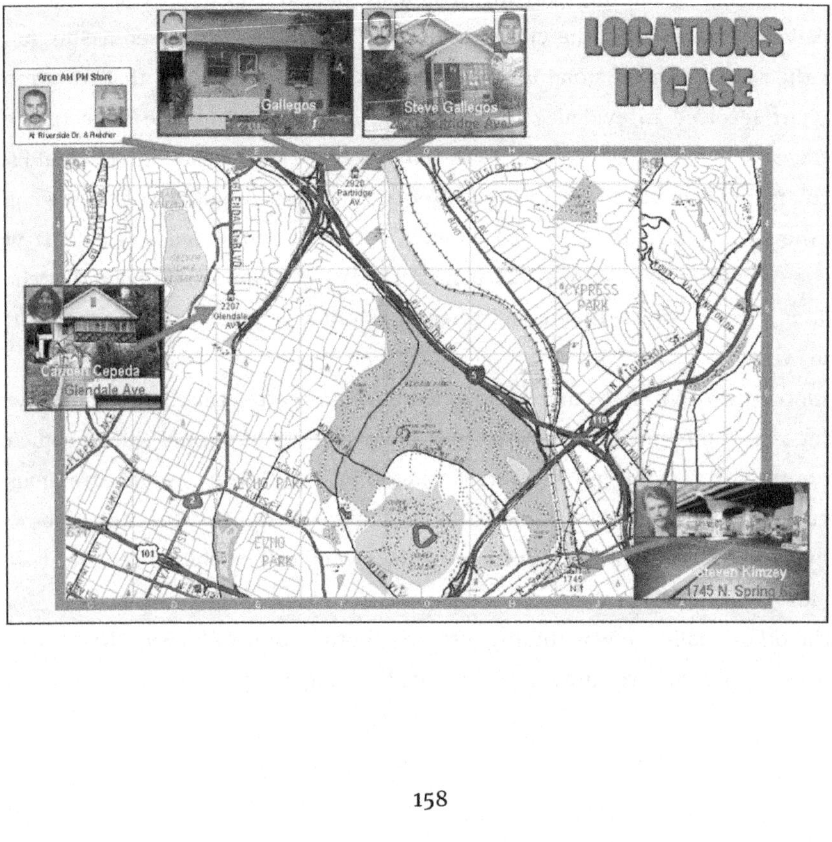

The individual photos were superimposed on the various locations. It was important that the jury understand that the Gallegos brothers lived next to each other in modest houses. Also it was important that the jurors saw how far Steve Kimzey was transported by Steve and Charles. With this map being made an exhibit, the jurors could refer to it during their deliberation if they had questions about the locations.

Darrell knew that the jurors would have to be able to follow all the details that Eva would testify about. The Defense wanted to make Eva look like an opportunist who would say anything to save herself, even if it harmed her old boyfriend Steve Gallegos.

CHAPTER 38 VISUALS SHOWING THE FACTS

Darrell used the below-left photo board to show the path that Steve and Charles took after they parked their car on the street and walked all the way up the stairs to the front door. Darrell wanted the jurors to visualize Steve carrying the shotgun up these stairs with his 350- pound partner Charles in front of him. These photos supported what Eva had told the detectives regarding how and where the killing of Carmen occurred.

CARMEN CEPEDA'S HOUSE

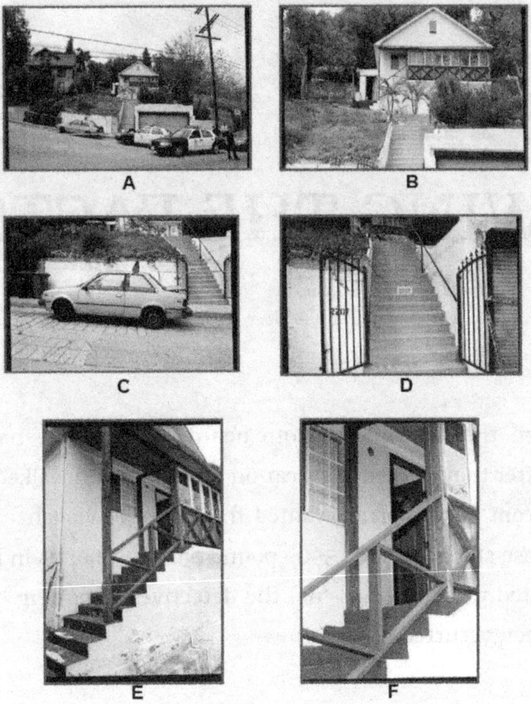

CARMEN CEPEDA'S HOUSE- INTERIOR

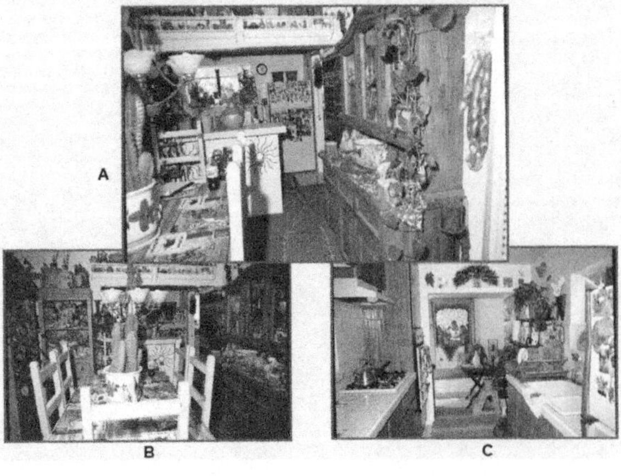

The other photo display to the right was used by Darrell to show that Carmen had fixed up the little house as though it was hers. This supported the claim that Charles was mad that Carmen was trying to take over the family home. The Defense wanted to depict Carmen as an obnoxious person who was a slob housekeeper. These photos would project a different image of someone who was trying to provide a clean and pleasant environment for her mother who was suffering from acute Alzheimer's disease.

Eva's testimony had to be supported by some form of corroboration. Darrell realized that the jury could find all sorts of corroboration for Eva's testimony. Darrell grouped several of the photos of Carmen's bedroom, so the jurors would have the same view that Steve and Charles would have as they entered Carmen's room. The first four photos provide a view of Carmen's body when it was covered by a bedspread. The jurors could see that Carmen was shot while she was peacefully sleeping and in no way posing a threat to anyone.

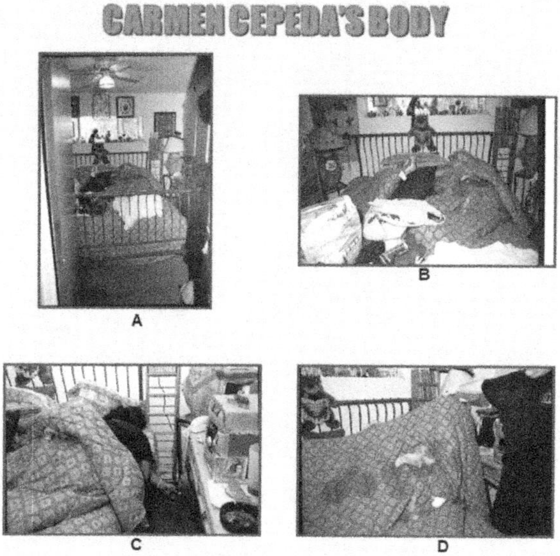

Darrell tried to use the photos that were less likely to be objected to by the Defense attorneys. The problem was that when someone is shot at close range by a shotgun, there won't be any pretty pictures of the victim's body.

Every photo told a story about what happened on the night of the shooting. The shell casings were found all over Carmen's bedroom floor. They supported Eva's testimony as to the number of times Steve shot at Carmen. Also, the two colors of shotgun shells became a major issue in the case. The prosecution contended that finding two separate colors of shotgun shells supported what Eva had said.

The Defense tried to spin it that the multi-color shells were indicative of a person who went to garage sales to buy various colored shotgun shells to reload. The Defense claimed that the fact that there were two different colored shells proved that the shooter was a poor burglar who couldn't afford to buy new shotgun shells. The Defense's twisted logic seemed difficult to follow.

CHAPTER 39 CELLPHONE RECORDS MADE EASY

The biggest challenge for Darrell was how to handle the cellphone calls. This could be highly relevant corroboration for Eva's testimony. She had told the detectives that she had been with Steve when he made phone calls to Charles at the time of the "Wake" and Funeral. The detectives got copies of both Steve's and Charles' phone records for the month of April 2002. Steve's cellphone number was (323) 309-1135 and Charles' cellphone number was (719) 964-4097.

Darrell realized that the jurors were going to have great difficulty understanding what the stacks of phone records really meant. So Darrell had three separate visual aids created showing the three crucial times that the phone records were relevant.

The first one which is below showed that Steve tried to call Charles' phone number three times between 7:20 p.m. and 8:12 p.m. but Charles never received a phone call during that period of time. The reason was that Charles had forgotten to turn on his cellphone. Darrell had a telephone expert come in to testify that the phone calls to his phone would not be reflected on his statement unless he had turned on his phone.

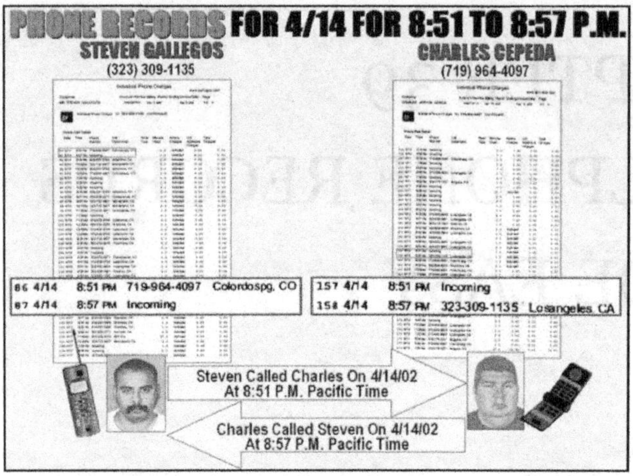

The next visual below shows what happened when Charles turned on his phone. He did receive a phone call from Steve at 8:51 p.m. and returned a call to Steve at 8:57 p.m. All of this corroborated what Eva had said about them trying to reach Charles and finally being able to reach him around 9:00 p.m.

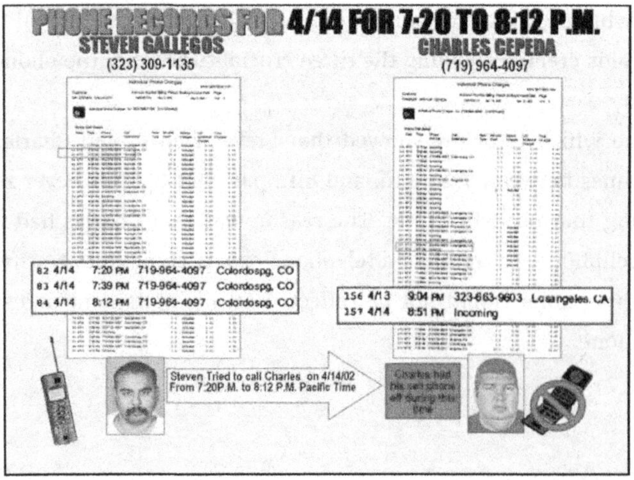

The final chart was similar to the others. It showed the phone calls that were made to Charles during the funeral. As to all these calls, Charles did receive them and talked to Steve. The Defense tried to create a Red Herring regarding the phone records. They pointed out that the statement referred to Charles' phone being in Colorado Springs. They made it appear that Charles was out of the state around the time of the Wake and the funeral.

Darrell had to have a telephone expert testify that the designation of Colorado Springs didn't refer to where the phone was being used but where the phone had been placed in service. Charles had been in the armed services assigned to the Colorado Springs area when he bought his cellphone. That explained the designation of Colorado Springs on the phone bill.

Darrell was trying to find every piece of corroboration of Eva's testimony and present it to the jury. Eva had mentioned to the detectives that Steve Gallegos had been stopped while driving Charles' car when Charles was sick and couldn't drive. A traffic officer had given Steve a ticket for driving without a license. Darrell asked the detectives if they could track down that traffic ticket.

Sure enough with some good detective work they were able to dig up the ticket, which showed exactly what Eva had said. The traffic ticket showed that Steve was driving Charles' Buick and he didn't have a driver's license. Darrell took all that information and placed it on a chart for the jury to see how this corroborated what Eva had claimed.

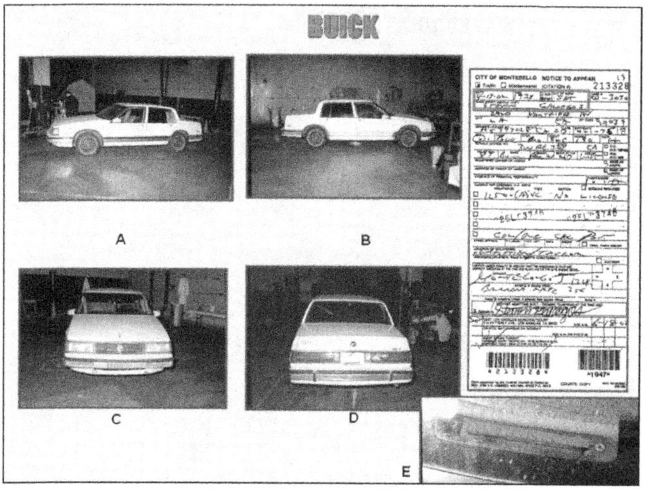

Darrell called one of the detectives to the witness stand to testify to what the two defendants had said in statements to the police. The detective testified that he had talked to Charles and asked him who he was with at the time of the murders. Charles adamantly stated that he was with Steve Gallegos all that evening. When the detective talked to Steve about who he was with on the night of the murders, he said some friends. Then the detective asked him if he had spent any time with Charles on that night. Steve said he was absolutely certain he was **not with Charles.**

Obviously, someone wasn't telling the truth. Just because someone lies doesn't mean they are guilty. However, Darrell knew that he would be able to use this lie to show Consciousness of Guilt, especially on the part of Steve.

After the prosecution rested its case, the Defense presented their side. There were several witnesses called by the Defense, but the main thrust of the Defense's case was to attack Eva's credibility. There was some anticipation that the defendants might testify. Steve was sufficiently confident that he could withstand the cross-examination by the prosecution. When the moment came for Steve to take the witness stand, he chickened out and remained at the counsel table.

As to Charles testifying, the judge asked him. Charles merely shook his head and uttered the word 'No.' Even though Charles wasn't a mental giant, at least he was smart enough to know that he was not a match for Darrell the Harvard graduate who was a law school professor.

CHAPTER 40 HOW TO ARGUE THE CASE

When it came time for Argument, the prosecutor had to think of what type of approach would be most effective to explain the case to the jury. Darrell was well educated. Would he be able to relate to jurors who weren't Ivy Leaguers? He knew that the entire case depended on whether the jurors believed Eva was telling the truth. Darrell wrote out 15 specific points in which unimpeachable independent evidence supported Eva's testimony. He had a chart prepared to list the various points. This was the draft of that visual that Darrell had started working on.

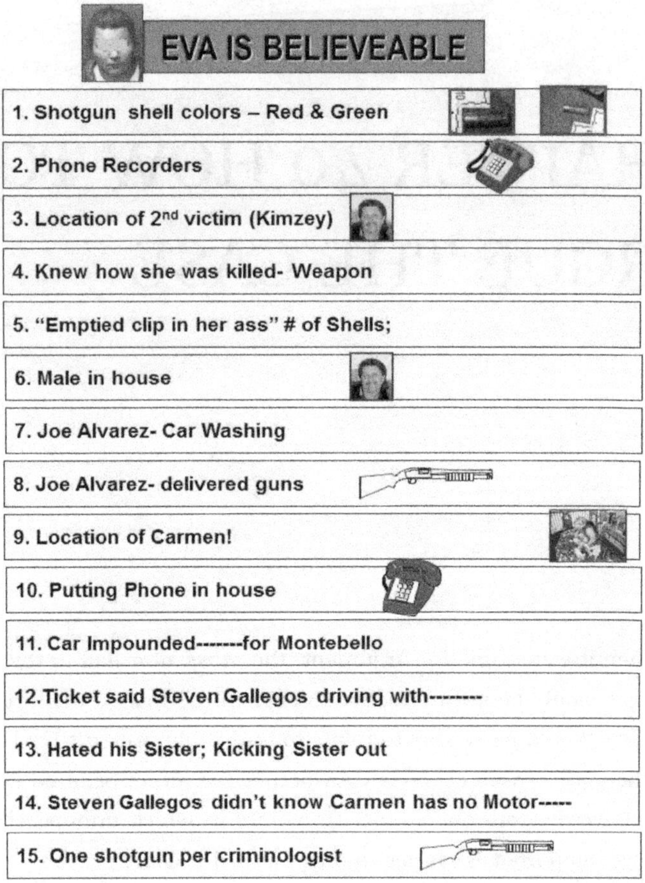

Darrell wanted to see how the Defense was going to argue their side of the case. He realized that the Defense had placed all their cards on the table trying to discredit Eva. Darrell decided to change his approach and not use the above chart. Instead he used the various visuals which had become exhibits during the trial. In this way, every time he made a point about Eva being credible he picked up an exhibit that corroborated that point and displayed it to the jurors. Besides all the exhibits that Darrell had the court receive into evidence, he did use one additional visual. That was the Charges Chart against the defendants that is shown below.

CHARGES AGAINST DEFENDANTS

Count	Crime	Date	Victim	Defendant
1	Kidnap to Rob	3/31/02	George Jimenez	Steven Gallegos
2	Kidnap for Carjack	3/31/02	George Jimenez	Steven Gallegos
3	Robbery	3/31/02	George Jimenez	Steven Gallegos
4	Carjack	3/31/02	George Jimenez	Steven Gallegos
5	Attp. Premed Murd	3/31/02	George Jimenez	Steven Gallegos
6	Robbery	4/1/02	Karine Martin	Steven Gallegos
7.	Murder	4/5/02	Carmen Cepeda	Steven Gallegos, Charles Cepeda
8.	Murder	4/5/02	Steven Kimzey	Steven Gallegos, Charles Cepeda
9.	Kidnap	4/5/02	Steven Kimzey	Steven Gallegos, Charles Cepeda
11.	Burglary	4/5/02	Carmen Cepeda	Steven Gallegos, Charles Cepeda
12.	Poss. Firearm	4/18/02		Bob Gallegos

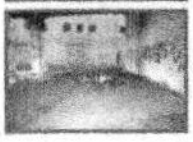

He wanted the jurors to think of the case in four separate categories. By using this chart the jurors could clearly see what charges fit into each group. Throughout his Argument he left this chart up on the blackboard so he could continually refer to it. This visual helped Darrell summarize the case and at that same time it acted like the glue holding all the evidence together.

CHAPTER 41 CONCLUSION

The jury got their final instruction and went out to deliberate. After several days of discussions, the jury notified the court that they had reached verdicts on all the counts except for two which included the burglary and the Attempted Murder of George Jimenez. This was great news for the prosecution. Even though there was no way of knowing what the verdicts were, however, these counts were the easiest charges for the jury to find the defendants not guilty of. So the inference was that the jury must have found the defendants guilty of something.

The judge didn't want a mistrial to occur, so he asked if there was anything that he could do to help them reach a verdict on those two counts. Some of the jurors spoke up that they were having trouble with the jury instruction regarding what constituted the elements of Premeditation and Deliberation as to the Attempted Murder of George Jimenez. As soon as they said that, Darrell knew that the jury had found Steve Gallegos guilty of the Attempted Murder but couldn't agree whether it was First Degree or Second Degree. This was a very astute jury to have recognized the complexity of that issue.

Darrell told the judge that he didn't have any objection taking the verdict and making the Attempted Murder only of Second Degree. When the court clerk read the verdicts, Darrell saw that he had been right in his analysis. The jury found both Steve and Charles guilty of all counts except that they didn't find that they had committed a Burglary when they entered the house and killed Carmen.

When a person enters a structure with the intent to commit a felony, that act is technically a Burglary. The prosecution's theory was that when Steve and Charles crossed over the threshold of the front door their intent was to commit murder, which is a felony. Therefore their action qualified as a Burglary. This legal theory is only important when there is no other way to make the killing a First Degree Murder. However, in this case it wasn't important since there was so much other evidence proving that the Murder was done with Premeditation and Deliberation, making it a First Degree Murder.

The jury also found Bob Gallegos not guilty of possession of a firearm, which referred to the shotgun that was given to his brother Steve to do the shootings. At the time of filing, it appeared that Bob Gallegos had given the shotgun to his brother, but at time of trial the evidence against him was even weaker. This was a confusing part of the case. There was little doubt that Steve Gallegos obtained the shotgun from his brother Bob. The big unresolved issue was whether Bob actually knew what that shotgun was to be used for. Darrell had no disagreement with the findings of the jury. This had been an extremely wise jury that had performed their civic duty in an admirable way.

The reason of adding this Gallegos and Cepeda case to this book was to illustrate how a prosecutor like Darrell Mavis worked tirelessly to see that justice was done. In this case the issue wasn't whether Steve and Charles committed two murders. The main issue was whether the prosecution could legally prove the necessary corroboration to support Eva's testimony. Darrell's meticulous preparation coupled with great police work certainly helped the prosecution.

Most of all, Darrell's brilliant visual presentation of the case made a big difference. There was no one telling Darrell what to do and how to do it. His dedication to detail wasn't rewarded by a bonus or a recognition plaque. Darrell didn't receive any satisfaction from the fact that Steve and Charles would spend the rest of their life behind bars. Darrell's only reward from all the tireless effort he put in to this case was to see the Criminal Justice System actually worked the way it is supposed to. Thank God for all the hard working 'Darrell Mavises' of the world.

JUVENILE INFORMANTS

People v. Noriega, Martinez & Ibarra

SUPERSTAR PROSECUTOR

Jeffrey Ramseyer

CHAPTER 42 LIVING IN CAMELOT

Once upon a time, a family moved to Yorba Linda in Orange County, California. This was considered as one of the safest and finest communities to raise children. Every parent wants to find a place to live where they don't have to be concerned about child molesters in the park who prey on young children. Parents don't want their children being bullied by gang members or their children having to dodge bullets from drive-by shootings. That's why parents are willing to struggle to secure good paying jobs so their family can afford to live in suburbia. The MacDonald family, which is the family we will be following in this story, moved to the city of Yorba Linda in order to raise their children in a sheltered environment.

Besides the safety aspect, the City of Yorba Linda is better known as the hometown of the 37th president of the USA. The President Richard Nixon Presidential Library and Museum is located in the center of town. Since the name 'Nixon' is so controversial, many people dismiss this community because of the city's most remembered son. The city's origins revolved around ranching, with its fruitful citrus orchards and cattle grazing on the rolling hills up until the late 1970s when it was transformed into a well-designed suburban residential community. Yorba Linda had been identified as one of the richest cities in the U. S. by the 2006 U. S. Census Bureau. They claimed this city had a median household income of $121,075, higher than any other city in 2006.

This city was fortunate enough to be developed with almost all new spacious homes, and it wasn't plagued with a deteriorating older section which would be a hotbed of criminal activity. When the community became incorporated in 1967, the issue of police services wasn't a major concern for the city fathers. As a matter of fact, the residents of Yorba Linda didn't even want to create their own police department. They decided to utilize the police department of the neighboring City of Brea to provide all the necessary police services.

The bottom line was the city of Yorba Linda was a totally safe community with little or no crime within its city borders. The civic leaders were proud of this fact and wanted to discourage any criminal activity from getting started. With a population of 60,000 residents, many considered it the Camelot of Orange County.

So what could possibly go wrong? Unfortunately, what transcends all communities rich or poor or urban or suburban is the juvenile drug epidemic. And often the more affluent the area, the more likelihood there will be illegal drug use. It often takes a large amount of money to support a drug habit, and the rich kids have access to such money, therefore they have more access to illegal drugs.

Another cause for the higher use of drugs in suburbia is the fact that the parents are often working longer hours and possibly commuting longer hours in order to have the wherewithal to afford the high price of living there. Often this requires both parents to work outside the home. The adverse result is that teenagers in the suburban community have plenty of unsupervised time. Frequently the parents are so consumed with their jobs that they don't spend the time to check on their children and learn who they are associating with.

There is a third factor which comes into play when children live in spacious homes: most of the children have their own private room where their behavior isn't seen by their parents or siblings. Within the confines of their private bedrooms, the teenagers can consume drugs without attracting the attention of the other members of the family.

Chad MacDonald

Chad MacDonald was one of those teenagers who grew up in Yorba Linda. He was born in 1980 in Detroit. His family yearned for a better life in sunny southern California. They moved and settled in Yorba Linda. All was going well for the family until one night before Chad's first birthday. His parents had decided to have a night out for dinner.

However, as they drove home around 2:00 a.m. Chad's dad crashed the family car into a power pole, which resulted in his dad's death and causing serious injuries to his mother, Cindy.

As a result of this unfortunate accident, the family's lifestyle changed dramatically since Cindy was disabled and unable to work. After a period of time, Cindy met another man and decided to remarry. In some ways this was great for her son Chad since he now had a male figure in his life. However, his stepfather came with his own set of problems, which revolved around alcohol and drugs. Although this had an impact on Chad's childhood, it didn't prevent Cindy from providing her son with an active teenage life. The family was active in Little League and all the typical teenager sporting activities. By middle school, Chad was one of the most admired kids in school, and in high school he had blossomed into a handsome, popular jock on campus.

Chad became the young man on campus that everyone knew and liked.

CHAPTER 43 METH TAKES OVER CHAD'S LIFE

Chad MacDonald seemed to fit the mold of the so-called 'good kid'; however, he was not immune to the influence of drugs. For whatever reason, he started experimenting with Methamphetamine (Meth). He liked the effect of the Meth, and it made him feel full of energy. Meth can cause intense pleasure called euphoria. The Meth stimulates the brain in the same way that a real accomplishment does, creating a rewarding feeling that motivates people to continue to use more and more.

The Meth Experience starts out with the rush, in which the initial response is the increase in the heart rate, blood pressure, and pulse that soars for up to 30 minutes. What follows is the high, in which the user feels aggressively smarter and becomes argumentative and will interrupt others and finish their sentences. Often during this high, the person becomes intensely focused on an insignificant item.

A number of Chad's friends were using Meth recreationally. At first Chad thought he could handle his usage, but he found that he felt better when he was taking more of the drug. Then he found himself in a situation where he couldn't get his hands on enough money to pay for his habit. He understood that he had to find a way to make enough money. He was 16 years old at the time, and he could mow lawns or work at a fast food place flipping hamburgers for the minimum wage.

He soon grasped that there were no legitimate jobs that would pay for his drug habit needs. The only answer was a job selling drugs. Dealing drugs was quite profitable in that Chad could buy Meth for $800 an ounce and sell it for $2240, netting a hefty profit of $1440 taxfree. All it required was dividing the ounce into quarter grams and selling them for $20. The profit that Chad made would go toward supplying himself all the Meth he could possibly crave.

In this day and age, many people believe mere recreational use of drugs is not a problem or cause one to become addicted. If one develops an addiction, there are numerous rehabilitation programs to help the user get off the drugs. As a user, Chad would be considered only a victim that needed help. Everyone had their own theory as to what got Chad started on Meth. His family believed that it was when his grandfather had a heart attack that Chad slipped into serious depression. Yet Chad's companions indicated that Chad was involved in drugs long before his grandfather's illness.

It may never be known exactly when and how Chad made that turn down the path to addiction. However, things changed when Chad crossed the line and decided to become a drug dealer of Meth. A dealer isn't looked upon as a poor victim but as someone who is exploiting others' unfortunate addiction. Society stigmatizes dealers, and the laws become much harsher on those who sell.

How big a dealer he was can be debated; however, the local police department had gotten word that he was a supplier on the high school campus. Since Chad had so many contacts at school, it was easy for him to develop a good business selling drugs.

But the downside was that he had only turned 17 years old. He didn't have any actual understanding as to how to protect himself from being caught by authorities. In other words, Chad was so naïve as to what a good dealer has to do to prevent detection. This is why the big dealers seldom get caught, because they don't have to make contact with the actual user. When users get arrested, the police find it easy to get them to talk. Most users are more than willing to give up the name of the dealer who sold them the drugs.

Chad in his adolescent drug dealing was so vulnerable and he didn't know it, or if he knew it, he wasn't covering his tracks. A 17-year-old drug dealer may think he knows it all, but he doesn't and he will do foolish things. Chad's pride and joy was his 1991Nissan pickup truck, which was the envy of his fellow students. Eventually, his truck became better recognized as the 'Meth on wheels courier service.' Pressure was applied to the police department to do more to stop the proliferation of drugs, especially the Meth epidemic plaguing the city. The police heightened their patrolling around the school hoping to discourage the dealers from selling.

On January 16, 1998, at 2:00 p.m. Chad was out driving around in his Nissan pickup truck, which everyone in town knew was his. He hadn't taken the one minute required to stick on the next year's license tags on his rear license plate. From a law enforcement standpoint, this was the perfect reason for stopping Chad while driving his truck. When the officer pulled behind Chad and turned on the red lights, Chad panicked, not realizing why he was being stopped.

Officer Watson walked up to the driver's door and in the most sincere voice he could produce he said, "Good afternoon." Chad was petrified and when the officer asked if he had the current registration, Chad asked to look in the glove box. He thumbed through the papers and didn't find anything. Chad was apologetic and stated he was sorry but he couldn't find it.

Chad figured that the officer would give him a warning and he would get the registration from his mother. The officer had received word at the briefing that this Nissan truck was being used to sell drugs in Yorba Linda, especially at the high school. The officer then asked the question, "Do you have any objection if I search your vehicle and its contents?"

At that moment in time, Chad had to make what was to be the most important decision of his 17-year life. He could say no to the officer, but he figured that would send up all sorts of red flags that he must have something to hide. He didn't want to make the officer mad. On the other hand, he could tell the officer to search the car and hope that he didn't find any drugs.

Chad figured it would be best to roll the dice and hope that the officer didn't conduct a very thorough search of the truck. However, for Chad this wasn't his lucky day. The officer was extremely thorough, and it didn't take long before he uncovered 10.99 grams of methamphetamine worth several hundred dollars, which was packaged in four plastic baggies hidden in a day planner.

Needless to say Chad, the 17-year-old amateur drug dealer, made the wrong choice and was busted. Chad didn't know what to do. He was scared since his mother had a heart condition as well as her disability from the accident, and she didn't need him to be in jail on a dope charge. He did what all young dealers do, and that is sell their life to become a snitch for the police. He said, "I will do anything to correct my mistake." A young suburban kid who may have been under the influence of drugs couldn't envision what he had agreed to do.

Chad's mother came to the police department to pick him up. In the process, the police explained to both Chad and his mother the facts of life. The police could have criminal charges filed against Chad, which definitely would give him a criminal record. However, if Chad and his mother agreed to him working as an informant, then the police wouldn't file any charges.

After some soul searching, Chad and his mother signed an agreement so Chad could work as an Informant for the police department. This is where most of the police informant situations become a giant misunderstanding. Once the Informant starts working, he soon finds that it isn't easy being an Informant. The reason is that the police don't want the little fish (small town dealer) but the big dealers or suppliers who are much harder to catch. Unfortunately, most Informants have little workable information in which they are able to land the big dealer. Chad's situation was no different than most.

The first encounter involved Chad working with the police to do a controlled buy. He wore a wire and bought a gram of Meth from a woman. Yet when the police did a search warrant of her place two days later, they came up empty. Chad gave information about a Meth lab which didn't lead to any arrests. There was only one suspect that was actually arrested due to Chad's information. The police weren't pleased with what Chad had come up with. Chad was sincerely trying to work off his case by giving information that he thought wouldn't burn him.

On February 19, 1998, he went to a juvenile court for a status check to see how he was doing as an Informant. The outcome of the hearing was to put his case over for 30 days to see if he would follow through with his promise to give the police a big dealer. However, that became a pivotal day for Chad for another reason.

Around 7: 30 p.m. he was driving his Nissan truck when a Brea traffic officer pulled him over for following too close.

When Chad was searched, he was found to possess 2 grams of Meth and some marijuana. He claimed it was part of a buy he was doing for the narcotics officers. The detectives had no knowledge of any such buy, so they told the Brea officer to arrest Chad for possession of drugs. He was eventually released to his mother, but the police were finished with Chad. He wasn't giving the detectives workable information; but worse than that, he was continuing to use Meth.

CHAPTER 44 HITTING THE BOTTOM

The 17-year-old Chad MacDonald was experiencing the meaning of being at rock bottom in his life. While partying day and night on drugs, his mind had to be in a fog of disillusionment. He thought if he hung out with a rough crowd of drug users maybe he could score the big dealer that the police wanted him to deliver. He went to a ramshackle house on Halcourt Street in Norwalk, California, that was a hangout for drug and gang activity. It was on a street with well-kept houses. It stood out with its bare front yard with no lawn and no shrubs. The house would definitely qualify as an eyesore. The backyard was littered with tall weeds that were surrounded by junk that included everything from old tires to a broken vacuum cleaner.

Norwalk Drug House

In order to get to the front door, one had to maneuver around an old sofa with junk stacked on top of it. Someone had placed a blue tarpaulin that covered the area around the front door where it joined the garage. The place was a dump, and since no one was supposed to be living there, the utilities had been disconnected. There was no running water to cook or clean up with. At night it was dark because there were no electric lights.

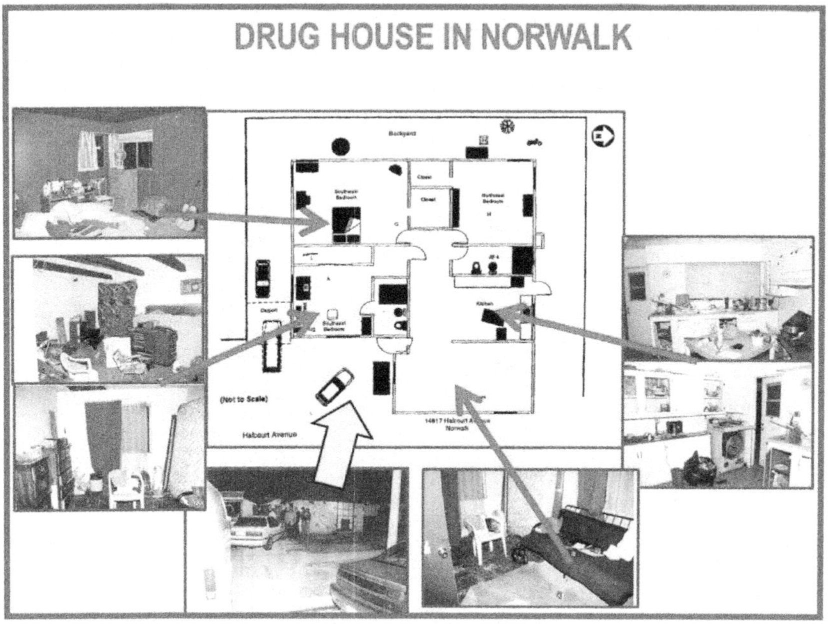

Someone had brought in a camp stove in order to be able to cook in the kitchen. The usual household amenities were meager if not non-existent. Some of the rooms had tool chests, as though someone was using the location to work on cars. Since there were no cushion sofas or chairs, the occupants had brought in plastic and beach chairs to add a cozy touch to the place.

For kids who had grown up in nice comfortable homes in Yorba Linda, it seemed strange that they would migrate to such a pigsty. That may be an indication of the strength of drugs. When the kids were under the influence, they would be unaware of their surroundings. When a kid is high on Meth, he doesn't need much else to make him happy.

Chad might have thought his true intention was to locate a big fish to turn into the police, but he truly seemed to relish partying with druggies. While visiting at the house, the woman he had turned in to the police came into the place and quickly told everyone that he was a snitch. Two of the guys confronted Chad with guns and accused him of being an informant. They beat him up, but he vehemently denied working with the cops. Luckily, Chad convinced them that she was wrong and that he was truly one of them.

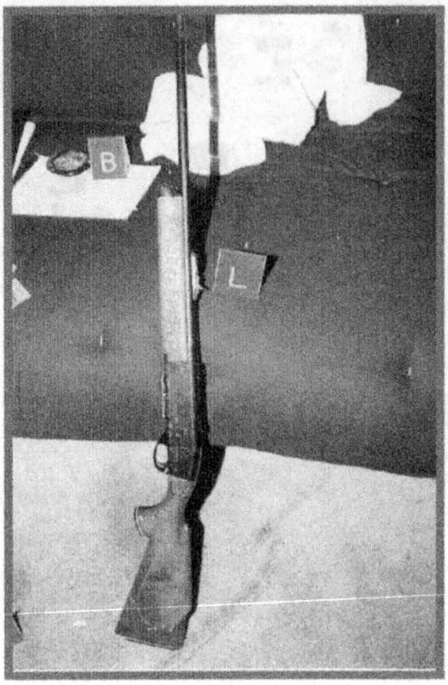

Chad was able to talk his way out of what could have been a deadly situation. He went to a motel to sleep off the effects of the Meth. By Sunday evening his girlfriend came over to the motel, and he was just thankful to be alive. Then for some unbelievable reason he talked his girlfriend into going with him back to party at the house in Norwalk where he had been almost beaten to death. Apparently, only a Meth addict would understand the craving that Chad felt in returning to such a nightmare.

CHAPTER 45 WHAT HAPPENS TO INFORMANTS?

When they arrived at the house, it contained only three persons who could be best described as low-life druggies. The oldest was Florence Noriega (28), who was the goddaughter of a prominent Meth supplier. It was hard to understand why she was living in such squalid conditions.

It was a strange mix of two kids from Yorba Linda with three low-life drifters from the inner city. The sets of values these five people had were quite different. Florence Noriega was a female and could project a pleasant appearance which was all deceptive. After Chad and his girlfriend were settling in with the others, Florence got up and walked over to the girlfriend and punched her in the face, then turned to Chad and called him a snitch. Almost immediately the two males Michael Martinez (21) and Jose Ibarra (19) began beating on Chad.

Florence Noriega (28)

Jose Ibarra (19)

Michael Martinez (21)

The one thing that the drug business can't afford is having snitches. The underlying rule is that I won't rat on you but you don't rat on me. If every druggie lived by those rules, then the police would never be able to infiltrate the drug business. Consequently, when someone becomes an Informant for the police, they must be severely dealt with by the drug organization. This is where the concept of "Deterrence" really comes into play in which an Informant has to understand the danger of being identified by drug dealers.

Florence searched both Chad and his girlfriend for a wire and found none. Next she demanded money from both and worked on a plan that she and Martinez take Chad to an ATM to withdraw money. This proved unsuccessful, and when they returned to the house Florence had Martinez take the girlfriend into the kitchen area while she and Ibarra worked on Chad. His girlfriend later indicated that she heard a horrible noise coming out of the living room, like a gagging noise as though someone was trying to breathe.

After Florence and Ibarra had strangled Chad to death, it was decided that Florence and Martinez would transport Chad's body to another location in south central Los Angeles. There they dumped Chad's body in a conspicuous place so he would be found and reported on by the news media. The message that it sent was one that was loud and clear: This is what happens to Informants. Strangulation sends a clear message that the snitches would suffer a slow torturous death if they ever worked with the police.

Alley in South Central LA

The Informant ends up dead in the most unflattering way. Every young person in the Yorba Linda area got the message. The word had been out for some time that Chad was into dealing drugs. The druggies in the area had figured out that Chad had been arrested on drug charges, so it was easy to infer that he had become an Informant.

The news media's photos of Chad's beaten-up, strangled dead body lying in a filthy alley was enough to scare any kid who ever thought of becoming an Informant. This one murder had caused law enforcement to lose their best source of information about drug activity. The bottom line was that illegal drug activity would flourish for a long time after people were discouraged from becoming an Informant for the police.

As to Chad's unceremonious death, it gave the dopers and dealers a gigantic win. This was the greatest form of deterrence to keep dealers safe from being arrested and prosecuted. It was ironic how nothing bad was supposed to happen to all the Chad types living in Suburbia. However, here was Chad lying dead in a drug- and gang-infested neighborhood far from Camelot.

Chad MacDonald Found Dead in Alley

CHAPTER 46 COLLATERAL DAMAGE

As to the fate of Chad's girlfriend, she remained at the house with Ibarra, who decided to rape her while his colleagues were disposing of Chad's body. When Florence and Martinez returned, it was time for them to take care of her. Why not kill her and dispose of her body in the same general area where they dumped Chad's body? It may have been the fact that they didn't want to strangle her like Chad. Since Chad's girlfriend had NOT been an Informant, there was no need to make her suffer.

Florence Noriega had told her companions to load the gun with five bullets. She indicated that it would take that many to make sure she didn't survive. They placed her alive in the trunk of their car. Then they started the long drive up to a very secluded area in the San Gabriel Mountains. One can only imagine the terrifying thoughts that were going through the mind of the girlfriend locked uncomfortably in this packed trunk.

CAR USED TO TRANSPORT BODIES

They drove her up to the San Gabriel Canyon above the city of Azusa. After traveling over a mile up this windy mountain road, they pulled over in a turnout near Morris Reservoir. The three druggies got out of the car and surveyed their surroundings. Because it was so late at night, there were no other people around. One of the guys went over to the trunk and popped it open. He ordered the girlfriend to climb out. Chad's frightened girlfriend turned her head so she could gaze at the kidnappers. She had difficulty bending her cramped legs.

With some effort on her part, she was able to stand up next to the trunk. The area was totally dark except for the headlights of the car. Since it was the first part of March, the weather was distinctly cold. This was such an isolated area that there weren't any humans for miles around. The only living critters would be some coyotes, a bear or two, and a few hungry mountain lions.

As this 15-year-old girlfriend stood on the embankment cold and frightened, her mind had to feel that she was experiencing an out-of-body experience. She wondered to herself, when was it going to end? Florence stepped over to the car and reached in and pulled out a gun. She had told her buddies to load it with five bullets since she had a belief that the girlfriend wasn't going to die easily. Florence walked over to the girlfriend and pointed the gun directly at her head. Without any hesitation or a word spoken her finger slowly pulled the trigger.

She shot the young woman once in the face, and the force of the shot knocked Chad's girlfriend down the embankment. Before Florence could shoot her again, the girlfriend had disappeared into the darkness. Florence and the two guys panicked and started looking for the girlfriend. Apparently the guys weren't Boy Scouts, since they had come unprepared without any flashlight. It was pitch black and they couldn't see a thing. They didn't want to go down the embankment, which was full of brush. They looked around the best they could in the dark. They even shouted out her name in hopes of hearing some type of cry or whimper, but all to no avail.

CHAPTER 47 WILL TO SURVIVE

One can only imagine what went through the girlfriend's mind. She had heard them kill her boyfriend. Then she found herself in the dark, standing like in front of a firing squad with a person shooting her in the face. All she could remember was the loud blast and feeling an intense pain coming from her head. Her body went flying backward down a slight embankment, landing on some rocks and weeds. She lay there not knowing what had just happened to her. As the blood started trickling down her face and feeling incredible pain, she knew that she had been shot.

CULVERTS UNDER MOUNTAIN ROAD

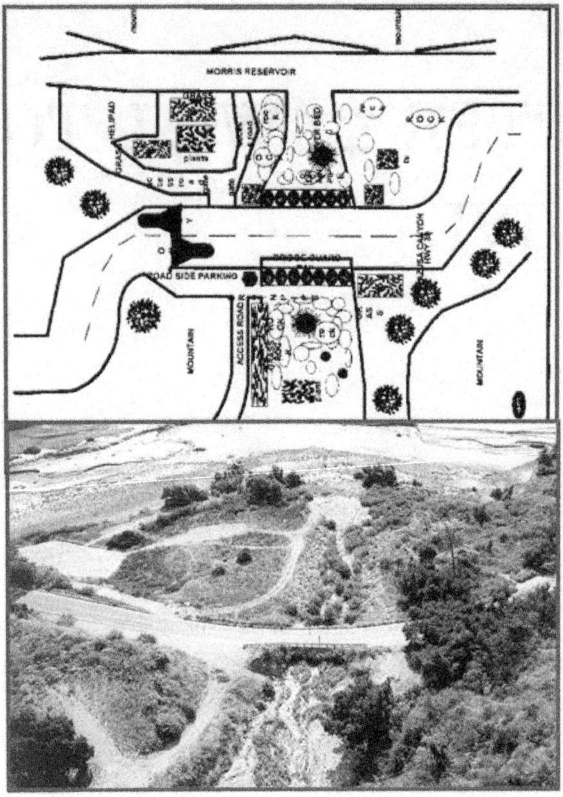

Needless to say, this young teenage girl had never been shot before, and being in a murky area she had no idea what to do. She could barely make out noise coming from several excited voices above the place she was at. All she wanted to do was yell out for help. However, after quickly assessing her situation, she realized that she was still alive and blood continued to drip down her face. Is this how one feels as they begin to die from a gunshot wound to their head? Maybe in minutes, she thought, this nightmare would be over and she would succumb to her injuries.

She felt like she was on her back and that she was partially in water. She was able to slightly move her legs and arms, which gave her hope. As she continued to hear voices overhead, she tried to listen to what they were saying. Not being able to make out the words, her thoughts turned to her basic instinct, which was fight or take flight. All she could think of was to try to escape from those evil people who wanted her dead. As she got up from being on her back, she wondered where she should hide for safety.

HIDING IN CULVERT

Water from mountain flows in this side of culvert

Water flows out of culvert on this side

The girlfriend crawled into this culvert

While she waited she continued to bleed

She heard the sound of a running stream and her feet seemed to be in water. Her eyes started to adapt to the darkness, and as she looked to her side she could see several large drainage pipes that ran under the roadway above. As the voices grew louder, she turned and splashed her feet through ankle-deep water. Where could she hide from those voices that seemed to be coming closer?

Her mind was spinning out of control as the pain from the gunshot was so intense; all she wanted to do was to die. Then she thought she could hide in one of the drain pipes. She waded through the drain water, and as she got to the opening of the pipe she leaned down and crawled in on her knees. The water in the pipe was ankle deep and flowing slowly. She crawled further in into the culvert and climbed over rocks and sticks that the water had washed down from the mountain.

When she felt she was a safe distance inside the culvert, she lay as flat as possible on the bottom of the corrugated pipe. She could barely hear the Meth heads cursing at each other for not finding her. She lay motionless as the cold water flowed over her warm body. Time drifted by as she listened intently to any sound coming from above. Eventually, there was the sound of the engine of a car and the muffled noise seemed to fade away. With her hands in the water, she pushed up her body and turned to sit upright against the side of the four-foot pipe.

As her anxiety subsided, she felt she was safe and somehow had dodged a bullet figuratively and literally. Then all of a sudden there was the sound of a car driving over the culvert. Were they coming back with a flashlight? Again she tensed up wondering whether she had done a wise thing crawling into the culvert. She felt like a sitting duck that could be easily shot since she was now trapped in the pipe. All of her senses were on heightened alert. She took a whiff of the foul odor of the musky water in the culvert. Her ears were sorting out a rainbow of sounds from the trickling of the water to the howling of coyotes echoing off of the mountain cliffs.

Chad's girlfriend didn't know what time it was, nor did she have any idea where she was. As she pressed her back against the cold corrugated pipe, she took her hand to feel the area of her face that had been shot. The blood seemed to have coagulated, although there was still a steady dripping of blood as she sat crunched over in the culvert.

A tug-a-war began in her mind. Should she crawl out and seek help before she bled to death? Or should she hunker down and wait for sunlight before leaving? Her fear of confronting the Meth heads again scared her enough to freeze her in place.

She waited until sunlight before she had the nerve to crawl out of the culvert. She crept up the embankment and sat alone on the edge of the mountain road. She gazed all around and saw beautiful high mountains silhouetted by clear blue sky. She thought this would be the perfect place to have a picnic with friends.

She recognized how isolated this location was as she waited and waited for any human being to drive by. Then she heard the sound of a car approaching, and there was a slight hesitation on her part. What if it was the people coming back to get her? When she could see the car wasn't the one used by her attackers she jumped up and started waving her hands. She was so desperate for help she stepped into the street so the vehicle would have to stop.

The motorist put on his brakes so not to strike her. He couldn't believe his eyes. Here was a filthy blood-soaked young woman who looked scared to death. She could best be described as looking like Death Warmed Over. He stopped and asked her, "Are you okay?" (Later he would grasp what a stupid question that was.) She could barely speak and started sobbing. The only sound she could make were the words, "HELP ME HELP ME PLEASE." With the help of the Good Samaritan, this tranquil mountain site turned into a major homicide crime scene even though she was still alive.

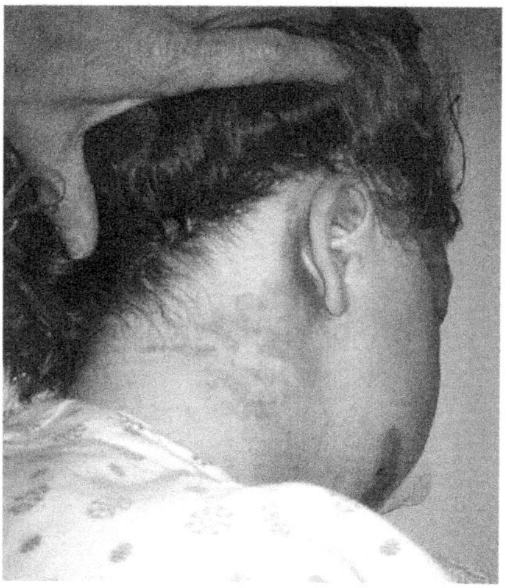

Chad's Girlfriend
Examined at Hospital

She was immediately transported to a hospital, where the doctors tried to treat her physical wounds. However, it might take a lifetime to heal the emotional trauma that she had experienced on March 3rd, 1998.

Because she had gone missing, her parents had made a Missing Person's report with the police. When she was found alive, the police prompted Cindy MacDonald to likewise make a Missing Person report for Chad. While Chad's mother was at the police department making the Missing Person's report, the word came in that a young male's body was found in an alley in south central LA. Within a short period of time, that body was positively identified as that of Chad MacDonald.

CHAPTER 48 NEED FOR SENSITIVE DA

The Sheriff Homicide detectives were anxious to interview Chad's girlfriend to get her story as to what happened to her and Chad. She explained how Chad was killed by the Meth heads because they knew he was an Informant for the police. The next question was whether this fragile young girl would be able to identify the Meth heads who had tried to kill her. The police went to investigate the house in Norwalk, where they conducted a search warrant. It didn't take long before they learned the names of the Meth heads. The girlfriend was shown photo line-ups of each suspect, and she was able to identify each of them. Then the suspects were tracked down and arrested.

Although this case was centered in Yorba Linda, which was in Orange County, it was the Los Angeles County DA's Office who prosecuted the case. The reasoning was that the Norwalk house and the place where Chad's girlfriend was shot were both within Los Angeles County boundaries.

The Los Angeles County Sheriff's Homicide detectives brought the case for filing charges to the DA's Office. The DA's administrators directed the matter to the Major Crimes Division due to the news media's interest and the outpouring of public concern. Needless to say, the DA's Major Crimes Division has some of the most seasoned and tenacious attorneys. By the time a prosecutor reaches the ranks of Major Crimes Division, they have lost their ability to be shocked or surprised at what some human beings will do to other human beings.

However, this case was going to require a prosecutor who could deal with the emotional trauma that Chad's girlfriend had gone through without causing her more distress. The most challenging issue would be Chad's mom, who wanted to blame the police for using her dear son to be snitch for them. Of course, the prosecutor would be thrown into the highly controversial situation of whether the police should use juveniles to help fight the drug problem in their community.

The DA's Administrator recognized that this case had special needs that required more than a highly skilled litigator. They needed a prosecutor with a degree of sensitivity as well as patience to listen to the parties involved. Fortunately, at that time Jeff Ramseyer was assigned to Major Crimes Division, and he had won praise from not only law enforcement but especially from victims and their families. It was a no-brainer that Jeff would be a perfect fit for the case.

Jeff had unique qualifications to handle such a case. He always saw the glass to be half full not half empty. He had a very disarming smile which made him likable with everyone he came into contact with. It wasn't because he didn't take his job seriously, but he always had a peaceful way of approaching everything. His closeness to his church may have been the reason he had a calming influence when things got tense.

Jeff's stature could be described as tall and slender topped off by a head of curly hair which framed his boyish good looks. He was in his late 30s without the slightest sign of a wrinkle on his face. He was like a person in constant perpetual motion. When he walked down the hallways of the CCB (Criminal Courts Building), he often would have his head buried in law books. He never wanted to waste time. The days he had to be in court he wore a sporty suit. However, around the DA's Office he would dress informally, usually with a sweater vest that gave him the preppy look.

He was proud of his family consisting of his wife and three lovely children. He enjoyed playing basketball and was always eager for a lunchtime basketball game. He was one of those people who could compartmentalize his business life from his personal life.

Jeff was finishing up another case, and when he got a verdict on it he shifted his attention to this new case. All he knew about the case was what he had read and heard from the news media. So he gathered up all the police reports and sat down and reviewed every aspect of the case. Then he methodically started conducting interviews with the detectives and witnesses.

It didn't take him long to assess the merits of the case and how he wanted to approach it. Based on the heinous acts committed on Chad and his girlfriend by the defendants, Jeff recognized this was a potential Death Penalty case. He wrote the case up for the DA's Office to consider asking for the Death Penalty. When he received the green light for the ultimate punishment, he knew that he would have to have all of his ducks in a row, since the case someday could be reviewed by the state Supreme Court.

Jeff's approach was to build a firm foundation of evidence which would support not only a conviction for murder but justify the Death Penalty. He knew that he would have to make sure that Chad's girlfriend was physically and mentally able to withstand the intense strain of testifying in court knowing these Meth-head gangsters were sitting only a few feet away. With all that the girlfriend had been through, she would be required to remember every despicable and terrifying detail of what the defendants had done to her.

Jeff needed her to be able to identify and explain exactly what each defendant did to her. Especially as to all the sexual acts committed by the two male defendants. It wouldn't be sufficient for her to testify that 'they' did it. Jeff spent hours patiently going over all the facts so she would be comfortable in discussing what happened to her and who exactly did it, and giving sufficient detail. He was able to build confidence in this 16-year-old girl in that she she could be able to recount her story before a group of 12 jurors in the presence of these cold-blooded killers.

CHAPTER 49 FINALLY THE TRIAL

On September 1, 2004, the trial commenced in the Norwalk courthouse, which is located at the east side of LA County. Unfortunately for Jeff, he lived on the west side of the County. The result was he had an extreme commute every morning crossing the second largest city in the nation. (He had to travel 20 miles through densely populated areas) Every morning Jeff arrived at the courthouse with a determined look to take on any of the challenges for the day. Jeff took the long commute in stride and was one of the early arrivers at the courthouse each and every morning.

Jeff knew how delicate the girlfriend's testimony would be. There was always the chance that one of the three defendants sitting in front of her might say something or give her a deadly stare which would cause her to freeze up on the witness stand. Jeff had the unique ability of connecting with all witnesses in his cases but especially with young people. Fortunately for Jeff, he was blessed with a youthful appearance. Few people knew that he was older than he looked. He had a laid-back demeanor that young people found comforting.

Jeff had prepared Chad's girlfriend to handle the stress of testifying before the jury. She was able to articulate her story and was able to positively identify each of the defendants. The Defense didn't do much in cross-examining, knowing any attack on the girlfriend could be counterproductive for them.

The next witness he had to deal with was Chad's mother, Cindy, who was more of a challenge, not knowing who she was going to strike out at next. She was highly critical of the Brea Police Department for using her son as a police Informant. Jeff needed her on his side for the prosecution of the case. Her testimony was needed to provide context to Chad's behavior and explain how and why he had become an Informant.

Chad's mother wanted the world to know how the police had taken advantage of her poor son, who was in need of drug rehabilitation, not incarceration. Jeff had to walk the fine line of getting Cindy to stick to the facts of her son's life and not get on a 'Soapbox' in attacking the police for using her son. Jeff knew that the jurors didn't need to become embroiled in the issue of whether juveniles should be used as snitches.

With all the diplomacy that Jeff could muster up, he tried to get Chad's mom to limit her comments to what was required for the criminal proceedings. Jeff tried to channel her wrath against the defendants in this criminal jury trial and avoided topics that would show her displeasure with the Brea Police Department

DNA FOUND ON PANTY

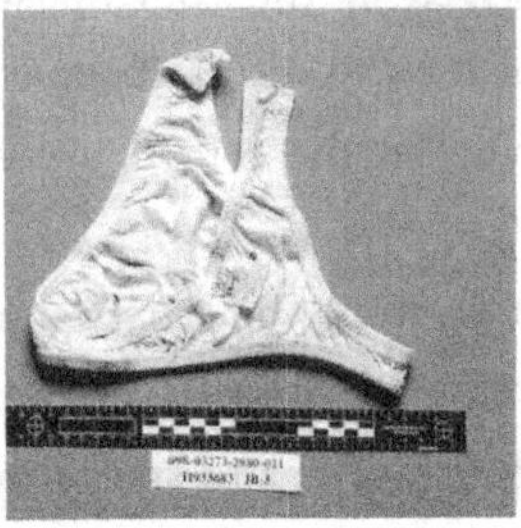

Panty '15' came back to Jose Ibarra

ITEM	DESCRIPTION	HLADQA1*	LDLR	GYPA	HBGG	D7S8	GC	D1S80
1	Blood from Chad MacDonald	1.1,4.2	A	AB	AB	AB	AC	22,24
2	Blood from Jane Doe	1.3,2	AB	AB	AB	AB	AC	24,30
3	Blood from Michael Martinez	2,3	B	AB	B	A	C	18,18
4	Blood from Jose Ibarra	4.1,4.2	AB	AB	B	AB	C	16,31
5	Blood from Florence Noriega	1.1,3	B	AB	A	B	C	21,22
12A	Vaginal Swab - Epithelial	1.3,2	AB	AB	AB	AB	AC	
12A	Vaginal Swab - Sperm	4.1,4.2 (1.1,2)[1.3]**	AB	AB	B(A)	AB	C(A)	
13B	External Vaginal Swab - Epithelial	1.3,2	AB	AB	AB	AB	AC	24,30
13B	External Vaginal Swab - Sperm	4.1,4.2 (1.1,2)[1.3]**	AB	AB	B(A)	AB	C(A)	18,18 [22,24,30,31]
14	Rectal Swab - Epithelial	1.3,2	AB	AB	AB	AB	AC	
14	Rectal Swab - Sperm	(1.1,2) 4.1,4.2	AB	AB	B(A)	AB	C(A)	
15	Panty Cutting (JB-5B) - Epithelial	1.3,2,4.1,4.2**	AB	AB	AB	AB	AC	
15	Panty Cutting (JB-5B) - Sperm	4.1,4.2	AB	AB	B	AB	C	

* = Results listed as HLADQA1 4.2 may actually be 4.2 or 4.3. The probe on the strips does not differentiate between the two types.
** = HLADQA1 type 1.2 may be present, but masked.
( ) = Weak results for types in parenthesis.
[ ] = Results in brackets are too weak to be conclusive.

Jeff had to build a solid case, and all the hours of hard work were paying off. He then focused on the forensic evidence to prove up the sexual assault on the girlfriend. He was able to prove that defendant Ibarra's DNA was found on the girlfriend's clothing.

DNA was also found on cigarette butts found at the Norwalk house which came back to defendant Ibarra as well as Florence Noriega.

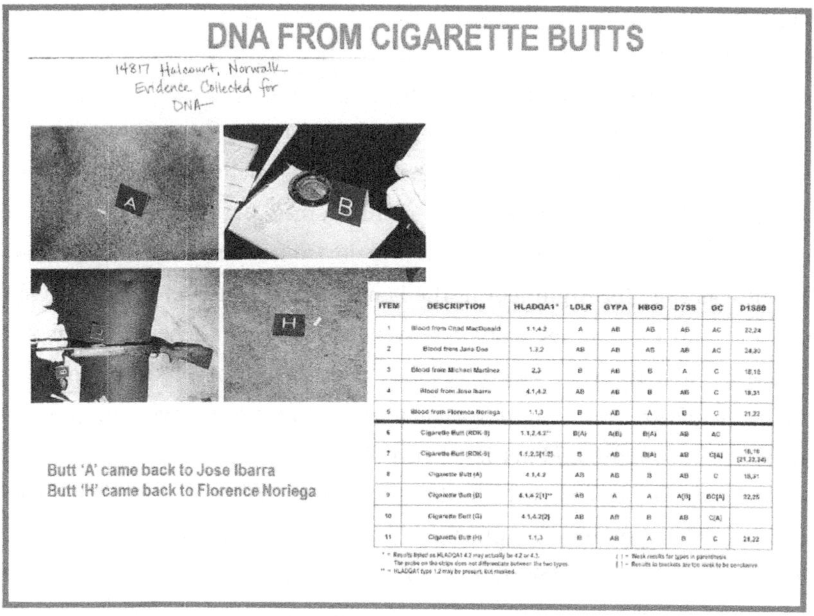

ITEM	DESCRIPTION	HLADQA1*	LDLR	GYPA	HBGG	D7S8	GC	D1S80
1	Blood from Chad MacDonald	1.1,4.2	A	AB	AB	AB	AC	22,24
2	Blood from Jane Doe	1.3,2	AB	AB	AB	AB	AC	24,30
3	Blood from Michael Martinez	2,3	B	AB	B	A	C	18,18
4	Blood from Jose Ibarra	4.1,4.2	AB	AB	B	AB	C	18,31
5	Blood from Florence Noriega	1.1,3	B	AB	A	B	C	21,22
6	Cigarette Butt (RDK-8)	1.1,2,4.2**	B(A)	A(B)	B(A)	AB	AC	
7	Cigarette Butt (RDK-9)	1.1,2,3[1.2]	B	AB	B(A)	AB	C[A]	18,18 [21,22,24]
8	Cigarette Butt (A)	4.1,4.2	AB	AB	B	AB	C	18,31
9	Cigarette Butt (B)	4.1,4.2[1]**	AB	A	A	A(B)	BC[A]	22,25
10	Cigarette Butt (G)	4.1,4.2[2]	AB	AB	B	AB	C(A)	
11	Cigarette Butt (H)	1.1,3	B	AB	A	B	C	21,22

* = Results listed as HLADQA1 4.2 may actually be 4.2 or 4.3. The probe on the strips does not differentiate between the two types.
** = HLADQA1 type 1.2 may be present, but masked.
( ) = Weak results for types in parenthesis
[ ] = Results in brackets are too weak to be conclusive

The trial evidence all fitted together like a puzzle, making for a well-presented case. The Defense took a slightly different approach by trying to imply that Chad's death was a mere accident which occurred when the defendants were trying to scare him from further cooperating with the police. They claimed their only intention was to frighten, not to kill, Chad.

Both sides argued their case to the jury. The prosecution relied on the testimony of the girlfriend. The Defense claimed that the prosecution hadn't proved their case beyond a reasonable doubt. All three defendants were found guilty of the murder of Chad MacDonald and the Attempt Murder of his girlfriend.

Both Florence Noriega and Jose Ibarra were convicted of the rape, but for some reason the jury didn't convict Michael Martinez on the rape charge.

The special circumstance allegation was found to be true, and the case proceeded on to the Death Penalty phase. This meant that Jeff needed to present any Aggravation evidence against any of the defendants. The prosecution was going to rely on the horrific facts of the crime to substantiate the claim of Aggravation. However, the Defense claimed that there was Mitigation because of the role played by Chad as an Informant.

One of the defense attorneys called Detective Griffin, who downplayed Chad's usefulness as an Informant saying Chad did not provide information that would have led to the arrest of either of his main sources. Brea's police chief was called as a witness to testify that Chad was a major source of Meth in the community. When it was time for Argument in the Penalty phase, the Defense attacked Chad's behavior. Ibarra's attorney said, "He went to Norwalk because he was arrogant, because he was reckless, and because it was a way to get drugs to further his criminal conduct. This youth was a purveyor of poison who even robbed his girlfriend of her youth and her innocence."

Jeff found this to be a stretch of the so-called 'blame game.' Would the jurors really buy this argument that Chad brought all this down on himself by deciding to get involved in drugs? Claiming that the defendants shouldn't receive the Death Penalty because the victim, Chad, wasn't pure as snow was a novel approach.

Yet it must have worked, since the case ended up with a hung jury as to each of the defendants (for Noriega and Ibarra it was nine for death and three for life, and for Martinez it was seven for death and five for life.) Afterwards, the DA's Office had to make a tough decision as to whether it should retry all three defendants on the Penalty Phase. After considerable reflection, it was decided that it wouldn't be worth another Death Penalty trial, which would require the girlfriend to relive all the events while testifying again. The end result was that all three Meth heads received a sentence of Life Without the possibility of Parole (LWOP), which may or may not have been sufficient for what they did to Chad and his girlfriend.

CHAPTER 50 WHAT HAVE WE LEARNED IN CHAD'S CASE?

As the trio took their county-jail-issued toothbrushes with them, they headed to their respective state prisons for the rest of their lives. The entire sad affair was finally over. Or was it? Most people would place their dislike on the three Meth-head killers and rapists who committed the unthinkable acts. However, throughout the trial Cindy's mother seemed to want to paint a picture that the cops were the bad guys, in that no responsible person in law enforcement should ever think of using a juvenile as an Informant.

Yet some people in the Yorba Linda community looked upon the entire sad experience as a lack of parental responsibility. Chad had had several scrapes with the law which his mother was well aware of. Chad's heavy usage of Meth for over a year before his death was full of warning signs that an observant parent should have recognized. His loss of over 20 pounds was a red flag of possible Meth usage. Once Chad was expelled from his high school and placed in a continuation school, the red lights and sirens should have been a wake-up call to his mother as to his involvement in and addiction to drugs.

The most interesting fact in this case was that when Chad was busted for a large amount of drugs, it was his mother who agreed that Chad could work it off by being a juvenile Informant. As a matter of fact Cindy, as the parent, signed the papers giving permission for her son to work as an Informant. However, Chad's mother didn't want to take any of the responsibility and spun the facts that it was the deceitful or tainted police who killed her son. Her argument was that the police took advantage of her vulnerable 17-year-old son. The police should never have used young people to catch hardened drug dealers. The role of the police was to protect young people, not to place them in harm's way.

It was interesting how Chad's mom verbally attacked and sought legal action against the Brea Police Department in two ways. First she was able to get the attention of a politician who went all the way to Sacramento to put forth new legislation severely limiting the use of juvenile offenders as Informants. As a result, the law in California was changed with the enactment of Assembly Bill 2816, which created Penal Code 701.5, which prohibits any minor under 12 to be used as a police informant and any minor between 13 and 17 could not be used as an informant without a court order. There is no doubt that this new law has had a major impact on the way law enforcement conducts narcotics investigations.

Nevertheless, within months of the verdict, Chad's mother hired a civil attorney to file a lawsuit against the Brea Police Department for using her son as a police Informant which resulted in his death. She sued them for $10 million. Her contention was that the police shouldn't use minors to try to work off criminal matters that they may have. The paradox of this was the fact that she had signed the agreement that her son could work off his juvenile drug case by being an Informant. Her lawsuit raised a myriad of issues.

This civil lawsuit dragged on for years, and it was finally settled by the city of Brea paying her side $100,000 to end the final chapter in the Chad MacDonald case. In reality, no one came out a winner in Chad's untimely death. Law enforcement lost. The three killers lost. There are those that feel that Chad's mother may have collected a few dollars, but she may have ended up the biggest loser of them all.

As to the criminal prosecution, there was no doubt that Jeff Ramseyer was the right person for this case, which seemed like a hand grenade missing a pin just waiting to detonate. He was like an orchestra conductor who was able to get each witness to come in on cue and to perform beyond expectation. He was the type of attorney needed in a sensitive case which could have quickly unraveled if one of the witnesses started sparring with fellow witnesses.

GREED CAN KILL

People v. Van Sickle & Rodriguez

SUPERSTAR PROSECUTOR

Jeffrey Ramseyer

CHAPTER 51 THE SILENT MOVIE THEATRE

It was a Friday evening in Hollywood on January 17, 1997, no different than any other. The hard-working people wanted to celebrate the fact that they had survived another grueling work week. They wanted to escape from their dreary, mundane lives, and they craved to be entertained by the magic of the silver screen. Tinsel town had an abundance of movie theatres they could visit to add some spice to their zombie-like lives.

Back in 1997 there was a plethora of box office hits. At the time, the most popular was *Titanic*, which was a blockbuster, followed by *Men In Black*, which was the favorite of the younger generation. But the most relevant movie of the day was *L.A. Confidential*, which showed the mob years of Hollywood. However, the movie *Boogie Nights* was a depiction of the drug culture occurring only a short distance away in the Hollywood Hills.

Nevertheless, there was a special avant-garde movie fan who relished viewing their favor oldies at the **Silent Movie Theatre** at 611 North Fairfax Boulevard, Los Angeles (Hollywood).

On that evening there was an unusual showing of the1927 classic movie ***Sunrise***, for which Janet Gaynor received the Academy Award for Best Actress. This tiny theatre had only 143 seats, and that night it was over half full of enthusiastic patrons.

The owner of the theatre, Laurence (Larry) Austin, was pleased with the turnout. He had come about his ownership of this ironic little theatre in the strangest way, but he persevered to keep it afloat. He realized that it was a struggle to make a living operating a movie house that only showed the old silent movies. Larry willingly worked the ticket counter but had to pay for a girl to work the concession stand. The projectionist also had to be taken care of. Fortunately for Larry, he had his longtime companion work as the projectionist, which saved on the labor costs.

Larry Austin
Owner & Operator of Theatre

The lights began to fade, and the theatre curtain was jerkily pulled open, revealing the blank silver screen. At that moment the elderly Larry Austin shuffled his way to the front of the theatre and stood in front of the audience. He slowly raised his hands in the air to get the crowd's attention. As the murmur of chatting patrons subsided, he cleared his raspy voice. He thanked the audience for attending and tried to create interest in the night's feature film.

In order to generate some degree of excitement, the organist faintly started playing background music of Pomp and Circumstance to gain the notice of the audience. Larry Austin continued to make his announcement as the house lights began to dim. Then Larry, with a giant grin on his face, said, "Without further ado have an enjoyable evening watching our movie ***Sunrise***."

For a senior citizen at 74, Larry spiritly walked back to the ticket booth to sell some more tickets to late arrivals. Larry was pleased with the turnout and could hear the organist amping up the music to highlight the special moments in the silent movie.

Larry was lucky in that he had a reliable organist who was in his 80s. Besides being talented, he truly enjoyed playing the background music to the silent films. Larry couldn't have been happier, since the turnout was good and his staff was doing their job while he sat in the ticket booth collecting money.

CHAPTER 52 THIS IS A ROBBERY

After the main feature, the second short film, which was titled ***School Days***, appeared on the screen. Although this wasn't the time for an intermission, a man in the back row of seats got up and walked a few steps out of the darkened theatre. He continued over to the concession girl, where he asked about purchasing tickets for future performances. She pointed over to Larry in the ticket booth as the person to see.

This man appeared younger than others in the audience. He was wearing a baseball cap and seemed a little different, especially with his request for future tickets. Larry didn't mind since he was always pleased to sell more tickets. The man walked through the empty lobby and stood next to Larry. As he talked about buying tickets for upcoming attractions, he pulled out a revolver from his waistband and pointed it directly at Larry. The organ music at that moment hit a fever pitch, making it impossible to hear anything other than the organ.

The young man said, "This is a robbery, give me all the money." Larry couldn't hear each and every word; however, his eyes were staring at the steel revolver telling him it was a ROBBERY. This caught Larry by surprise, so he took several moments to process what was happening. He had just counted the cash for the evening and really didn't want to hand over the few hundred dollars. It was hard enough just to pay the staff and all the bills. When the robber repeated his demand for the money, Larry looked at the gun and comprehended that the money wasn't worth his life.

With a slight reluctance, Larry handed over to the robber a fistful of cash. Larry felt relief as the man grabbed the money, since he had complied with his wishes. What followed next surprised everyone. The man dropped the money and started shooting his gun at Larry. He shot him at point-blank range, hitting Larry in the head and several times in the torso. After the second shot, Larry's body spun around as his legs gave way from under him.

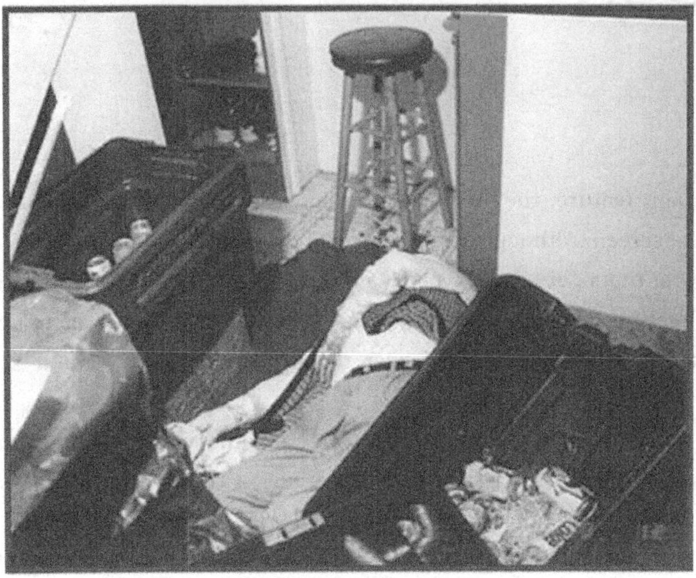

**Victim Larry Austin
Lying on Box Office Floor**

Larry's body came to rest on the dirty floor of the ticket booth between two ice chests full of sodas. His light-blue dress shirt turned to crimson red from the blood of his gunshot wounds. The tile floor became a pool of blood too slippery to walk on.

The robber had dropped the stack of bills, which landed near Larry's shoes. As the money lay there, it became saturated with blood, giving the appearance of truly 'blood money.'

Money Dropped
Next to Victim

The robber spun around and looked at the concession girl. Her expression was one of shock and surprise and she stood there frozen in fear. His cold eyes locked in on her eyes as he pointed the gun directly at her. What was she supposed to do? Should she give him the concession money? Before a word could be spoken, he squeezed the trigger and bullets went flying at her. What had she done to deserve this? The gunfire knocked her off her feet falling to the floor. She sustained two gunshot wounds and landed on the floor that was covered in Larry's blood

CHAPTER 53 TIME TO ESCAPE

Within seconds the robbery was over and it was time for the robber to escape. All the robber had to do was walk out the front door and he would be on the sidewalk of Fairfax Boulevard, where he could easily disappear into the darkness. What was peculiar was the fact the robber didn't take the easy way out but ran back into the darkened theatre with his gun in his right hand. The second feature film was still playing on the screen as he scurried down the right side aisle.

Interior of Theatre

He slowed down and turned to the audience so they could see his entire face, and he fired his gun into the ceiling. This shocked the theatre goers, who had no way of knowing whether this was part of the entertainment for the evening. The audience didn't know how to react. Should they run for an exit or should they try to climb under the theatre chairs? There was a moment of panic, but before they could process what to do the shooter had run out the side exit door that went to the patio and back gate. In less than a minute, the owner of the theatre had been mortally wounded while the concession girl was critically injured

.

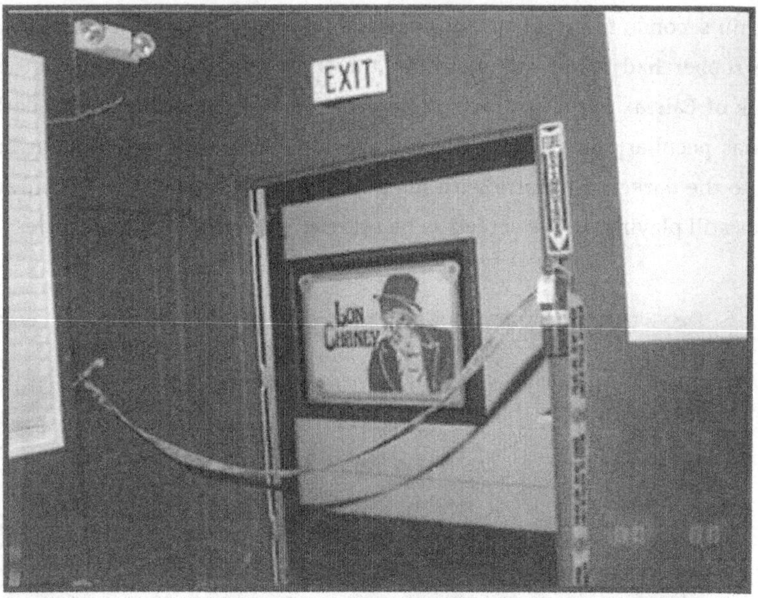

Theatre Exit to Back Patio

LAPD was called, and within minutes officers converged on the little theatre. They could see the two shooting victims were in need of medical attention. Should they close off the neighborhood to look for the suspect? Before long the police surrounded the crime scene and order was restored.

Police Responding to Silent Movie Theatre on Fairfax Blvd.

The homicide detectives eventually arrived, and they seemed perplexed as to what had happened. Initially, the facts didn't add up since the large bundle of cash was lying on the floor next to the owner. Why would a robber leave the large amount of cash? Further, why would the person go back into the theatre and shoot into the ceiling?

The detectives began to scratch their heads as to the motive for the shooting. The detectives' main source of information came from the projectionist, James Van Sickle. He described being in the projection booth when he heard a noise that sounded like a shooting. He stepped out of his projection area of the theatre and saw Larry, his companion and boss, lying on the box office floor. A short distance over was the concession girl lying bleeding on the floor. He didn't get a look at the shooter and couldn't provide a description.

When the detectives spoke to the members of the audience, they were able to give a fairly good description of the suspect. They all agreed that the suspect was a thin male in his early 20s and he appeared to be Hispanic. This information was broadcasted to the officers in the field but was too vague to be useful.

After talking to some people in the audience, it was believed that the shooter had been seated in the back row on the right side. When the detectives checked that area, they found a plastic bottle of pink lemonade.

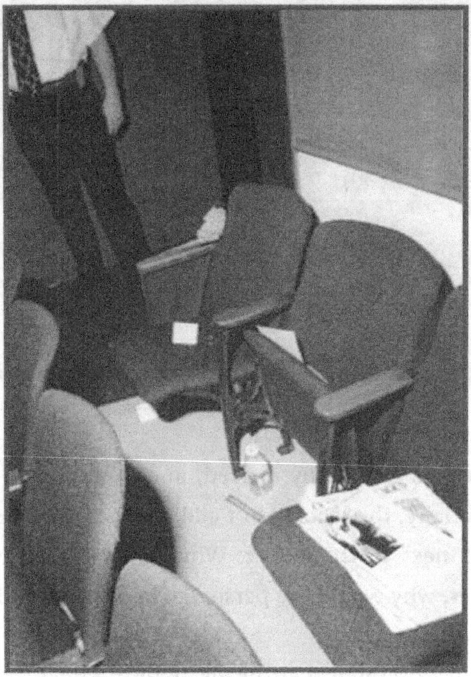

Where Shooter Was Seated

The detectives had never dealt with a robber who drank pink lemonade. After collecting whatever evidence was available, they sent it for forensic testing. The Latent Print detail was unable to lift any prints off of the lemonade container.

CHAPTER 54 HISTORY OF THE SILENT MOVIE THEATRE

In the 1930s, talky motion pictures started to replace the silent movies. Within a short time, all the studios had converted over and there was no market for the old silent films. The studios started to clean out their film libraries and get rid of all their old non-talky movies. However, there had been hundreds of these old movies made since the conception of filmmaking. These silent films showed the evolution of the movie industry from acting to editing. So much of Hollywood's history was contained in these old movies.

John Hampton and his wife lived in Oklahoma and showed the old silent movies in their backyard. As the talkies came into vogue, he realized that the old silent movies had lost their appeal to the mass audiences. He wanted to do something to preserve them. So he decided they would move to Hollywood with plans to show the old silent movies in a little theatre.

He found a building on Fairfax Boulevard which he and his wife were able to convert into a little theatre. By 1942 they formally opened what was called the Silent Movie Theatre, which only showed silent films. Because of WWII the little theatre closed for business and didn't reopen until 1946. During this period of closure, Mr. Hampton was acquiring more of the old silent movies from the studios.

After the War, the Silent Movie Theatre became popular for film buffs. Here people could see the old Laurel and Hardy clips that many people had grown up watching. The theatre would rotate some of the old movies in order to encourage more patrons to frequent the theatre. Clara Bow and Charlie Chaplin were often seen in the back row viewing their old movies.

Mr. Hampton continued to acquire more films and spent hours trying to repair the old ones. Above the movie theatre on the second floor, Mr. Hampton had built racks and racks to store his classic silent film library. Next to the film vaults were the living quarters for the Hamptons, which consisted of a large bedroom with kitchen and bathroom. The living area wasn't luxurious but allowed Mr. Hampton a short commute to work by merely walking down the stairs to the ticket booth.

The real benefit for Mr. Hampton was that he could spend long hours trying to repair the old films. It may have been the long hours and fumes from the editing glue that cause his health to fail. Laurence Austin was an old film buff and spent time assisting the Hamptons running the little theatre. When Mr. Hampton died, Mrs. Hampton was in poor health and needed help running the movie house. Larry Austin was able to aid her in keeping the theatre open.

Mrs. Hampton eventually moved into a convalescent hospital, and Larry took over the daily operation of the theatre. There was some controversy as to how

Larry acquired the ownership rights to the theatre and the library of old films. Most people had believed that all the property would stay in Mrs. Hampton's name. There was a police investigation, and Larry seemed to have the blessing of Mrs. Hampton in reopening the theatre under his control. Some people questioned the manner in which Larry acquired the theatre, since in 1983 he had been convicted of embezzlement from another company he had worked for. As a result of this conviction, he served 22 months in prison.

Even with Larry Austin's questionable past, he seemed to know how to maintain the theatre and was able to operate it reasonably well even up to his death. Nevertheless, even Larry needed help to operate the theatre. James Van Sickle was hired to help with the business of the movie theatre.

In 1990, Larry was having the theatre painted and one of the painters was James Van Sickle. Even though Larry was twice the age of Van Sickle, they became close companions who lived upstairs in the apartment that the Hamptons had occupied.

Their relationship was described as stormy. Possibly to keep Van Sickle around, Austin hired him to be the projectionist. Van Sickle continued in that position for a number of years. However, there were times that Van Sickle would move out and stay in the city of Paramount. At one point Austin accused Van Sickle of robbing him and made a formal police report.

Projectionist Ready

It was interesting that even Van Sickle had a jaded past, starting with an attempted murder charge in Compton. When the victim failed to appear in court, the charge was dropped. Later, in 1989, he was convicted of sales of narcotics and was sentenced to state prison. He also had a forgery case in Torrance. Even with all these criminal matters, Austin would take Van Sickle back and permitted him to continue to work as the projectionist at the theatre. Austin dropped the robbery charges against Van Sickle, and everything appeared to be going well on the surface.

CHAPTER 55 MAKE IT LOOK LIKE A ROBBERY

However deep down inside, Van Sickle was growing tired of Larry. Since Larry was 74, Van Sickle had hopes of inheriting the entire theatre business upon the demise of his friend Larry. He became impatient and wanted to speed up the process, so he concocted a plan that he would hire someone to kill Larry Austin and make it look like a robbery. Van Sickle had prepared a handwritten Will that made it appear that Larry had given everything, including the movie theatre and the film library, to him upon Larry's death.

Since Van Sickle didn't want to be a suspect in Larry's passing, he needed a solid alibi. So his plan was to have someone shoot Larry in the ticket booth while Van Sickle would be working as the projectionist in a separate part of the theatre. Van Sickle started thinking about who could he hire to do the actual killing. Obviously it had to be someone who had the stomach to kill a person in cold blood. This hit man had to have a gun and be a good shot with the weapon. Also, it goes without saying that he needed someone who wouldn't rat on him. In other words, the killer needed to be trustworthy.

It appears that the most challenging requirement was deciding how much to offer the killer for doing the job. Van Sickle knew that there wasn't a fixed rate of pay for hit men. He thought to himself, if he were being hired as a hit man, how much would he demand? He understood that if he inherited Larry's ownership of the entire silent film library it would be worth over a million dollars. That was when he settled on the amount of $25,000, which he felt was fair compensation for shooting his buddy Larry Austin.

Months earlier, Van Sickle had worked part-time at a company where he met Christian Rodriguez, who was a 19-year-old young man. He knew that Christian was always in need of money. He was one of those young people who was always looking for the 'big break' to climb up to get in the fast lane to live the 'good life.' Van Sickle contacted Rodriguez to see if he was interested in making $25,000. Rodriguez didn't take long to respond. He said he would be willing to do whatever it took to get that type of money.

Van Sickle tried to explain it in the simplest terms that he could earn $25,000 for five minutes of work. He would be given a handgun, which he would point at an old man and pull the trigger. Rodriguez may have been more impressed that someone was going to trust him with a .357 magnum than the fact he would have to kill someone. He didn't have any hesitation to do that for $25,000. Since he was so willing to do the job Van Sickle then added that he wanted him to also kill the concession counter girl. Maybe Van Sickle noticed some reluctance by Rodriguez to kill another person, so he said he would throw in another $5,000. At that point young Rodriguez could only think of $30,000 and what he could do with that amount of money.

Van Sickle went over the details with Rodriguez, explaining that the killing needed to look like a robbery. This seemed like the perfect crime. No one at the theatre had ever met or seen Rodriguez before, so no one would be able to later identify him. Since Van Sickle would be working as the projectionist, he would have a solid alibi. They had planned the shooting to occur when the music was the loudest during the show. They also had planned to have Rodriguez run through the theatre shooting the gun so everyone would be able to see that the robber was a youthful Hispanic male.

The week prior to the robbery, both Van Sickle and Rodriguez were paging each other back and forth as though they were anticipating something was about to happen. On January 17, 1997, everything was ready to pull off their plan. That night Larry was working at the ticket booth. The concession girl was Mary Gillum (pseudonym), who was 19 year old and was familiar working the snack bar.

As planned, Rodriguez bought his theatre ticket and took a seat in the back row. He wanted to blend in with the other members of the audience, so he brought with him a bottle of pink lemonade (it is unknown if that is the favorite drink of most hit men).

Rodriguez remembered he was to wait until the organ music reached a high point. As the second feature was beginning, the music became louder. That was the time Rodriguez made his move to enter the lobby to do his dastardly deed. He used a .357 magnum; possibly he wanted to emulate Clint Eastwood in the ***Dirty Harry*** movies. (However, Clint really used a .44 magnum)

Rodriguez fired at point blank range, hitting Larry in the face. The .357 magnum is a powerful weapon that can make large holes in its victims.

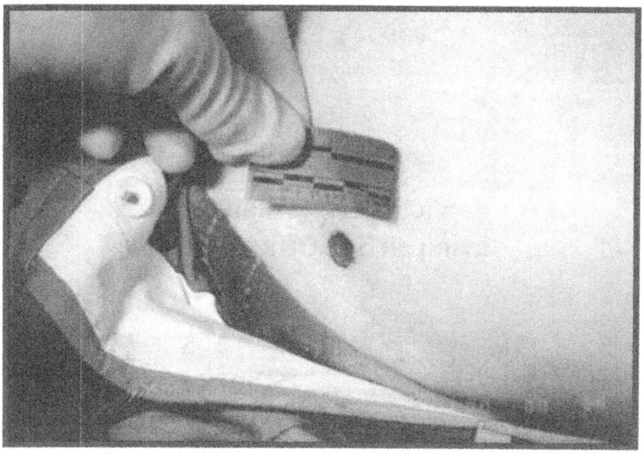

Size of Bullet Hole in Larry Austin

Rodriguez didn't know how many times he needed to shot people in order to kill them. He looked at Larry on the floor and pointed his gun at his body and pulled the trigger several more times. Eventually, he didn't see Larry's body make any movement and he assumed he had shot him enough.

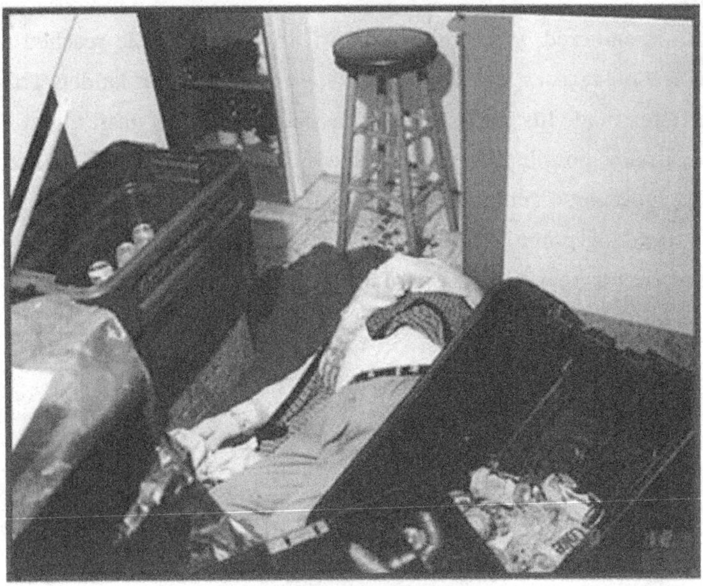

Victim Larry Austin
Lying on Box Office Floor

After Rodriguez had shot the Concession girl, he remembered that he had been told to go back in the theatre to make his escape by way of the back door. He ran down the right aisle and turned around so everyone would get a good look of him. He raised his gun to the ceiling and fired the .357 to get everyone's attention.

Right Aisle of Theatre

After the shooting in the theatre, Rodriguez ran out through the patio back gate. Looking back over their well-planned killing, they had to be pleased that it appeared that they had pulled off the 'Perfect Murder.'

No one suspected that Van Sickle was involved. He put on a fine performance, appearing distraught over the tragic death of his lover and business partner. As a matter of fact, he gave a very touching eulogy about his old friend Larry Austin at a fundraiser for the Silent Movie Theatre.

CHAPTER 56 WHO'S A SUSPECT?

Even with all the astute preparation , several things didn't go completely as planned. The concessions stand girl, Mary Gillum, fortunately survived the two gunshot wounds she suffered. The other disappointment for Rodriguez was the fact that Van Sickle didn't pay him the $30,000 he had been promised. Van Sickle's excuse was that he hadn't received the inheritance as of yet. Van Sickle claimed he had found a handwritten Will made out by Larry giving him the Silent Movie Theatre plus the million dollar silent-film library.

However, when Van Sickle told one of Austin's old friends about finding this Will, Larry's friend thought that was particularly strange based on the volatile relationship between the two men over all those years. Larry's friend was so suspicious of such a Will, he went to the police to let them know of his skepticism.

The detectives had suspicion about this so-called 'Robbery.' They couldn't figure out why a robber would go to all that trouble just to leave the money on the floor in the ticket booth.

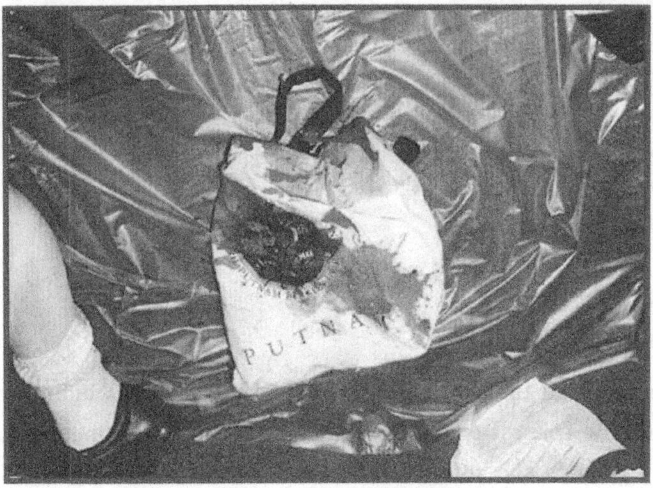

Bloody Bag in Box Office

This didn't mean that Van Sickle was involved, but the detectives had an uneasy feeling about the motive for the shooting. Since they weren't coming up with any good leads on the case, they were willing to follow up with this new information about the Will that gave everything to Van Sickle. The detectives recognized that Van Sickle had a solid alibi since he was working as the projectionist. But because Van Sickle had a shady past, the detectives thought at least he was capable of being somehow involved.

The idea that Van Sickle might be implicated was like trying to take a square peg and put it into a round hole. Van Sickle didn't fit the description given by the members of the audience of a young Hispanic male. Since Mary Gillum had survived, the detectives asked if Van Sickle could have been the shooter. Mary knew Van Sickle since they both worked together at the Theatre. She was definite that Van Sickle didn't and couldn't have done the shooting.

When Mary's condition improved the detectives recontacted her and asked her to work with a forensic artist to possibly come up with a composite of the killer. Since Mary had gotten such a good look at the shooter, she and the artist spent time together in which she was able to give a detailed description. The end result was a well-drawn composite which the police provided to the news media to show the public.

Unfortunately for Rodriguez, a friend of his saw the composite and noticed that the features matched Rodriguez. She notified the police that she thought the composite closely resembled Christian Rodriquez. With that information, the detectives now had the names of two people—Rodriguez and Van Sickle—who could possibly be involved. At this point, the detectives wondered if they could somehow connect these two individuals.

The detectives didn't have any firm evidence that either was involved. However, since Rodriguez resembled the shooter, the detectives decided they had enough to arrest him and bring him in for questioning. When Rodriguez was booked, they found in his wallet a card that had several phone numbers on it. At the bottom of the card was the number (310) 634-0137. They didn't think much of it at the time, but they kept the card as possible evidence.

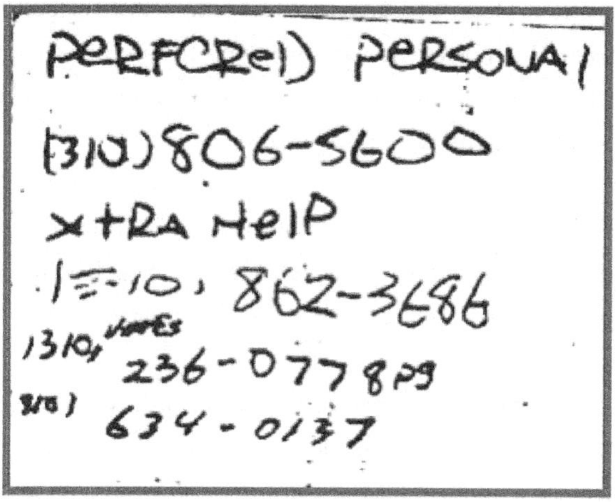
PeRFCRel) PeRSONAl
(310) 806-5600
xtRA HelP
(310) 862-3686
(310) VartEs 236-0778 pg
(310) 634-0137

While conducting their investigation, the detectives came across a Rental Application that Van Sickle had filled out in which he listed his phone number as (310) 634-0137.

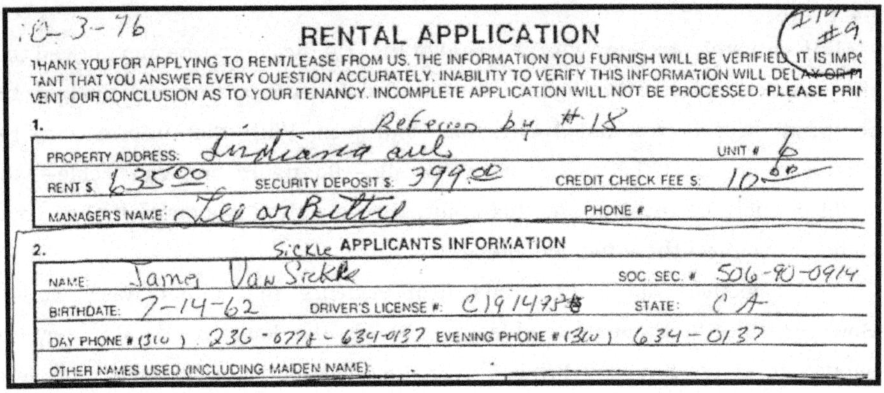

10-3-76

RENTAL APPLICATION

#9

THANK YOU FOR APPLYING TO RENT/LEASE FROM US. THE INFORMATION YOU FURNISH WILL BE VERIFIED. IT IS IMPO-TANT THAT YOU ANSWER EVERY QUESTION ACCURATELY. INABILITY TO VERIFY THIS INFORMATION WILL DELAY OR PR-VENT OUR CONCLUSION AS TO YOUR TENANCY. INCOMPLETE APPLICATION WILL NOT BE PROCESSED. PLEASE PRI

1. Referred by #18

PROPERTY ADDRESS: Indiana ave. UNIT # 6

RENT $ 635.00 SECURITY DEPOSIT $: 399.00 CREDIT CHECK FEE $: 10.00

MANAGER'S NAME: Leo or Bettie PHONE #

2. Sickle APPLICANTS INFORMATION

NAME: James Van Sickle SOC. SEC. #: 506-90-0914

BIRTHDATE: 7-14-62 DRIVER'S LICENSE #: C1914738 STATE: CA

DAY PHONE # (310) 236-0778 - 634-0137 EVENING PHONE # (310) 634-0137

OTHER NAMES USED (INCLUDING MAIDEN NAME):

This was the type of connection the detectives were looking for. Why would Rodriguez have Van Sickle's phone number in his wallet? The inference was that they knew each other. Next, the detectives obtained the various phone numbers that both men used. When they started reviewing these phone records, they could see a pattern of phone calls. Bingo! They were in communication with each other just before and right after the day of the murder.

Now the detectives wanted to talk more to Rodriguez. One of the detectives advised Rodriguez of his Miranda rights by reading it from a Miranda Card. The detectives asked him if he understood his rights, to which Rodriguez responded, "Yea." The detective asked him about his age and Rodriguez indicated he was 19 years old.

Shortly thereafter the two detectives started asking if he knew Van Sickle. To their surprise, Rodriguez laid out how he was hired by Van Sickle to shoot this guy in this old theatre. He explained all the planning and what role was played by both of them.

After obtaining the incriminating statements from Rodriguez, the detectives wanted to see if they could get any of the persons in the audience to identify Rodriguez. The detectives prepared a photo lineup including Rodriguez's photo in it. They showed it to several of the parties in the audience that night, and they were able to identify Rodriguez as the person running through the theatre. With Rodriguez's 'cop out' and now the identification, the detectives were pleased that they would be able to make a case against Rodriguez.

Then the detectives turned their attention to see if there was some way to build a case against Van Sickle. Through certain channels, the police were able to wire an informant who knew Van Sickle. The informant met with Van Sickle and asked him about what happened to Larry Austin. They were able to record Van Sickle explaining why he couldn't do the shooting of Larry. He didn't want to appear to be involved. This statement proved to be useful in prosecuting Van Sickle since his jury wouldn't be hearing the highly incriminating statements made to the detectives by Rodriguez.

When the detectives arrested Van Sickle, he refused to waive his right and speak to them. That may be because Van Sickle had past dealings with the police and knew it wouldn't be in his best interest to talk to them.

CHAPTER 57 LET'S TALK TO THE DA'S OFFICE

The detectives prepared their reports of their investigation and submitted them to the DA's Office for filing of murder and attempted murder charges. Initially when the case was reviewed by prosecutors, it was decided that charges should be filed against both Rodriguez and Van Sickle. Since the news media had been closely following the developments on the case, the DA's Office realized that this case would generate considerable attention. Because of all the premeditation and planning in this case, the DA's Office decided to pursue the Death Penalty against both suspects. Within short order the case was transferred to the exclusive Major Crimes Division, where the case could receive the attention and time that would be required.

Jeff Ramseyer was the prosecutor who was assigned the case. You the reader already are familiar with Jeff from the previous case we have discussed. I, the author, decided to include this case in this book because it illustrates what talented attorneys make up this elite group of prosecutors. Therefore it is not necessary for me go into the qualifications of Jeff as an outstanding prosecutor.

Jeff soon recognized the challenge of the case was that there was substantial evidence against Rodriguez but there was much less evidence against Van Sickle. Although Rodriguez's statements incriminated Van Sickle, the prosecutor knew the law would not permit Rodriguez's statement to be used against Van Sickle. As

Jeff immersed himself more into the facts of the case, he realized he wouldn't be able to use the same jury for both defendants. If he had to have two separate trials, there was the problem that in the second trial the Defense attorney would be able to play up any inconsistency the witnesses made in their testimony in the first trial.

To prevent that from happening Jeff was able to convince the judge to have one trial consisting of two separate juries. What it meant was that most of the witnesses would have to testify only once before both juries. However, when a witness was testifying as to evidence that pertained to only one of the defendants, that defendant's jury would remain as the other defendant's jury left the courtroom. An example was when the detective testified to Rodriguez's confession detailing how both of them planned the killing, only Rodriguez's jury would hear about that and Van Sickle's jury would be removed from the courtroom.

Several months after Jeff was assigned the case he came by my (the author's) office. He said, "Ron, you won't believe this case I've got." He gave me a good-natured grin, so I was in wonderment as to what he was talking about. Over 40 years with the DA's Office, I thought I had seen just about every conceivable case. He started out by asking me if I had heard about the 'Silent Movie Theatre Murder.' I indicated I had read in the newspapers something about a Silent Movie house but I couldn't figure out what it was all about.

That's when Jeff said, "That's the problem. Everyone gets confused with all the crazy facts about all these characters." That's when I asked him to start at the beginning and explain the relevant facts of the case. Jeff had a way of explaining things in simple terms. He wasn't one of the attorneys who had to always try to impress you. He explained that there were only three basic characters that I had to know about. As he started to discuss the characters in the case, I took a yellow tablet on my desk and wrote the names AUSTIN, VAN SICKLE, and RODRIGUEZ.

CHAPTER 58 TIME TO PREPARE FOR TRIAL

After 15 minutes I understood the roles of the various parties. Then I asked Jeff what evidence he had against the two defendants. That was when Jeff said, "Ron that's the problem. I have enough to bury Christian Rodriguez, but I am wafer thin on evidence against Van Sickle." He went on to tell me that they knew Van Sickle was the brains behind the shootings from the detailed statement that Rodriguez gave to the detectives.

The key piece of evidence was the fact that Rodriguez had Van Sickle's phone number. I asked Jeff for copies of the note that Rodriguez had in his pocket and the Rental Agreement with Van Sickle's phone number. I told Jeff that we could make a visual display showing the two pieces of paper on the same poster board.

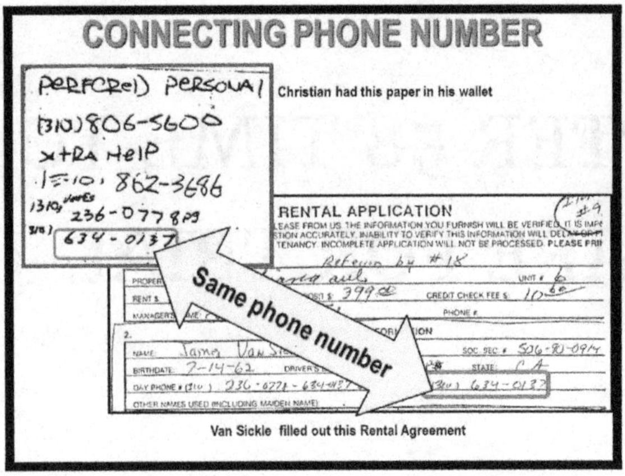

Then Jeff explained that the strongest evidence was the number of phone calls made between Rodriguez and Van Sickle. He gave me a stack of phone records and showed me page after page of phone calls between the two. I told Jeff that we needed to place all the relevant information about the frequency of the phone calls on one visual.

In that way the jurors would see that these guys were in constant contact shortly before the shooting and immediately afterward. Jeff tried to develop a Timeline that would more graphically show the increase in the frequency of the calls around the time of the murder and shortly thereafter. After many drafts, Jeff finalized the chart as shown below.

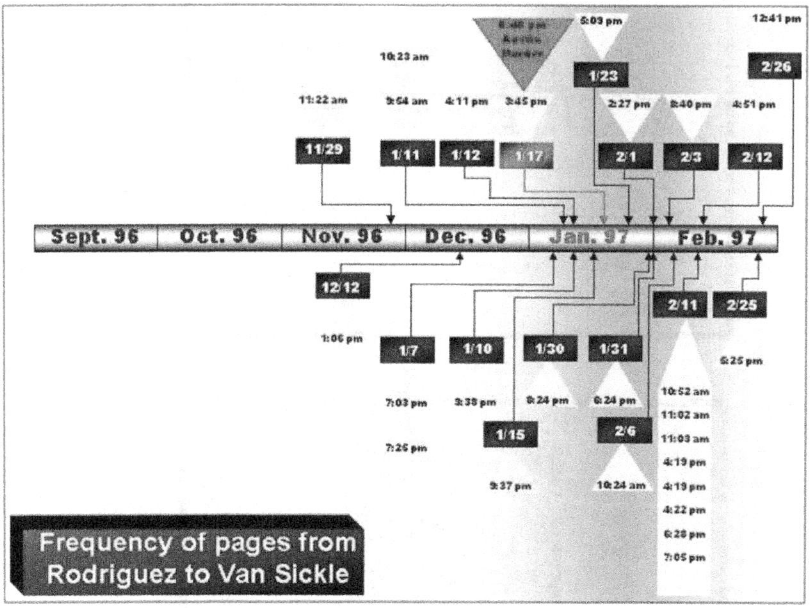

Here he was able to show that around January 7th a pattern emerged in which the two defendants were making frequent pages and phone calls to each other. Also, as the investigation began to expand, the defendants were in constant contact with each other. The phone records by themselves couldn't convey the information that was essential to the case like this Timeline chart.

The judge had agreed to have two separate juries in one trial. That meant that both defense attorneys needed to have two separate set of exhibits. For Jeff's Opening Statement, I prepared the two sets of photo poster boards that showed the location of the Silent Movie Theatre on Fairfax Boulevard.

One of the photo boards showed where Larry Austin was shot in the ticket booth. Then there were photos showing where the robber left the money at the crime scene. Jeff wanted to make sure that the jurors understood that this wasn't a real robbery but an execution.

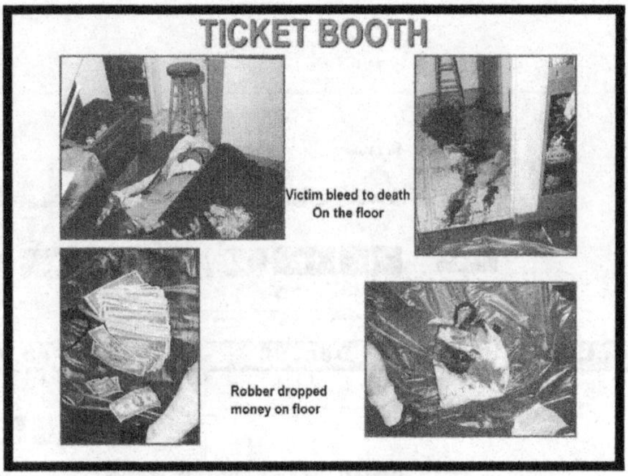
TICKET BOOTH
Victim bleed to death
On the floor
Robber dropped
money on floor

SILENT MOVIE THEATER- INTERIOR
Posters on the wall of old Silent Movie Stars

For the trial, Jeff wanted additional photo boards that he could show to the witnesses when they were testifying. This graphic consisted of three photos showing the interior of the theatre. Each witness could use it to show the jurors where they were seated when the killer ran through shooting into the ceiling.

One diagram was made by the city engineering department that showed the floor plan of the first floor of the theatre illustrating the entrance-lobby area; the projection room; the actual theatre; and finally the patio area in back. Lower on the chart was the layout of the living area with the long storage area for the silent movie library.

SILENT MOVIE THEATRE DIAGRAM

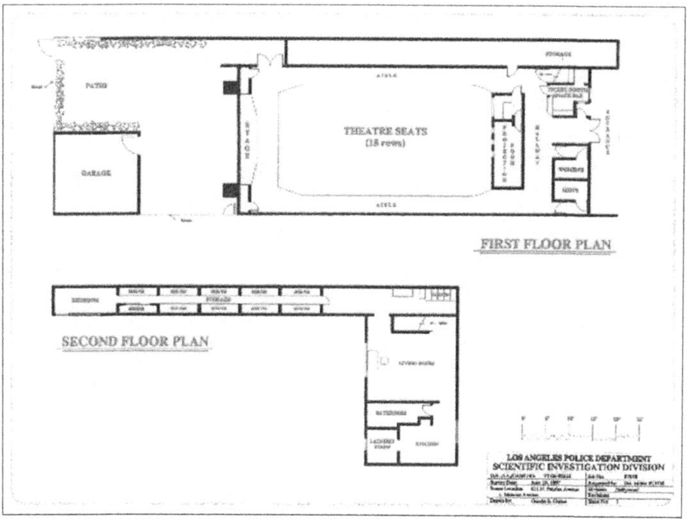

Also for trial, a photo board was created which illustrated the path that Rodriguez ran down to escape. This visual was used so the audience witnesses could show how close Rodriguez was to them when he ran out. This would help the jurors understand why some witnesses were better able to identify Rodriguez then others.

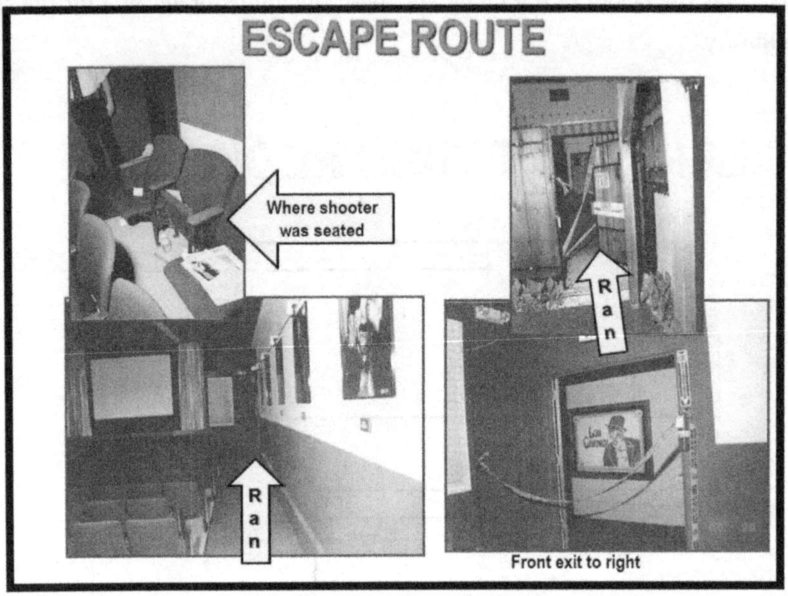

Finally for Jeff's Argument to Rodriguez's jury, Jeff wanted a way to convey to his jury what evidence had been presented to them. Jeff liked to list the prosecution's points in arrows and have them pointing to Rodriguez's name.

Most of the points involved the paging or phone calls between the two defendants. The other point was the finding of the business card in Rodriguez's pocket that had Van Sickle's phone number. This Argument chart was one way to see the cumulative effect of the evidence against Rodriguez.

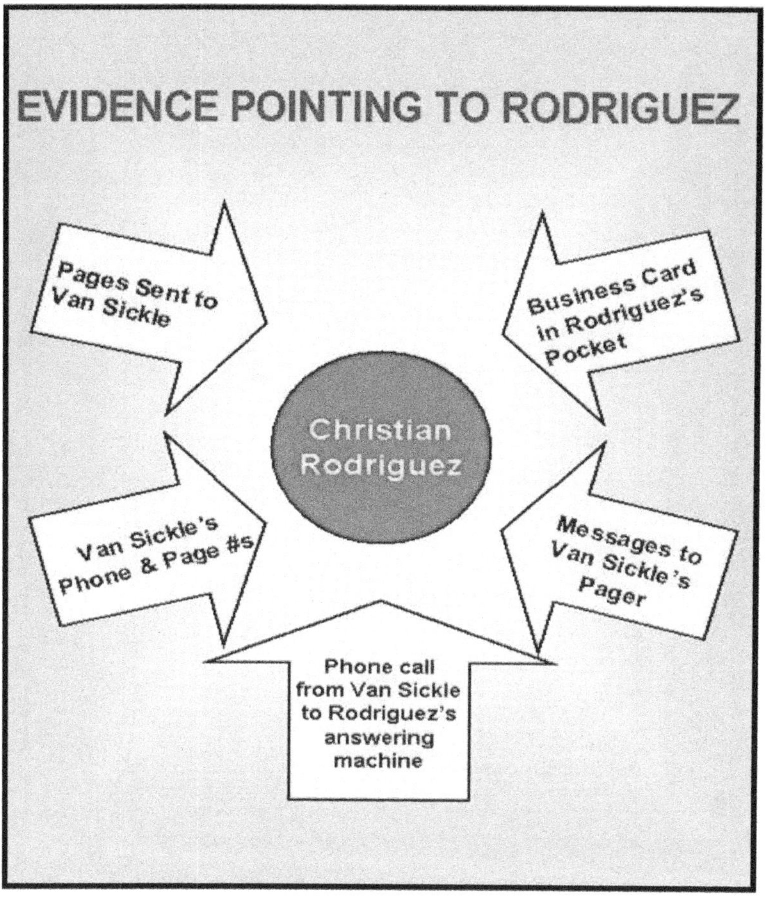

CHAPTER 59 NEED TO UNDERSTAND THE LAW

Jeff knew that the big challenge was convincing Van Sickle's jury that he was guilty. Jeff used witnesses to testify that there was no way that Larry Austin would have bequeathed his entire estate to Van Sickle. Jeff needed to have the jury focus on the LAW and see how it applied to Van Sickle. There were several legal concepts Jeff needed to explain to the jury and make sure they understood them and followed them.

FIRST DEGREE MURDER

All Murder that is <u>Willful, Deliberate & Premeditated With Express Malice Aforethought</u> is MURDER in First Degree.

- **WILLFUL = Intentional**
- **DELIBERATE = Formed/ arrived at after careful thought, weighing of considerations for/ against**
- **PREMEDITATED = Considered beforehand**

He used several Jury Instruction charts to convey to the jury that there were two ways that they could find that this killing was in fact a First Degree Murder. They could use the theory that there was "Premeditation and Deliberation." Or they could use the fact that this killing was a form of "Lying in Wait" and that is another way to prove First Degree Murder.

LYING IN WAIT FINANCIAL GAIN

DEFINITION OF LYING IN WAIT

1. A substantial period of watching & waiting for an opportune time to act.
2. A concealment by ambush or by some other secret design to take the victim by surprise even though the victim is aware of the murderer's presence.
3. The killing must occur during the same time period, or in an uninterrupted attack commencing no later than the moment the concealment ends.

To establish lying in wait no particular period of waiting & waiting is necessary provided its duration is such as to show a state of mind equivalent to premeditation & deliberation.

SPECIAL CIRCUMSTANCES FOR FINANCIAL GAIN

Penal Code §190.2(a)(1)

To find that the special circumstance of murder for financial gain is true, each of the following facts must be proved:

1. **The murder was intentional, and**
2. **It was carried out for financial gain.**

Once the jury had found there to be First Degree Murder, then they had to decide if the Special Circumstances were true. One Special Circumstance was that the murder was done for "Financial Gain." This was where Jeff discussed how much Van Sickle had to gain by claiming he was the beneficiary of Larry's Will. But what was confusing for the jurors was the fact that another Special Circumstance was the one regarding "Lying in Wait." It was worded exactly like the legal concept of 'Lying in Wait' which could be used to prove First Degree Murder.

Jeff explained how several of the jury instructions overlapped but they should not become confused with those jury instructions.

CHAPTER 60 CONCLUSION OF CASE

In Christian Rodriguez's case, the jury deliberated for a short period of time and came back with a guilty verdict for First Degree Murder regarding the killing of victim Larry Austin and Attempted Murder as to victim Mary Gillum. Also, the Special Circumstances of Financial Gain and Lying in Wait were found to be true, which meant that he was sentenced to Life in Prison without the Possibility of Parole.

However, defendant Van Sickle's case resulted in a lengthy deliberation. It took the jury six days to arrive at a guilty verdict just like in the Rodriguez case. After receiving the conviction against Van Sickle, the case moved on to the Death Penalty phase. During this stage of the proceeding, the prosecutor pointed out that Van Sickle had a prior felony conviction. Also, Jeff argued that Van Sickle was the one who developed this Murder for Hire scheme and hired someone to carry it out. He stressed that Van Sickle did this to his lover and companion who had given him so much over the years.

The same jury deliberated for several days to decide whether the Aggravating factors substantially outweighed Mitigating factors. Eventually, the jury announced to the court that they were deadlocked and the judge declared a hung jury. The jury was divided seven for Death and five for Life. Afterwards, the DA's Office decided that it wasn't likely that they would be able to get all 12 jurors to decide on Death. As a result, the Penalty phase was not retried, and the judge sentenced Van Sickle to Life Without the Possibility of Parole.

Both defendants appealed their conviction. Defendant Christian Rodriguez claimed the evidence was insufficient to support findings he waived his Miranda rights before the detectives started asking him questions. The appellate court considered all the surrounding events, which included a written statement saying that he was making all these statements of his own free will. Even though the detectives' tape recording of Rodriguez's interrogation didn't contain the word 'waived those rights', the court was satisfied from the record that he implicitly waived his Miranda rights.

As to Van Sickle's appeal, he claimed that there wasn't sufficient evidence to support the finding he aided and abetted defendant Rodriquez in the murder and there was no evidence he had the knowledge or intent that Rodriquez would personally commit the murder. The appellate court reviewed Van Sickle's contention and denied his appeal.

At time of sentencing, Jeff described this crime as one totally based on GREED. Van Sickle was greedy and wanted to be the sole owner of the Silent Movie Theatre. The film library was worth at least a million dollars. Van Sickle was willing to kill a friend in the process. Also, he was willing to kill a 19-year-old girl co-worker for no real reason except that she might be a witness to the crime.

It was supposed to be the "Perfect Crime" but ended like an old Hollywood movie with so many twists and turns to keep the audience on the edge of their seats. It had all the ingredients of a delightful movie in that there was suspense, violence, and in the end the bad guys got caught and were sent away for Life. However, in one respect this case was different from a Hollywood movie. Here the main character, Larry Austin, didn't get up and go home at the end of the day.

You might be curious as to what happened to the old Silent Movie Theatre. After Larry Austin's death, the theatre was closed for a while. Eventually it was purchased by a Charles Lustman, who did considerable remodeling and reopened the theatre showing specialty movies. Generally one day a week is set aside for the old 'Silent Movies.' As a matter of fact, when the theatre reopened it showed one of Charlie Chaplin's silent films to a packed audience. Only time will tell what more chapters will be written about the Hollywood Silent Movie Theatre.

The prosecutor, Jeff Ramseyer, did a remarkable job in getting Van Sickle, the mastermind, convicted. Some prosecutors would have plea-bargained the case by giving Christian Rodriguez a lesser sentence to get him to testify against Van Sickle. However, Jeff did it the hard way by not agreeing to any deals. He ended up getting both the mastermind of the crime as well as the trigger man convicted and sentenced to Life Without the possibility of Parole. Jeff's hard work and tenacity was done in the tradition of the DA's Major Crimes prosecutors.

What made Jeff such a special unique prosecutor will never be known because shortly thereafter he passed away from a heart attack at the young age of 39. One evening he was doing what he always enjoyed doing, playing basketball at his church, when he was stricken. His death shocked everyone in the Los Angeles Criminal Justice System. At his funeral, the church was overflowing with judges and attorneys from both sides of the aisle.

He was truly loved by all and has been greatly missed. A mother of another murder victim wrote a letter about Jeff to the district attorney stating, "Except for my son, I have never met such a compassionate, sensitive, generous and honest person. But most of all, he listened.... In addition to preparing a great case, he was sensitive, compassionate, and generous with his time and honest, both in and out of the courtroom."

I, the author, remember Jeff well and enjoyed working with him. He was not only very bright but truly a wonderful person to deal with. From early morning to the end of the court day he would greet you with a smile. Besides his pleasant demeanor, he had a steely resolve to do the right thing. When I am asked who Jeff reminds me of, the first person who comes to mind is **Paul Walker,** the movie star of the ***Fast & Furious*** movie series. Both were the same age at the time of their premature death, same height and most of all had the same smile that seemed infectious. The question was, how many more movies could Paul Walker have made? The same is true of Jeff Ramseyer, who was a gifted litigator. How many more criminals would he have convicted for their crimes? We will never know how much more good Jeff would have done. Both talented men will long be remembered.

When I attended his funeral, it was standing room only. I stood next to a dozen judges at the rear of the overflowing chapel, and everyone stood there with tears in their eyes shaking their heads saying, "Why? He was so young."

In his short life, Jeff touched so many cops and attorneys and had gained the respect of the entire Los Angeles County Courts. We can only hope there will be more Jeff Ramseyer types who will work for the DA's Office.

Jeff Ramseyer's legal career was like a bright comet that didn't go unnoticed from his flash of energy and enthusiasm. However, like a comet, the bright glow was quickly extinguished way too soon.

AN EYE FOR AN EYE

People v. Rodriguez & Torres

SUPERSTAR PROSECUTOR

Michael Camacho

CHAPTER 61 WHAT A WONDERFUL DAY

The month of May is one of the favorite times of the year. Those living on the East Coast enjoy the spring season for its colorful flowers covering their gardens. Just by walking outside one notices the refreshing scent of rhododendron and dogwood. Your thoughts are more optimistic after the rain, mud, snow, sleet and all the dreary days which seemed like a long cold winter.

However, on the West Coast the month of May is time to hit the beaches, maybe not going into the surf but walking the strand enjoying the fresh sea air and firing up the old barbecue that has been sitting idle for months just collecting dust.

Students look forward to this time of year since many are graduating and others are just thankful to be out of school for a couple of months in order to forget all those long nights memorizing boring facts and cramming for tests.

Even the lovers in our midst use May to prepare for their grand weddings with all the invitations, seating arrangements, ordering flowers, selecting the music and all those frustrating dress and tuxedo fittings proving you should have selected something a size larger.

The month of May was named for the Greek goddess Maia who was the goddess of fertility. This month contains several popular holidays such as Mother's Day, Memorial Day as well as Cinco de Mayo. Also it is the month for the Indianapolis 500 car race and the Kentucky Derby. The first day of May is celebrated in comes countries by having children dance around the Maypole holding onto colorful ribbons. Other countries use May first to be a day honoring those who labor. However, in old English May was called the 'month of three milkings' referring to a time when cows could be milked three times a day.

Strange that nothing of great importance ever seemed to happened on May 11th, unless you consider the birth of songwriter Irving Berlin as being important. He did give us several songs we still sing, such as *God Bless America*, *White Christmas*, *There's No Business Like Show Business*, *Alexander's Ragtime Band*, and you can't forget *Puttin' On the Ritz*. (Isn't it amazing how useful the internet can be?)

The only other event that stands out for May 11th is that BF Goodrich manufactured the first tubeless tire in 1947, and of course you all remember that the first flush toilet was patented on this day in 1792.

Yet for some people in the Los Angeles area the date of May 11, 1999, is indelibly etched in their mind because of a heinous crime that was committed in their midst. Even though the crime was sensational, the news media showed no interest in it. I, the author, have been hesitant to tell this horrendous story since it shows the total depravity of mankind. However, it may be time to tell these repugnant stories in order to educate some of the 'do-gooders of the world' who believe that all persons in prison can be rehabilitated.

Yes, some can change their stripes, but what the 'do-gooders' ignore is that there are vile people in the world who need to be isolated from the good hardworking people in society. After reading this story, I wonder if anyone's opinion changes as to the popular concept that ALL Criminals Need a Second Chance.

I feel obligated to warn you the reader that this story is not for the faint-hearted. It all starts out innocent enough. Two guys were trying to figure out what to do on May 11, 1999. These guys lived in the city of La Puente, which is to the east of Los Angeles. They had an older vehicle which permitted them to cruise the streets of their home turf. The one was Nicholas Santino **Rodriguez** (21), better known by his friends as "Slick Nick." His pal was David Daugherty Torres (23), who was slightly older but was more of the follower type. Both were members of the La Puente gang, which was made up of various cliques. They were proud to be part of the notorious 'Blackwood' clique.

Nicholas Rodriguez
aka Slick Nick

These homies realized that their old jalopy was almost out of gas and didn't have a current registration. They were in need of better 'wheels' with a full tank of gas and up to date registration so not to be pulled over by the cops. Most of all, they were short on cash so they decided that they would have to commit a carjacking and in the process rob the victims of their money.

Self-Carwash in La Puente

As they drove around on this Tuesday morning, they passed by a self-service car wash and noticed a young man scrubbing away on his new car. He was trying his hardest to clean up his car without getting his clothes dirty or wet.

Although this didn't occur on Santa Monica Boulevard, this setting conjures up thoughts of Sheryl Crow's catchy song "***All I Wanna Do***"

The good people of the world
Are washing their cars on their lunch break
Hosing and scrubbing as best they can in skirts in suits
They drive their shiny Datsuns and Buicks

...

All I wanna do is have some fun

Until the sun comes up

Over Santa Monica Boulevard

Rodriquez told Torres to drive around the block so they could check out the car. Rodriguez wasn't thinking about washing their grubby old car. He most likely never washed a car on his lunch break while wearing a suit. Although these guys were thinking 'all I wanna do is have some fun,' they most likely weren't humming Sheryl Crow's tune.

CHAPTER 62 WE NEED A CAR

Paul Nunez (pseudonym) didn't own the car, but he was doing his best for the owner to make the blue 1995 Ford Contour shine in the sun. When the guys pulled back around, they parked in the rear of the carwash. From that vantage point they could see that Nunez was alone and frantically trying to scrub the water spots off the windshield.

Paul Nunez Washing this Car

They both quietly slipped behind him, and Torres stepped to the side to get his attention. Paul was startled since he was concentrating on the stubborn water spots on the windshield. It was similar to when someone steps into what you consider is your personal space. Paul, not wanting to appear confrontational said, "Hi, man." Before he could say anything else, Torres stuck a gun next to his chest and uttered, "Give me your money."

Paul stood there shocked, not knowing how to respond. There was a few seconds delay and Torres grew impatient and handed the gun to Rodriguez. To speed up this robbery, he started to go through Paul's pockets for money or valuables. This turned out to be a waste except for the facts he got the keys to the car.

Both Rodriguez and Torres, would-be robbers, were disappointed not coming up with anything of value. Torrez climbed into the squeaky-clean car and placed the key in the ignition and turned it. Torres continued to try to start the car without any luck. The guys yelled at Paul as to what was wrong.

This Car Had a Kill Switch

Not knowing what to say, he tried to explain that he always had difficulty starting this car. Out of disgust, Torres grabbed some CDs from the seat and several other things in the car's console. He climbed out of the car and in frustration went over to Paul and hit him as hard as he could in the face.

Paul was small in stature, so he went flying backwards. Then Paul heard the words, "Waste him, waste him." His mind did a nanosecond risk assessment and decided on turning and running as fast as his legs would carry him. He leaned down to make himself as small a target as possible, and as he passed by a cinder block wall he ducked behind it.

As Paul's adrenalin receded, he reflected on just how smart it was for him to push the kill switch on the car so the robbers couldn't steal it. He wondered whether jeopardizing his life for a Ford Contour may not have been the smartest decision he ever made. At least he saved the car from being a 'killing machine,' however, he paid the price with a giant headache.

Our robbers were disappointed in not getting the car or any real useable items. Yet they felt comfortable being in their barrio, where they had earned the respect of all the gangsters in the neighborhood. They continued driving around in their old jalopy and approached Cadbrook Dr. with its older tract homes that had been lovingly remodeled by the Hispanic residents.

The area might qualify as the lower rung of the so-called Middle Class. This was a place where those from south of the border would establish a foothold in their dreamland. Their years of hard labor paid off in allowing them to have a modest house to call home. These people cherished their humble abodes and often fortified them with wrought iron fences and metal bars on their windows.

As Slick Nick and Torres turned the corner, they noticed several young teenagers standing on the sidewalk talking to each other. They quickly evaluated the group and sized up these kids as an easy robbery target. Although there were four young teenagers and just two of them, Slick Nick knew that their handgun was the great equalizer.

La Puente Barrio

The kids were dressed as wannabe gangsters. They had on the baggy pants and long white T-shirts. The kids wanted to look fashionable, which was why they dressed that way. Many of the kids in the barrio try to emulate the older gangsters. These kids were 15 and 16 years of age and had no affiliation with any gang. The main reason to mimic a gangster image was to appear tough and able to defend themselves.

But this type of thinking didn't work with Slick Nick. He didn't have any fondness for wannabes. He interpreted the gang look-a-like appearance to mean they most likely had some drugs on them or at least some drug money. For Nick, they were the perfect target to rob.

CHAPTER 63 NEED TO ROB

Where Car Stopped
Location of Shooting

Torres pulled the car up to the curb and stopped next to the group. Nick stepped out of the vehicle and shouted out to the kids that he wanted meth and some money. The teenagers looked at each other wondering 'What's this guy talking about?' Each side was staring at each other but no one was acting. At that point, Slick Nick pulled a handgun from his waistband and pointed it at the crowd of guys. He reiterated his request for drugs and money.

The kids shrugged their shoulders and began to disassemble. They claimed that they didn't have any drugs or money. Slick Nick thought they were being disrespectful so he threatened them again, saying if they didn't give him money that he was going to kill them. This time the kids shook their heads indicating they didn't have anything. For Slick Nick, that was too much of an insult. He had asked them nicely and they had turned him down. He felt he had no alternative, since he was a "Man of his Word." Nick slowly raised his handgun to the shooting position. When no one came forth he aimed at the crowd as he pressed his finger against the trigger. The sound of the blast caused the teenagers to freeze in their tracks.

Their eyes were wide open with fright not knowing what to do. Two of the teenagers took off running. One of the young men looked back to see his friend fall to the sidewalk. He seemed to be fixated on the gun now pointed at him. The other young boy begged for his life but Slick Nick didn't seem to have a sympathetic ear and callously shot him. Nick pulled the trigger a second time and the teenager was propelled backwards as he stumbled to his side.

Teenager Shot During Robbery

By then two young men were lying dying on the sidewalk. This would seem to be enough carnage for a normal killer, but Nick wanted to inflict more mayhem on these victims. He slowly walked over to where the victims were bleeding to death. With the gun firmly gripped in Slick Nick's hand, he pointed it at both victims and proceeded to empty his gun into their bullet-riddled bodies.

This brutal act of overkill shocked the others, who had just witnessed their friends being executed before their eyes. They stood frozen to the sidewalk. Should they run or fight?

Suddenly Slick Nick pivoted to his right and gave a deadly look at the victims' colleagues. Then he raised the gun to shoulder height and pointed it directly at them. At that moment in time, both men could see that death was about to befall them if they didn't run for their lives. As Nick pulled back the trigger, there was the sound of a hollow click. Rapidly he continued to pull the trigger with no results.

As the two friends of the victims ran as fast as their feet could carry them, they looked for a safe haven. Although these guys were the luckiest victims in the world, they weren't in the mood to rejoice quite yet. Slick Nick had emptied his gun in shooting their friends. Nick's act of wasting his ammunition had saved these teenagers' lives. Now Nick had an empty gun which was proving to be useless.

Nick came to his senses and remembered why they had stopped the kids in the first place. Robbery was their objective. Either money or a small quantity of meth was to be their reward. Both Nick and Torres rummaged through the pockets of the dying victims, trying to find something of value. They noticed that one of the victims had a silver necklace chain with a cross of Jesus. Unfortunately, this sacred cross didn't provide any protection to the young man who was bleeding out on the sidewalk.

Cross Ripped off Victim's Neck

This necklace may have been the only fruit of the robbery; however, they must have again been disappointed. In disgust, Nick threw the cross into the street. They both jumped back into their old car wanting to get away before the police arrived.

Slick Nick and Torres were upset that their attempted robberies weren't working out as intended. Now they were faced with a robber's dilemma of having to commit robberies with a gun that didn't have any live ammunition. This was going to make their job of robbing people more difficult. All they could do now was threaten people with an unloaded gun.

CHAPTER 64 THE RIDE TO HELL

They drove away from the area where they had shot the two youths. But as they were driving around, a deputy sheriff came up from behind and turned on his red lights. These guys were petrified that they were going to be arrested for the two murders that they had just committed. They didn't know what to do. They had a handgun, and they could easily kill the deputy when he attempted to approach the car.

There was only one problem, and that they had wasted away all their bullets. They turned to look at the Sheriff's black-and-white unit and noticed it was a one-man unit. There were two of them and only one Sheriff's deputy. Could they take down this single deputy? As the deputy got out of the car and started to approach their car, they noticed that he was a big burly guy who hadn't missed any meals.

As they were trying to assess their situation, the deputy in a deep voice stated, "Do you guys know that you don't have your current license tags on?" In hearing that, Rodriguez and Torres felt a revelation had occurred. They looked up at the sky and wanted to praise the Lord. Then the guys switched from thinking of killing the deputy to feeling so appreciative that the good deputy brought it to their attention to put their new tags on their license plate.

To show their sincerity, they said that they would park the car on the street and not drive it until they had attached the new tags. The deputy was pleased with their cooperative attitude and directed them to where they could park their car. Everyone was happy with this resolution of the problem.

The car was locked up in a parking lot and the deputy drove off. Was this one of the luckiest days of their lives? It all depends how you look at it. Now they didn't even have a car to drive around to rob people. They found themselves standing on a street corner waving at people to stop to give them a ride. They didn't know where they really wanted to go but just needed to get out of this area.

At that moment in time, Beto Salas and his girlfriend, Delilah Espinosa, (pseudonym) were riding in a white Toyota driven by one of their friends. Beto was a member of the "La Puente" gang, which had several affiliate gangs that made up the main gang. Beto noticed Rodriguez and Torres waving at cars on the street corner. They looked like fellow gang members of the bigger "La Puente" gang.

Beto Salas Delilah Espinosa

He told the girl who was driving to slow down, which she did. He could see that it was Slick Nick from the affiliate gang called the "La Puente Blackwood Street." So he told her to stop the car so he could find out what was happening. Slick Nick told Beto that they needed a ride out of the area. Beto wanted to be helpful and indicated they might be able to drive them wherever they needed to go.

At first all the guys acted like homies and were very congenial with a lot of gang talk. The guys were all standing near the back of the car while the girls were doing small talk in the front seat. For some unknown reason, Slick Nick became hostile toward Beto over something involving their respective gangs. Nick used his fist to strike Beto, who fell against the car. The two women turned to see what the altercation between the two guys was all about. As the hostility ramped up, the female driver of the car jumped out and went running toward several stores.

Car Beto & Delilah Were in

Since the back door was still open, Nick pushed Beto inside the car as the fighting continued. Nick seemed obsessed with hitting Beto and had lost interest in robbing people. Nick yelled at Torres to get in the front seat. At the same time, Nick shouted at Beto's girlfriend to slide over into the driver's seat. Delilah did as she was told and started driving away.

For the next several minutes Delilah continued down the main street as her boyfriend was being pounded in the backseat.

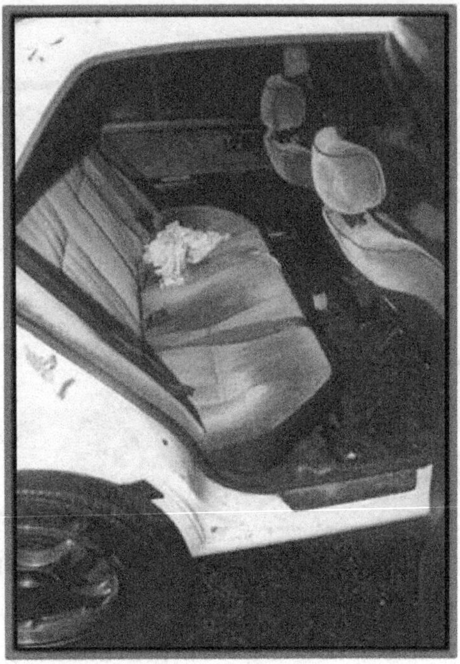

Beto & Nick in Backseat

As they were driving down the street, Rodriguez accused Beto of shooting one of Rodriguez's fellow gang members. Rodriguez's "Blackwood Street" gang wanted revenge for the shooting of one of their own. In order to place fear into Beto and his La Puente gang, Nick explained that they had to torture and mutilate anyone who had harmed one of their fellow gang members. Since Beto was the only person present, he would have to receive the brunt of the torture.

Slick Nick felt obligated to do something to Beto to teach him and his gang a lesson for what someone in their gang had done. Nick then realized that they didn't have any more bullets left to shot at Beto. He didn't know what to do. He also mentioned that gangs occasionally will gouge the eyes out of traitors to their gang. So he told his partner, Torres, to look in the glove box to see if there was anything in there that could be used as a weapon.

Delilah & Torres in Front seat

One can only imagine what Beto's girlfriend was thinking as she was driving around the streets of the city of La Puente while Torres was madly rummaging through the glove box of the car looking for some type of weapon. Torres pulled out of the glove box a map, a registration card, and bunch of repair slips for the car. There weren't any tools or knives in the glove box that could be used as weapons. The only thing Torres found at the bottom of the glove box was some type of can opener.

CHAPTER 65 DOING THE UNTHINKABLE

He passed the metal object that looked like a can opener to Nick and said, "That's the best I could come up with." Nick grabbed it and said, "That will have to do." As Nick was holding Beto down in the backseat, he leaned over Beto's head and jabbed the sharp end of the can opener into Beto's eye. Beto let out a horrific scream as Slick Nick continued to gouge out Beto's eyeball. The eyeball rolled down on to the dirty car mats in the back seat.

Eyeball on the Backseat Floor

The intense screaming frightened Delilah, who couldn't see what was going on; she continued to drive through the pleasant residential city of La Puente. This intense cruelty to a human being was unimaginable. Nick wasn't finished inflicting pain on Beto, who was wincing in unbelievable pain.

Nick took the can opener and inserted it in Beto's other eye and began to twist it until the eyeball came out of the eye socket. This time Nick grabbed the eyeball before it fell to the floor. Then Nick leaned forward and handed Beto's eyeball to Torres, who was in the front seat, and told him to give it to Beto's girlfriend, who was driving the car. With shock and disgust she glanced at the eyeball, then it was tossed out the car window.

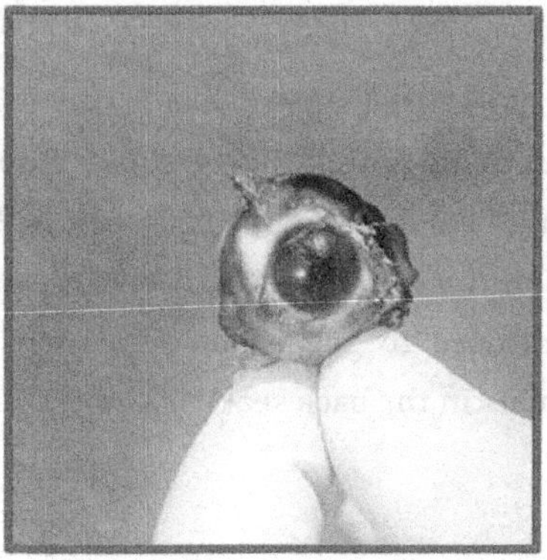

Eyeball that was handed to Delilah

During this entire process of gouging Beto's eyes out, Beto was conscious and was screaming in tremendous pain. It would appear that Slick Nick had accomplished his objective, which was to teach Beto's gang not to mess with the Blackwood gang members. All Nick had to do was get out of the car and let Beto's girlfriend take him to an emergency room where he could receive medical attention. Beto would be blind for the rest of his life, and he would be a walking, talking example of what happens to any person who disrespected the Blackwood gang.

CHAPTER 66 HEADING FOR THE HILLS

Apparently Slick Nick couldn't quite comprehend that an alive Beto was a much more effective poster child for 'Don't Mess with Blackwood.' For whatever reason, he felt compelled to permanently dispose of Beto. Nick ordered Beto's girlfriend to drive up to the Turnbull Canyon area. This is a bushy, hilly area covered with thick chaparral. There is a windy road that connects the communities of Hacienda Heights to the City of Whittier. This narrow two-lane road winds through the canyons and valleys and is seldom traveled by anyone who is in a hurry.

Turnbull Canyon Road

Especially after dark, this is a very deserted area. Occasionally, some foolish people use it as a lovers' lane to view the lights of the city. But more often it becomes an excellent dumping ground for dead bodies. Because of its steep embankments, the corpses that are rolled down into the ravine are merely devoured by the hungry wildlife.

Delilah was only slightly familiar with Turnbull Canyon so she drove slowly, not knowing what was going to occur to her and her boyfriend, Beto. The further she drove, the more she became aware that there was no one around to help her. She felt that she was on her own and she didn't want to do anything that would agitate Nick to focus his rage on her. As she continued to drive, she could hear her boyfriend cry out in intense pain. She couldn't figure out what these guys' game plan was.

Turnbull Canyon Road Shoulder
Where Delilah stopped the Car

All of a sudden Nick yelled at her to pull over and stop. His loud shout startled her, and she glanced around and all she could see was a dark, lonely road with no other human beings in sight. With the headlights of the car as the only source of light, she tried to find a wide enough area on the dirt shoulder so she could pull over. She came upon a wide shoulder area and gradually came to a stop.

Beto continued moaning as Nick and Torres tried to figure out what to do. Even though Beto was now 'blind as a bat,' the guys knew that if they let him go he still could identify them. Now it seemed like an easy decision to kill Beto. However, the more difficult decision was how could they go about killing him?

True, they had a handgun, but it was of little use since they had wasted all their ammunition when they continually fired at the two teenage victims lying on the sidewalk. Nick was realistic enough to know that the can opener used for eye gouging was not a practical tool for killing someone.

Nick was wearing a so-called Muscle Man T-shirt, which was near and dear to him. As a last resort, he yanked off his shirt and immediately wrapped it around Beto's neck. As Slick Nick tried to strangle Beto, his moaning turned to gagging. No matter how hard Nick pulled on the shirt, Beto continued to make sounds of life.

In a fit of exasperation and rage, Nick took the unloaded gun and bludgeoned Beto in the head with it. After repeatedly beating Beto on the head, eventually there was no more movement of life. Although Nick was physically tired from all the violence, he knew that they needed to get rid of Beto's body.

Torres came back to help Nick pull Beto's body out of the backseat of the car. Next to the car was a high berm of dirt that they had to drag Beto's dead body over so they could roll his body down into the ravine. While dragging Beto, one of his shoes and a sock came off. When they got him on the crest, they pulled all his clothes off. Their thinking was that if he had no clothes on the body couldn't easily be identified.

These two Blackwood gangsters looked down on Beto's tattered dead body. Their victim lay naked on the dirty ground without any eyes and with a head that had been beaten in. The victim's entire body was bloodied and bruised from the prolonged torturing. Did they feel some satisfaction as to what they had accomplished?

As they both stood at the top of the ridge, they took their shod feet and kicked Beto's body over the edge of the steep embankment. At first the body gently rolled over, and then it gained momentum as it cartwheeled down the vertical-sided ravine. Eventually they lost sight of Beto's body and they turned and walked away.

CHAPTER 67
RECOVERING THE BODY

The next day when the Sheriff's Homicide detectives were investigating the killings, they were brought to the location in Turnbull Canyon. They didn't know where Beto's body had been dumped. They noticed a shoe and sock on the side of the road. They climbed up over the dirt berm to check out the spot. A short distance closer to the cliff they noticed numerous shoeprints in the soft dirt. Immediately they stopped and started looking over the embankment.

As they peered down into the ravine, they couldn't see any evidence of a body. At that point, they brought in a Search and Rescue team that rappelled down the hillside. After lowering themselves halfway down into the brushy ravine, they came upon a naked body caught in the underbrush.

Apparently what happened was that Beto's body had rolled down the steep canyon wall, but somehow it got caught on the underbrush part way down the hillside. The Search and Rescue team lowered a metal wire stretcher tied to a long rope they attached to a winch on the front of their trucks. The team members in the ravine carefully rolled the corpse onto a body bag.

Sheriff 's Search & Rescue Brought up Beto's Body

Carefully they secured everything on to the stretcher. They signaled the members on top to started pulling the rope up. The winch was used at first, but as the body reached the top they reverted to pulling by hand so not to drag the stretcher through the loose soil. At the top, the homicide detectives opened the body bag to examine the body. From looking at the face, they could tell that his eyes had been gouged out.

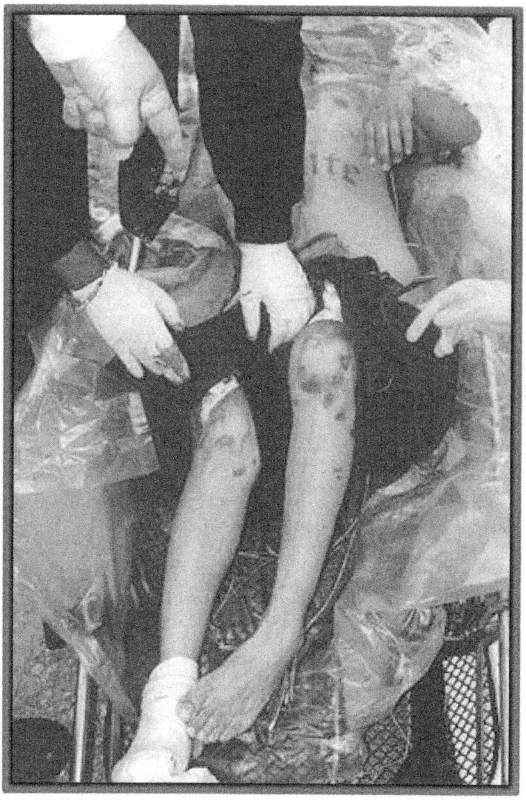

Beto's Body Pulled out of Ravine

His chest was emblazoned with the word "Puente," which was the name of his gang that he was so proud to be a member of. Later the Coroner-Medical Examiner determined at the autopsy that Beto was alive when he was being tortured by Nick and Torres.

CHAPTER 68 HOW TO GET AWAY

To understand the complete picture we need to return to our story of what Nick and Torres did after discarding the body. Slick Nick and Torres ordered Beto's girlfriend, Delilah, to drive them back down Turnbull Canyon Road into town. Needless to say, Delilah was totally traumatized from seeing what they had subjected her boyfriend to. All along she didn't know what they were going to do to her.

What she didn't realize was that neither suspect had a valid driver's license, so they needed her to drive the car. (They certainly didn't want to break the law by driving without a license.) It seems outlandish how vicious lawbreakers would be afraid of driving without a valid license. Earlier in the day, a deputy Sheriff had stopped them from driving their old car without a valid registration. That deputy had warned them not to drive unless they had a valid driver's license.

While Nick had been torturing Beto, the original girl who had been driving Delilah and Beto around in her white Toyota contacted the Sheriff's Department. She reported that two guys had kidnapped her friends in her car. An all-points bulletin had been put out to all law enforcement to stop the white Toyota. When Nick and Torres returned to the streets of La Puente, a deputy Sheriff who was patrolling noticed that the car fit the description of the wanted vehicle.

The deputy started following the car. The suspects were paranoid enough from committing all the killings, but when they saw the patrolling black-and-white behind them they panicked. They screamed at Delilah to continue driving and try to take evasive action. The deputy was able to maneuver through traffic without losing them. The guys were frantic. Even though they had a gun which should have been able to protect them, it was of no use since they didn't have any ammunition to fire at the deputy.

Finally, Deliliah pulled down a street that turned out to be a dead-end street. The guys told her to stop, and before the car came to a complete stop both jumped out, landing on their feet. Since both suspects were well-educated gang members, they knew to run in oppose directions, thereby creating a dilemma for the deputy, who was all by himself. Their tactic worked like a charm as they both disappeared into the dark of the night. Both were able to escape initial capture.

Slice Nick was able to avoid authorities for just one day. By the next day he was in custody. If he had been more successful in his robbing attempts, he might have had enough money to make it to Mexico. There he would be home free and unlikely to ever be extradited back to the USA. Eventually, Slick Nick would be looking at charges that would make him eligible for the Death Penalty. Since the country of Mexico doesn't have the Death Penalty, they will not extradite any person to the USA if that person may be facing the Death Penalty.

As to Torres, he fared slightly better since he wasn't quickly apprehended. Only after Torres was highlighted on the TV show "America's Most Wanted" was he captured.

CHAPTER 69 TIME FOR TRIAL

Without a doubt these two defendants fit the description of being very "Bad Dudes." But the question was, what evidence would be available for a prosecutor to use in court? Because both suspects were so dangerous, some of the witnesses were scared to death to testify against them. This fact alone could be a serious impediment in any attempt to prosecute either Slick Nick or Torres.

The case was assigned to one of the very top and experienced prosecutors in the Los Angeles DA's Office by the name of Mike Camacho. His reputation was that of a serious-minded attorney who was always thoroughly prepared. Prosecutor Camacho reminded one of Teddy Roosevelt's famous sayings, "Speak softly and carry a big stick." Camacho might speak softly; however, his well-organized approach is like a big stick over every defendant he prosecutes.

Because of his unique skill set, he excelled in trying gang cases. He knew how to handle frightened witnesses who needed some form of reassurance. But most of all, he was a great communicator with jurors. He knew what techniques to use in order to convey the facts and law to the jury.

When the Rodriguez and Torres case was assigned to Camacho, he reviewed all the police reports and met with the detectives to go over the evidence. Although all the crimes in this case occurred on just one day, the combination of charges involved three completely separate incidents. Camacho knew that his first challenge was orientating the jury to all the charges. Camacho wanted the jury to understand all of the charges that they would have to consider. The defendants were charged with 19 separate crimes. He needed to categorize them so the jury would think of them in distinctive groups. The first group was the Car Wash robbery and the attempted carjacking. The next logical grouping involved the attempted robbery and murders of the two teenagers on Cadbrook Drive. Finally, the last group consisted of the carjacking, kidnapping and ending in the murder of **Beto**.

People v. Rodriguez/Torres
BA189759

CT.	CHARGE	VICTIM	DEFENDANT	FIREARM ALLEGATION
1	Firearm Possession	N/A	Torres	N/A
2	Assault w/ Firearm	P. Nunez	Torres	Use of Firearm
3	Robbery	P. Nunez	Torres	Use of Firearm
4	Assault w/ Firearm	P. Nunez	Rodriguez	Use of Firearm
5	Robbery	P. Nunez	Rodriguez Torres	Use of Firearm N/A
6	Attempted Carjacking	P. Nunez	Rodriguez Torres	Use of Firearm N/A
7	Attempted Robbery	C. Garnica	Rodriguez Torres	Discharge of F/A N/A
8	Attempted Robbery	S. Salcido	Rodriguez Torres	Discharge of F/A N/A
9	Attempted Robbery	T. Garnica	Rodriguez Torres	Discharge of F/A N/A
10	Attempted Robbery	J. Gonzalez	Rodriguez Torres	Discharge of F/A N/A
11	Murder Robbery-Murder Multiple-Murder	T. Garnica	Rodriguez Torres	Discharge of F/A N/A
12	Murder Robbery-Murder Multiple-Murder	J. Gonzalez	Rodriguez Torres	Discharge of F/A N/A
13	Carjacking	D. Espinosa	Rodriguez Torres	N/A N/A
14	Kidnaping for Carjacking	B. Salas	Rodriguez Torres	N/A N/A
15	Kidnaping for Carjacking	C. Marquez	Rodriguez Torres	N/A N/A
16	Mayhem	B. Salas	Rodriguez Torres	N/A N/A
17	Torture	B. Salas	Rodriguez Torres	N/A N/A
18	Murder Kidnap-Murder Torture-Murder	B. Salas	Rodriguez Torres	N/A N/A
19	Firearm Possession	N/A	Torres	N/A

In order to illustrate the grouping, prosecutor Camacho had the various categories listed in different colors on a poster chart that all the jurors could see on one page. This allowed Camacho to discuss the facts of the case in the various groups. Each grouping had a different set of witnesses that would testify to that particular incident.

The next thing he needed was a map of the crime scenes to orient the jury where all the events occurred. It was important for the jury to know how close some of the events occurred to each other. The jurors needed to know where the remote area was located and where the defendants discarded Beto's body. Camacho used this type of visual in his Opening Statement to explain each location of the defendants' crime spree.

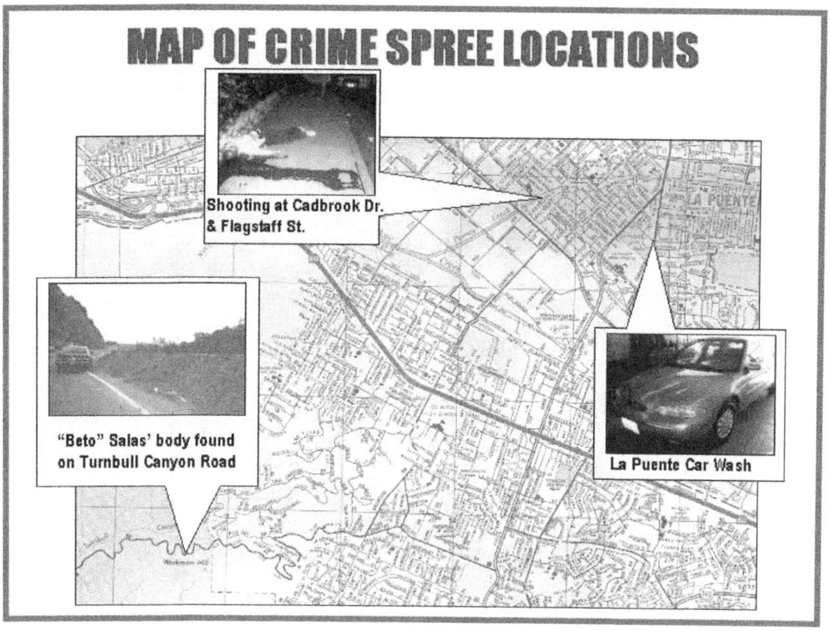

The visual aids of the Charges Chart and Map Locations assisted the jurors to better understand what could be a very confusing case. Then prosecutor Camacho recognized that he also needed some type of visual aid that would allow the jurors to better understand where everyone was seated in the car.

What made it even more confusing was the fact that Beto and Slick Nick were seated in the backseat but their exact position changed during the lengthy beating. It was known that the girlfriend was forced to drive and that Torres was in the front passenger seat, but it had to be left vague as to the seating arrangement in back.

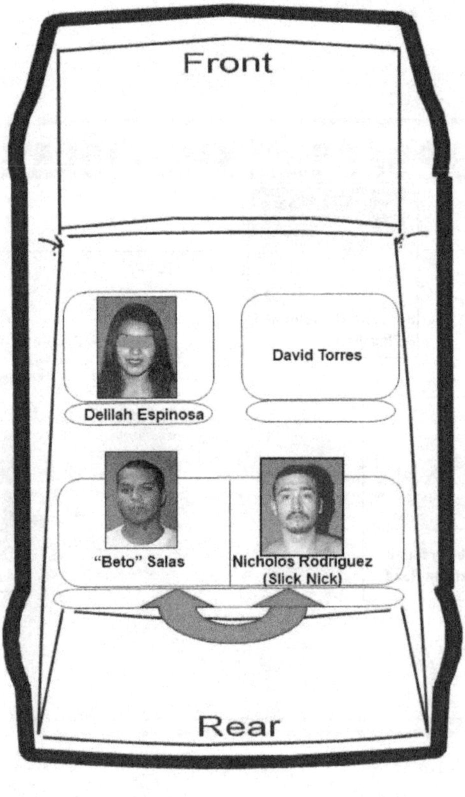

It was very hard for Delilah Espinosa to testify to the torturing of her boyfriend, Beto. Needless to say, any person would be apprehensive in testifying against such brutal defendants. However, her composure and testimony were exemplary and she did the best she could in remembering the events. During the entire incident, she didn't know whether she would ever survive this ordeal. During her testimony, Slick Nick continually stared at her. If looks could kill, Delilah should have died on the witness stand. It was a miracle that she was able to withstand the intense pressure placed on her. The prosecutor's preparation and support of this witness paid off as she came through like a champ.

After all the testimony from both sides was complete, it was time for Argument. The prosecutor summarized what all the witnesses had testified to. The Defense tried to show that the witnesses were wrong in their identification. However, Delilah remained steadfast as to her identification of both. She had driven around with the defendants for more than an hour, so her identification wasn't based on a mere instantaneous look at them. The handing of an eyeball to her was a memorable event that she wasn't about to soon forget.

After both sides had argued their case, the jurors started deliberating. It did take the jury some time to review all the evidence. Finally, the jury stated that they had verdicts. Ultimately, both defendants were found guilty of all the charges. The jury also found the special circumstances of multiple murders and the kidnap-murder and torture-murder to be true.

CHAPTER 70 DEATH PENALTY PHASE

After the jury convicted them, the Penalty Phase of the case began. Both defendants got on the witness stand and asked to be executed. Slick Nick said that he was not afraid to die. He tried to be "Mr. Macho" in that he wasn't afraid of anything, even the Death Penalty. They both basically confessed during the Penalty Phase but blamed it on the fact that they were suffering from being under the influence of methamphetamine and alcohol. That was the excuse the Defense gave for both. However, prosecutor Camacho argued to the jury that neither defendant deserved any sympathy for what they had done. He said that their drug use shouldn't be a justifiable excuse for their actions.

Nicholas Rodriguez
Slick Nick

The jury deliberated and came back recommending the death sentence on Slick Nick. However, the jury didn't recommend death for Torres. When it came for sentencing, neither defendant showed any remorse for the killing of three people on this one-day crime spree. As to the killing of Beto Salas, the judge sentenced Slick Nick to the death penalty.

As to Torres, he was sentenced to Life Without the Possibility of Parole. As to the other murders, both defendants received the sentence of Life Without the Possibility of Parole (LWOP).

Prosecutor Camacho's thoroughness and tenacity had paid off. As a result, two extremely vicious and treacherous criminals would never be able to terrorize the streets of our community.

CHAPTER 71 WHAT HAVE WE LEARNED?

Man's inhumanity to man has no limits. Police officers or prosecutors are subjected to seeing the worst side of mankind. They see crimes that are so grotesque that one wonders how could one human being come up with the thought of doing something so brutal. But this Rodriguez case involved a human being actually committing unthinkable acts. The person had to actually take time to plan and perform acts that were exceedingly cruel and sadistic.

The question becomes, how could a human being gouge both eyes out of a person who is alive? What thought process is going through this person's mind that makes him think this is an acceptable thing to do? What form of pleasure is derived from such acts?

Some people will say that such a person must have been under the influence of alcohol or drugs in order for them to do such a vile act. How many intoxicated people are able to perform eyeball removal of both eyes with a can opener? The answer is that being under the influence can't justify this atrocious behavior.

For others, the simple answer is that anyone who would do such an act has to be a sick person. Our society believes that sick people aren't to be put in prison but are to be placed in mental institutions until they recover, at which time they are to be released to return back into society. Most reasonable people would say that merely labeling Slick Nick as being a sick person doesn't give us the result we want.

However, many "Do-Gooders" will explain that Slick Nick was suffering from some type of mental illness that caused him to act out in a violent fashion against another. They make it sound perfectly normal and that society should understand that Mr. Rodriguez's bad behavior was merely isolated. They would say that psychological therapy over time would be able to reprogram Slick Nick's demented mind.

"Do-Gooders" want to believe everyone can be rehabilitated. There are those who are a little more skeptical. They believe that there are a limited number of evil people who have malignant hearts living among us. Should we try to rehabilitate them? Should we put them in mental institutions? Should they be imprisoned? Should they be executed?

You the reader will have to decide for yourself what should be done with the Slick Nicks who do exist in our society.

DEFENDANT ATTACKS DA

People v. Bravo

SUPERSTAR PROSECUTOR

Michael Camacho

CHAPTER 72 SETTLE IT WITH A GUN

It was September 14, 2000, and it was a hot evening and a great time to drink a frosty Corona beer. Juan Carlos Bravo and some of his friends were drinking on the sidewalk in front of an apartment complex at 867 Williams Street in Pomona, California. Juan was with his friend Jorge Guerra, and they were talking about girls and macho things when a young lady came by and started joking with them. Her name was Yolanda Toledo (pseudonym), and she was very friendly since she was no longer married and had dumped her most recent boyfriend. In other words, she was available and looking for new male companionship.

Apartment House on Williams St. in Pomona

After chatting for a while, she invited Juan and his friend Jorge up to the apartment where she was living with her friend Maria Gomez. For several months Gomez had lived in apartment "C" with her three children. It was approaching 2:00 a.m. and the courtyard of the apartment house was almost deserted. The only sound was the crickets creeping in the ivy planter near the community mailboxes. All the residents had turned in for the night except for those in apartment "C." Inside were some who still wanted to drink whiskey and chased it down with beer. Juan and Jorge were feeling no pain and had mellowed out with some drinks. The more they drank, the more they tried to impress the girls as to how tough they were. The senoritas giggled and laughed as the guys told stories about all the fights they had been in and of course won.

Everyone was enjoying the brag session until the phone rang. The call was for Yolanda Toledo from her ex-boyfriend Felix Rincon (pseudonym). He told Yolanda that he knew where she was and he was going to come over to talk to her. He abruptly hung up, and Yolanda placed the phone back on the table. Her face turned an ashen gray, and she appeared to be frozen with fear. The guys noticed her mood change and asked her what was wrong. She continued to stare at the phone on the table and didn't respond to the guys. Juan stepped over to her and shook her shoulder and asked, "Are you okay?" In a faint voice Yolanda said, "He's coming over." Yolanda knew that Rincon, her old boyfriend, had a violent temper and he would start trouble if he found the guys in her apartment.

Minutes later a second phone call from Rincon was received, and that was when Yolanda said to the guys that he sounded as though he was very close. A loud knock on the apartment door broke the silence, and everyone inside the apartment looked at each other. Yolanda went to the door to look through the peephole to see who was outside. She became frightened, so Maria rushed over to secure the door.

She realized that the door wasn't completely locked, so she tried to secure it. At that point, the person outside the door either pushed or kicked in the door. The person who came in was Francisco Ramos who was a close friend of Rincon. Yolanda quickly tried to defuse the situation by instantly introducing the young men to each other. Everything seemed cool, and there appeared to be no problem.

Ramos, who was the one who had forced his way inside, walked back to the front door and signaled to someone to come in. Within moments, Rincon rushed into the apartment to join his friend Ramos. Rincon had a gun in his hand when he entered the apartment. Yolanda knew that there was an explosive situation that was about to erupt into trouble. She jumped between her old boyfriend Rincon and Juan Bravo. She appeared to be trying to protect Juan from being shot at.

With one blow Rincon struck her head with the gun, knocking her down on her knees. This was enough of a distraction to give Juan enough of an opportunity to pull his gun and point it at Rincon. Now both Rincon and Bravo had their guns pointed at each other. The two started cursing at each other. Both yelled at each other, "Where are you from?" Yolanda realized that within seconds someone was going to be seriously injured or killed.

Livingroom in Apt. #C

When you have two guys pointing loaded guns at each other, it is predictable that there will be a shooting. However, in this case no one was able to say exactly what happened next. From this point on total chaos broke out in which guns began blazing and people shrieking blood-curdling screams. The ex-boyfriend, Rincon, was able to get off several shots in the apartment. At the same time, Bravo tried to find some cover to protect himself. He fired in the direction of Rincon, hoping to hit him. He was either able to hit him or at least scare Rincon into running out of the apartment.

As the gunfire settled down, the other guy, Francisco Ramos, remained inside the apartment. He was not armed and quickly tried to assess the situation. After his buddy Rincon had run out, leaving him behind, his first instinct was to find a way to exit the apartment. Crawling on his hands and knees, he slowly maneuvered himself around the apartment furniture. As he neared the front door, he tried to stand up in order to open the door. Reaching the front door knob, he twisted it to open. However, somehow the apartment door wouldn't open.

Apt. Broken Front Door

Apparently, when his buddy Felix Rincon made his escape, the door jammed. Ramos turned around to assess the situation when he saw Juan Bravo looking directly at him. Ramos flashed a stupid grin on his face like he was saying, "I 'm trying to leave, just give me a second." At that point, Ramos used both hands to grab the door knob and with all his might pulled on it, but nothing happened.

Bravo in a menacing voice directed Ramos to get out or he was going to shoot. Ramos turned his head looking at Bravo in dismay as to what to do. Bravo being a man of his word squeezed the trigger several times and Ramos as though in slow motion fell to the floor right in front of the door.

Yolanda had been holding on to Bravo's leg during all the shooting. Was it out of protection or fear? She didn't know for sure, but she loosened her grip. Without anyone holding him back, Bravo took several steps toward Ramos lying on the floor next to the front door. Bravo positioned himself directly over Ramos and took his gun and pointed it at the victim's head. Without saying a word or showing any expression on his face, he fired several more times at point-blank range. One of the gunshots found its mark directly in the back of Ramos' head.

CHAPTER 73 TIME FOR KILLER TO LEAVE

Bravo looked back at the two women, who were standing in utter disbelief as to what had just happened. No one spoke a word in the stillness of the apartment. Smugly, Bravo tucked his smoking gun into this waistband as he kicked the victim's body away from the door. He yanked on the door knob and gradually pulled the door open. He took a giant step over the lifeless body of the victim. With some maneuvering, he was able to avoid the blood oozing from the victim's nose and mouth.

As he exited the apartment, he confidently strolled out into the courtyard. Holding his head high, he strutted like a pint-sized bantam rooster going on a stroll through the chicken coop. The noise from the gunshots had awakened several of the apartment dwellers. Various apartment lights were being flipped on so the residents could figure out what all the noise was about. Bravo didn't seem phased by all the lookie-loos staring out of their apartment front windows. He exhibited a 'no fear' attitude as he slowly disappeared into the darkness of the night.

When the police arrived at the apartment, they found Ramos dead on the floor inside the apartment door. The two women remained in the apartment, and the officers tried to calm them down to see if they could explain what had happened. At first the police didn't know what to think. Was it a murder or was it a justifiable homicide as a result of self-defense? The police called out the CSI team to look for any type of forensic evidence.

The detectives could see that the apartment's floor was covered with shell casings. Most of them appeared to be fired from a 9mm Beretta. Although two guns had been used, neither was recovered at the crime scene. The CSI technician went from room to room locating shell casings. Initially, the technician photographed where they were located and later removed each one by placing them in an evidence envelope with instructions as to where each was found.

Apt. #C Dining Room

As the technician methodically went about her job, the homicide detectives continued their investigation by talking to anyone still at the crime scene. Most of the people around the apartment didn't want to become involved, and they basically claimed that they hadn't seen or heard anything. That was when the detectives started talking to the two women who had been inside the apartment. Yolanda knew most of the guys and initially didn't want to say anything to get them in trouble. However, Maria Gomez was more cooperative with the police since she had young children who were in the apartment at the time of the shooting.

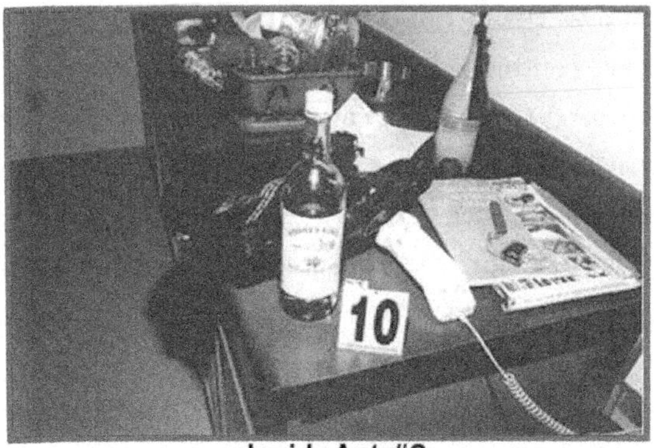

Inside Apt. #C

She indicated that originally she didn't see what started the shooting since she was in the bedroom with her three children. When she heard the first shot, she stuck her head slightly out of the bedroom door to see what the commotion was all about. She explained to the detectives that she could barely make out the four guys who were scurrying around in the living room looking for cover. From her vantage point, she couldn't tell who was doing the shooting. She could hear kitchenette chairs being knocked over and furniture tossed about. Then there was a lull and she heard the sound of someone slamming the front door and the faint sound of footsteps running away.

She related to the police that a few seconds after the initial shooting the apartment was deadly silent. That was when she eased her way out of the bedroom and along the short hall. As she got to the edge of the living room, she could see Juan Bravo and his friend crouched behind some furniture. She clearly saw Bravo holding a gun in his hand and appeared to wave it at some person who was crawling toward the front door.

All she could remember was that the guy got to the door, which was closed and tried to rise up to open it. From where she was standing, she couldn't see what was blocking the door. That moment of silence ended with a loud popping sound as Bravo fired his gun several times at the guy by the door. This guy spun around in midair as his legs buckled, causing his body to fall in slow motion to the floor.

To Gomez's surprise, she watched Bravo rise up slightly and slowly walk to the door, where he stood over the victim. As the victim's body steadily curled up into the fetal position, Bravo continued to point the gun at him. When he was within an arm's length, he squeezed the trigger, causing the sound of a piercing gunshot. The victim's head struck the floor with a thud and slightly bounced back up.

Maria Gomez tried to hold back tears as she graphically described the execution of Ramos. The detectives recognized that Gomez had cooperated enough and they could finish their questioning later. They indicated that they wanted her to come by the police station to look at some photos to see if she could identify the shooter.

She later went to the station, where she was shown a photo lineup in which she was shown six photos. It didn't take her long to positively identify the photo of Juan Bravo as the shooter of the victim Ramos.

Yolanda explained that everything had deteriorated when her ex-boyfriend, Felix Rincon, came inside the apartment. She admitted that Rincon had a gun and may have shot it. However, both women indicated that there were many shots fired and possibly Rincon was injured in all the gunfire.

As a result of that information, the police contacted the local hospitals to see if there had been any recent gunshot patients. Without too much effort, the police discovered a person by the name of 'Rincon' was seeking treatment for several gunshot wounds which required hospitalization.

As the investigation continued, the detectives reviewed what evidence they had uncovered. They couldn't determine what type of case they had. Since none of the witnesses could state who initially started the shooting, the detectives didn't know if they had an assault with a deadly weapon or a self-defense shooting. No one could say whether it was Rincon or Bravo who fired the first shot.

Rincon wasn't going to cooperate with the police. Therefore it may never be known who the first shooter was. However, the detectives were more concerned with the dead body of Ramos. The detectives realized that they needed to break the case into two separate shootings. The first one, between Rincon and Juan Bravo, was somewhat murky as to who was the bad guy. The second shooting was between Juan Bravo and Francisco Ramos, who was unarmed and was not an aggressor. This second shooting incident was what the detectives needed to focus on. They knew that Ramos was shot with a 9mm semi-automatic, most likely a Beretta.

The detectives were hoping that they would be able to tie the murder weapon to Juan Bravo. However, the detectives hadn't recovered any such weapon to be compared to the collected shell casings. Both women were definite in their identification of Bravo as the shooter of Ramos, so the detectives submitted their reports to the DA's Office for a criminal filing of the charge of murder against Bravo.

Although the filing DA would have preferred some forensic evidence, he still agreed to file a murder count against Bravo. Since Bravo wasn't in custody, an arrest warrant was issued.

WANTED FOR MURDER

Juan Bravo

Seven months passed without any arrest of Bravo. The murder weapon hadn't been found or used in any recent crimes. The detectives worked every lead as to Bravo's whereabouts, but there was no break in finding him. The detectives continued to mention at the police roll calls that they still wanted the patrol officers to be looking for defendant Bravo. There had been information that he was still hanging out in the Pomona area.

CHAPTER 74 MOBILE HOME PARK

The Bravo case investigation changed late on the night of April 15, 2001, when most people were more concerned with having their IRS tax returns mailed before midnight. That night would be the turning point in the Bravo case, in which the remaining pieces of the puzzle would come together. Officer Dailey (pseudonym) was an officer for the Pomona Police Department who was working patrol. He was wearing his uniform and driving a black-and-white one-person police car. He was carrying a Glock .45-caliber semiautomatic firearm.

Shortly before midnight he was patrolling the west side of the city. He had driven by the U.S. Post Office and noticed that there was still a postal employee standing near the drop-off box assisting people who were mailing their tax returns. It seemed everyone was all smiles knowing that they just made it in time to file their returns.

Los Brisas Mobile Home Park in Pomona

As Officer Dailey drove westbound on Holt Avenue, he passed by the imposing Catholic Church with its magnificent Spanish mission bell tower. He had to reflect on better times when the city of Pomona was considered the orange capital of California. The city of Pomona was revered for its fine churches and art deco FOX movie theatre. It was the train hub where most of the oranges were shipped from and traveled all the way to the east coast where they were enjoyed.

Officer Dailey wasn't nostalgic for the good old days since he was too busy trying to keep the lid on a city that had lost its grandeur to many gangbangers and dirtbags. He made a right turn down the long driveway to the Las Brisas Mobile Home Park. The area had been hit by numerous burglaries at all times of the day and night. His police cruiser's headlights illuminated two guys walking alone down this empty street. At this hour none of the mobile home residents were out and about. This long driveway doesn't have any outlets to other housing areas.

The two individuals looked in the direction of the bright headlights and apparently recognized that it was a police car. Suddenly they turned and quickly started to walk in the direction of the entrance to the Mobile Home Park. As they were walking they continued to look back over their shoulders at the police unit.

Officer Dailey, being a seasoned police officer, became suspicious. In his mind he wondered what these young men were doing there. It was late at night, and there was no one around and no car parked nearby. Further, the officer was well aware of the numerous burglaries that had been reported in this mobile home park. What made the officer's suspicion rise even higher was the fact that they started walking swiftly away from his police unit.

The officer's training had taught him that he didn't have any probable cause to arrest either individual, but he did have ample reason to detain both of them to check out what they were doing in the area so late at night. Officer Dailey picked up his radio mic and called the police dispatcher to indicate that he was going to check out the two individuals to see what they were up to.

As he pulled closer to the two men, the one person with a baseball cap ran and tried to climb over a cinder block wall covered by vines. The other man stayed in the middle of the street. Officer Dailey pulled a little closer and stopped and got out on the driver's side. He yelled at the two to stop, which they did, and they started to walk toward the officer. Officer Dailey asked them if they lived at the Mobile Home Park.

It was dark and a deserted area where he was confronting the two individuals. The officer was outnumbered so he used the driver's door as a barrier to protect himself if they tried anything. Both men were in front of him. He had the patrol unit's lights on the detainees. He asked for identification from the one suspect. His name was Sergio Escobar (pseudonym) and he handed the officer a California Identification Card with his photo on it. (This Card was later recovered to the side of the police unit.)

CHAPTER 75 RECOGNIZED MURDERER

Officer Dailey had that detainee return to the front of the patrol unit and wait there. Then he looked at the other detainee. That person had a baseball cap with the letter "P" on it. The officer recognized that was the symbol typically worn by members of the Cherryville street gang.

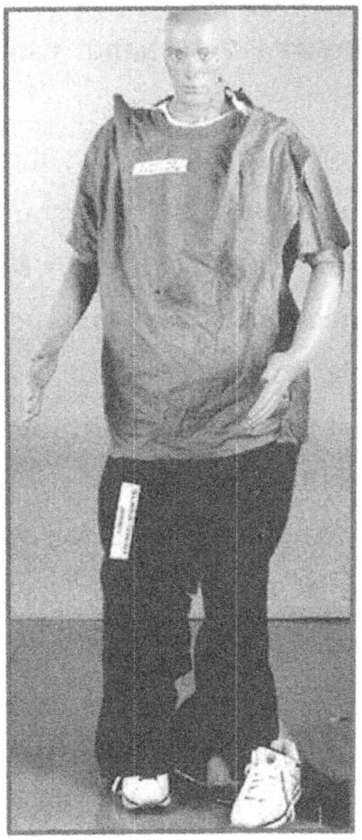

Escobar's Clothing

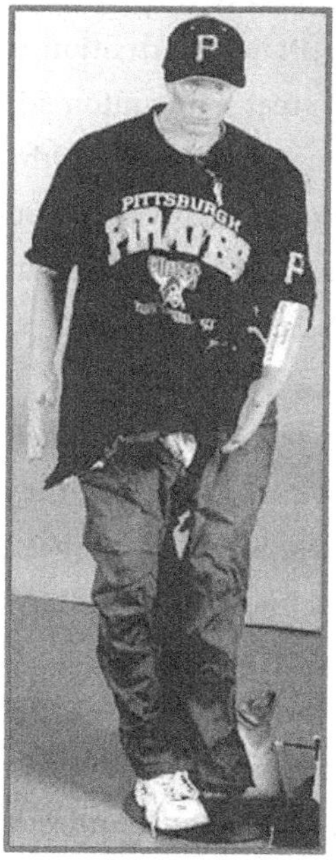

Bravo's Clothing

As the second detainee stood in front of the police unit, Officer Dailey was able to get a good look at his face. His mind was trying to remember if he recognized him. Initially he thought to himself that this second guy looked very familiar. The guy with the baseball cap turned his head to look directly at the officer and that was when it all came together. As the officer focused on him, he knew the person to be Juan Carlos Bravo, who was wanted for the Murder of victim Ramos.

This was a frightening moment for Officer Dailey who was working alone and coming face to face with a Murder suspect. How should he react? Without giving it any thought the officer pulled out his gun and stepped backwards in order to place more distance between himself and the Murder suspect.

Besides the headlights, it was totally dark, and as the officer backed away he had no cover between him and the suspect. As the officer's eyes remained fixated on Bravo, he couldn't make out much because he had dark clothing on. What caught the officer's attention was that Bravo kept his hands down by his pants pockets. Bravo slowly moved to within four to six feet of Officer Dailey. He kept mumbling something unintelligible. Office Dailey could hear words from Bravo stating, "I'm going to fucking kill you." After intently listening to what Bravo was saying Officer Dailey's attention was directed to Bravo's right hand, which was holding a blue steel semi-automatic gun.

This is the moment of truth that all police officers fear. How should he respond? There are those who would say that the mere fact that a person who is stopped by the police and is holding a handgun is not a justification for shooting at that person. Even after that person has already tried to run away and the officer has recognized the person as a wanted Murder suspect. These armchair quarterbacks would say that the officer should not start shooting until the person has actually pointed the gun at the officer and pulled the trigger.

Those people would state that the officer should instruct the person to throw down the gun and give him a reasonable amount of time to comply with the request. However, in the real world the officer doesn't have the luxury of having time. Officers have to make split second decisions.

If in fact the suspect doesn't drop the gun but in that split second fires at the officer, it may mean sudden death for the officer. But in this case Officer Dailey didn't want to take any chances, so he fired his service firearm. He realized he needed to get some cover, so he darted behind the driver's door of the police unit. As he fired and moved backwards he stumbled and fell to the pavement.

Through the driver's door window of the car Officer Dailey could see the top of Bravo's baseball cap. Although Officer Dailey was on the pavement he continued to fire upward in the direction of where Bravo was standing. By this time he had fired four to six shots and he was able to regain his footing and took cover at the rear of the trunk of his police unit.

Officer Dailey could hear Bravo yell, "You're fucking dead." As he positioned himself behind the car he looked through the rear window and could see Bravo standing in front of the car. The officer could hear Bravo firing at him as the police car continued to be pierced with gunshots. All the officer could do was to continue to fire in the direction of the front of the police car in hopes of striking the suspect.

This meant firing through the police car's rear window. The officer knew he was too vulnerable standing behind the police car, so he fired one more volley of shots, after which he took off running as fast as he could to the edge of a cinder block wall behind the police car.

CHAPTER 76 BACKUP FINALLY ARRIVED

The officer immediately crouched down behind the wall and tried to take a deep breath when he noticed a backup unit had appeared. It was Sergeant Baker who arrived first and ran over to Officer Dailey to determine if he was all right. Officer Dailey checked himself out and determined that he had not been hit by any gunfire. Sergeant Baker told him to wait by Sergeant Baker's police car. Officer Dailey retreated back to the Sergeant's unit.

Sergeant Baker continued to look in the direction where officer Dailey said he had shot at the suspect. Sergeant Baker couldn't see anyone standing, but he noticed something moving in the grassy area. He cautiously went to check it out and found Juan Bravo lying wounded on the turf. He immediately handcuffed him and waited for the paramedics to arrive. In the meantime he started looking around in the immediate area where Bravo was hiding. Several steps away he found a semi-automatic 9mm Beretta with an extended clip.

Bravo's 9mm handgun

Bravo's 9mm
Extend Clip

Later he examined the weapon and found that it was loaded with various unspent bullets, some of which were hollow point. These hollow points can be extremely deadly because they flatten out when they strike a person's body and continue to tear up the tissues and organs inside.

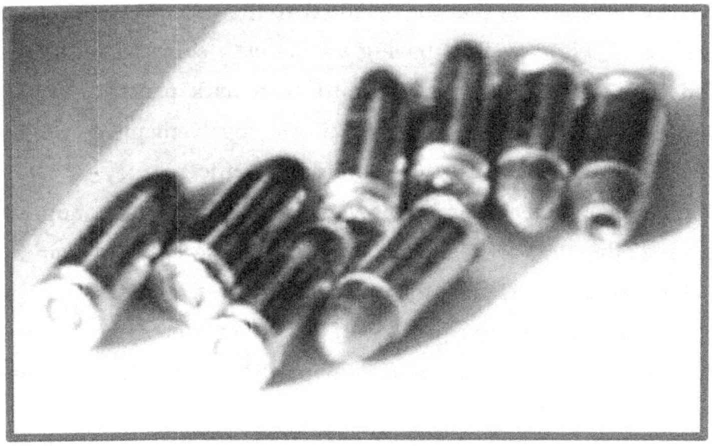

Hollow Point Bullets

After the shooting scene was secured, the CSI team came out to locate and collect all the expended shell casings. Later analysis determined that the Beretta handgun was operative with its extended clip. When Officer Dailey's police car was later examined it was determined that a 9mm bullet had entered the front of the police car and the slug was recovered from the crime scene. That would corroborate the fact that Bravo did in fact shoot at Officer Dailey from the front of the police unit.

The other party, Sergio Escobar, who had been standing with Bravo when Officer Dailey had stopped them, was found in the Mobile Home Park lying on a couch suffering from some type of gunshot wounds. He was taken into custody for questioning as to his involvement in the shooting.

After all the dust had settled, it was clear that Juan Bravo had shot at Officer Dailey at least one time, missing Officer Dailey but striking his police unit. Officer Dailey fired 21 rounds and had struck Bravo two times in his right arm, two in his right thigh, and two in his right buttocks. The shootout occurred over a short period of time and in an extremely dark area. Officer Dailey was able to piece together what each subject did by their clothing.

Officer Dailey remembered that the person with the gun was wearing a baseball cap with the letter "P" as well as having a shirt with some lettering on it. The other person had a baggy dark gray t-shirt with dark pants. By using these descriptions, Officer Dailey was able to explain the involvement of each detainee. Juan Bravo was arrested for an attempted murder on Officer Dailey.

Since Bravo was an active member of the local Pomona street gang called the Cherryville gang, the DA's Office decided to assign the case to their Hardcore Gangs Division. As a result, the Bravo case was given to prosecutor **Michael Camacho**. (Camacho was in the process of being transferred to Major Crimes Division, but he had too many cases in Pomona that he had to finish up before moving downtown.)

CHAPTER 77 ASSESSING THE CASE

The prosecutor now had two separate cases against Juan Bravo. After reviewing the police reports and interviewing the witnesses it was clear that the original case involving the shooting of Ramos was definitely not a strong case. The women inside the apartment claimed they didn't see who and why the shooting began.

However, there was now new evidence that connected Bravo to the Ramos shooting. Several of the shelling casings at the Ramos murder scene matched up with the 9mm handgun recovered next to Bravo at the shooting of officer Dailey. This certainly strengthened the fact that Bravo did some of the shooting at the apartment.

As to the case involving the shooting at Officer Dailey, there was no difficulty connecting Bravo to it since he was found lying injured at the crime scene. Although it was dark, Officer Dailey was able to definitely say that it was Bravo who had the handgun and was shooting at him. By trying the two separate offenses together, it gave the jury a picture that the defendant was a person who was not afraid of using a gun. It indicated that he was a violent person.

Prosecutor Camacho recognized that if he consolidated the two cases he had a stronger case overall. Therefore he had the two cases joined. However, he knew that combining two separate shootings that happened over six months apart could be confusing for the jury. That was when Michael Camacho contacted me, the author, to come up with some type of visual that would make it clear what witnesses went with which shooting.

DDA Camacho used the chart below in his Opening Statement to the jury, so they clearly understood there were two separate crimes involved in this case. The crimes were placed on both sides while the defendant and the gun were placed in the middle. This was done so the jurors would realize that the connecting piece of evidence between the two incidents was the 9mm Beretta handgun.

The trial was hotly contested. The Defense had to come up with two separate Defenses to the two separate crimes. As to the apartment shooting, the Defense tried to convince the jury that the defendant shot in self-defense. This most likely was true as to the boyfriend who entered the apartment and had started the shooting. However, the defendant continued to shoot at the other person, who was unarmed and not a threat to anyone. Therefore the self-defense claim was no longer valid. Prosecutor Camacho had to rely on the earlier statement of the witness that the defendant went over to Ramos, who was crawling out the door when he shot him in the head.

At the trial, the defendant took the witness stand and testified that it was Felix Rincon who had started the shooting and he was just trying to defend himself. As to Ramos, the defendant testified that he told him to leave and as he was approaching the door Ramos turned and Bravo saw a dark object in his hand, so Bravo shot at him. There was evidence that Ramos did have a dark brown glove on one of his hands. Bravo testified that he remained in the same position in the apartment at all times and at no time did he approach Ramos and shoot him when he was down.

As to the shooting at Officer Dailey, the defendant testified that the officer started shooting at him first, so the defendant had a right to defend himself. He said that the officer asked him if he had a weapon and Bravo told the officer that he did. Bravo claimed that he was reaching down to get his gun out, but before he could do it the officer started shooting at him.

The defendant said that he was shot in the arm and dropped this gun and it fell to the ground. He kept yelling at the officer that he was down. Bravo testified that he thought that the officer was going to kill him so he decided to make a run for it. Bravo saw his gun so he picked it up with his left hand and shot into the hood of the car to scare the officer. He kept running and was struck and dropped the gun again. He tried to hide in the grass but was shot at again. Then Bravo said that a short time later Sergeant Baker came over to him and handcuffed him.

The case was argued to the jury, and afterward the jury started their deliberations. They had to decide on two separate crimes. Eventually they returned with an unusual verdict. As to the shooting of Ramos in Gomez's apartment they found it to be Voluntary Manslaughter and not a murder as argued by the prosecution. The jurors didn't think that Bravo had a right of self-defense as to shooting at Ramos, although he may have had such a claim against his shooting of Rincon. The jury found him not guilty of shooting at and injuring Rincon.

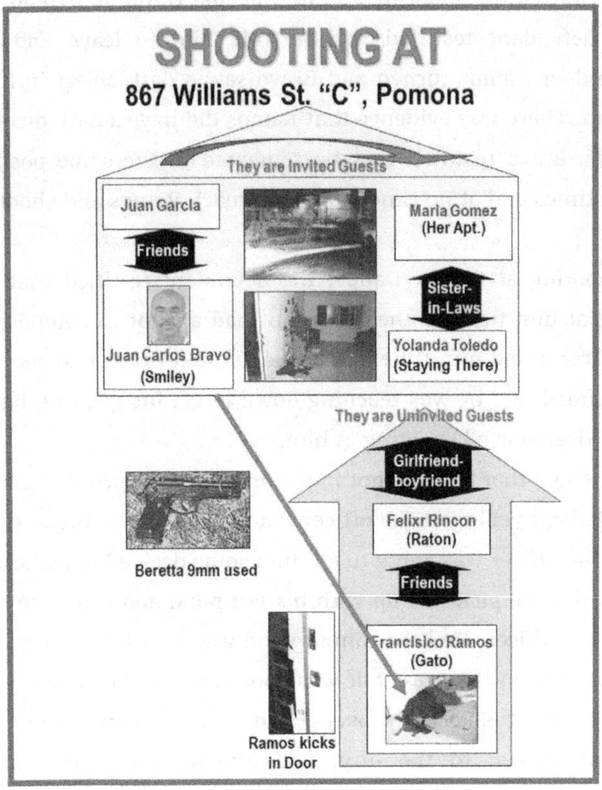

In the second incident involving the shooting at Officer Dailey, the jury didn't agree with the self-defense argument, so they convicted the defendant of Assault with a Firearm on an Officer, opting not to convict him of the Attempted Murder. The verdicts seem to be a compromise.

In analyzing the jury's decision, it appeared that the jury felt that the killing in the apartment was not started by the defendant even though he may have overreacted to the situation. As to the officer shooting, the jurors felt that the defendant had suffered enough since the officer shot at him 21 times while the defendant was only able to shoot at the officer once. Also, the defendant was the one who suffered injury as a result of the gunfight.

CHAPTER 78
ATTACKING DA

At the time for sentencing, the judge imposed a lengthy prison sentence for defendant Bravo. It was an uneventful hearing. The Defense attorney was shuffling together some of his legal papers. Prosecutor Camacho had pulled the bulky folder toward him on the counsel table. He began to write on the outside file jacket the exact prison sentence that the judge had imposed.

As everyone was finishing things up in the courtroom, the defendant quietly without any notice stood up. His hands were chained to his waist. Without saying a word he moved slightly to his left side near prosecutor Camacho. With all the energy Bravo could muster, he did a kickbox with his shod feet striking the prosecutor on his right side, knocking him to the floor. This came as such a surprise that Camacho, the prosecutor wasn't able to take any type of defensive posture.

The courtroom staff was shocked. They are used to hearing about violence but never are a part of it. Fortunately for prosecutor Camacho, he wasn't injured. He had to assess the situation and recognize the vulnerability a prosecutor is subjected to.

Six months later the defendant was prosecuted for attacking prosecutor Camacho. The case was transferred from the Pomona Branch courthouse to the downtown courthouse. A different prosecutor tried this second case. The witnesses called to testify were the original judge, prosecutor Camacho, the courtroom clerk, and the court reporter.

In this case, the Defense attorney's approach was that Michael Camacho wasn't acting as a public official since the sentencing hearing was over and the prosecutor was merely making notes in his file. In this second trial, the jury wasn't as willing to give the defendant any compromise verdict. Within 15 minutes, the jury came back with a guilty verdict of assaulting a government official.

This second case may have sealed defendant Bravo's fate in that it appears he will be spending the rest of his life in prison. His propensity for violence cost him dearly.

RACIAL KILLING IN OUR NEIGHBORHOOD

People v. Barron

SUPERSTAR PROSECUTOR

Michael Camacho

CHAPTER 79 TONY IS KNUCKLES

There are cases that make one wonder where society went wrong. Was it a failure of the institution of the family or the failure of our school system? Or can we blame it on religion and the total lack of a moral compass being instilled in young people today? Another possibility would be to blame it on the "Pop Culture" that reveres violence through the music and video games that young people are exposed to.

This present case stirs considerable philosophic debate since it involves a 16-year-old boy who took it upon himself to impose the Death Penalty on various people in his community. His primary reason for killing was simply that he disliked black people so much that he felt compelled to kill them. Most killers are motivated by some type of personal reason, such as revenge. Seldom is the motive outright racial hatred.

However, for this 16-year-old, his main goal was to gain the respect of his homies. His name was Tony Barron, and he went by a moniker of "Knuckles — sometime "Nuckles" for short. He lived with his grandparents in the city of Pomona in the 12th Street Gang area.

His sole ambition in life was to be recognized by all gang members. He wanted the rival gang members to respect him out of fear. In order to be noticed he had his moniker graffitied all over the neighborhood.

Tony Barron
aka Knuckles

Tony Barron was proud he had mastered the art of spray-can writing in order to let other gang members know that he and his 12th Street Gang were in charge of the southern part of the city of Pomona. His task every day was to find surfaces to spray his graffiti on. Garage doors and walls were great places to cover with one's own graffiti. In short order, Tony took his spray can and artfully painted "P 12 ST KNUCKLES." It wasn't sufficient to do it once but to spray it on as many walls as possible. He felt a sense of pride in seeing his name sprawled all over the community. He believed that everyone would admire him for all the hard work he had done by painting up the neighborhood with his Gang's name.

12th Street Gang Graffiti on Garage Doors

Part of the challenge for graffiti taggers is to spray can without being caught by the homeowners. If neighbors or owners caught him in the act, he would merely run off and come back later to finish off his so-called artwork. Often homeowners in frustration would immediately paint over the graffiti, but that didn't deter Tony. At times he had to return in the dead of night to secretly finish up his writing.

On December 15, most people were frantically getting ready for Christmas. This can be a joyous time of year; however, it can also be a hectic time. There is the rushing around to find the perfect gift for children or uncles and aunts. With all the thought that goes into the selection process, in all likelihood the gift will be immediately be returned after Christmas for a simple refund. (Thanks to 'online shopping,' one can do their Christmas shopping at home, thereby missing all the crowds and long lines.)

It is also a stressful time not knowing whether to send out Christmas cards or not. As the years go by fewer and fewer people send Christmas cards. At one time this was the only way to learn what your friends and family members have been up to. Today Facebook has taken over the job of Christmas cards since that tells the world what you have been up to over the past year.

One of the new debates for families is to decide whether to have a real Christmas tree or pull an artificial one out of the attic. Some members of the family want to have the sweet pine scent to put them in the Yuletide mood. The artificial Christmas tree advocates try to act like conservationists since they are saving a poor tree from being cut down. (Somehow they overlook the fact that it was grown in a Christmas tree farm) These people also take the high road in claiming that real trees can cause house fires when they dry out.

It is astonishing how Christmas time can so divide a family. Is there a correct way to celebrate such a holiday? Many communities have given up on Christmas since it has become such a divisive issue. Some people have stricken from their vocabulary the words "Merry Christmas" and replaced it with "Happy Holidays." In order to be politically correct, the 'nativity scenes' have had to be packed up and tucked away in the attics in order not to offend other religious groups and definitely don't want to appear to be leaving out the atheist in our community.

The public schools have erased Santa Claus from the holidays, and Christmas carols which were engrained in our memories are now taboo. As we were growing up in small-town America, we weren't aware of how many people in the world we were offending with our merriment. Back in 2001, the City of Pomona wasn't placing such a prohibition on Christmas, and even in the downtown area there were Christmas street decorations.

CHAPTER 80 DON'T MESS WITH THE GRAFFITI

Now back to the morning of December 15, most of the residents of the city of Pomona were going about their normal duties. In the back of their minds they knew that Christmas was just around the corner. Undoubtedly, Tony Barron was aware of Christmas chores that needed to be done. But on this day he was out surveying his neighborhood to see that everything was in order.

To his surprise, somebody had been messing with the graffiti he had earlier sprayed throughout the community. Someone had the gall to spray an "X' or run a line through his writing. This was such a hostile act of disrespect. He surmised that rival gang members had done these terrible acts. This required a swift and emphatic response. The only appropriate punishment for such a major act of disrespect would be the Death Penalty.

The burden was on him to find out who was the person or persons who had disparaged him. It was up to him to impose the capital punishment on the culprits. So Tony and one of his fellow gang members started riding their bikes around to see if they could catch whoever was doing it.

He and his friend decided to wait at a certain location where they had recently done graffiti by spraying their gang name and their moniker. They waited in a darkened area between several garages. While waiting, they saw two figures dressed in dark sweatpants and hoodies standing next to the garage door that had their graffiti on it. One of the guys leaned over with a spray can in his hand. Then he seemed to shake the spray can, making the sound of a metallic ball rattling inside the can.

12th Street Graffiti Crossed Out

The teenager made a motion of spraying a line across the graffiti. The other person chuckled out loud and took the spray can in his hand and started spraying a line through the name "Knuckles." The two guys stepped back to see if they needed to paint the line darker as they seemed to giggle at what they had done.

Immediately, without any conversation, Tony and his pal sprung out of their hiding place and came around the corner and startled the two guys. As Tony pulled his gun out and pointed it at the guys, their eyes got as large as saucers. The scent of the spray can mist was in the air.

At first the guys seemed frozen, not knowing in which direction to go. Eventually they realized the spray cans in their hands were no match for Tony's .22 cal. revolver and homie's .38 cal. revolver. These Olive Street gangbangers would have been interested in any form of mercy that Tony was willing to consider. Both guys turned to their left and started running out of there. Neither one of them had tried out for 100 meters sprint on their school track teams, but they took off so fast that they could have qualified. Tony and his buddy took off after them.

Tony wasn't going to give them any slack for crossing out his name as he continued after them. As hard as it is to hit a moving target, especially when you are running, Tony and his pal must have been skilled marksmen. Just as they got to the corner, one of the Olive Street guys went down. His name was Yanez, and he had been hit dead center.

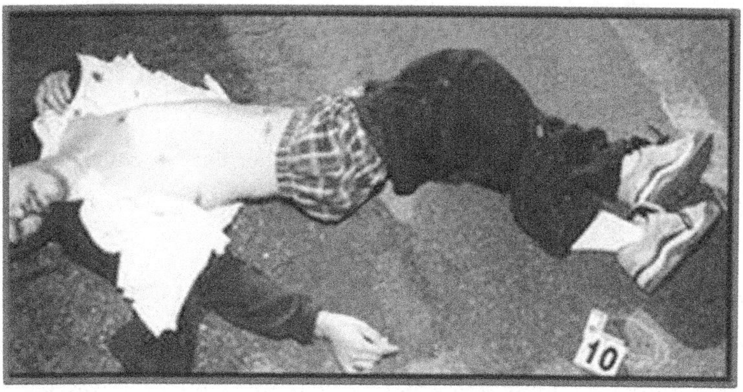

Yanez Was Shot near Garage

But the other rival, named Fuentes (pseudonym), must have been more nimble on his feet and cut through the alleyway passing between two garages. They figured he would reappear at the end garage. Tony held up his gun and pointed it to the corner thinking Fuentes would appear. Sure enough, a person came around the corner, at which time Tony fired at a partial outline of a person.

Unfortunately, it turned out to be a woman named Leautland-Garcia who was walking to her car. She could best be described as a totally innocent bystander. She wasn't involved in gangs or graffiti. Most likely the only thing on her mind was Christmas shopping or having family and friends over for the holidays.

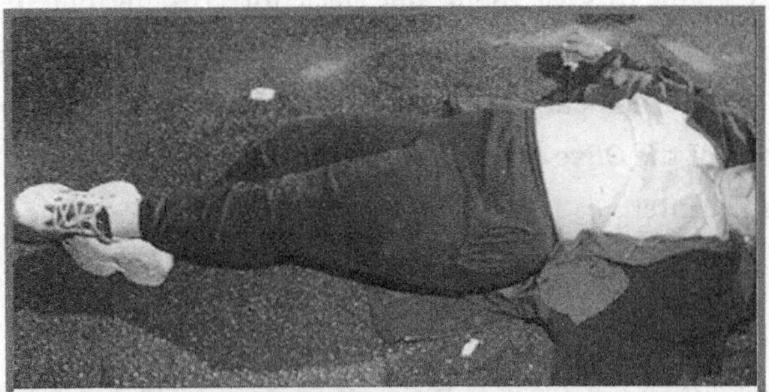

Leautland-Garcia
She was Shot walking to her car

She had no warning or time to prepare for her death. As her lifeless body fell onto the dirty alleyway, she was coming face to face with her maker whether she was ready or not.

Fortunately for Fuentes the graffiti artist, he was the luckiest one that night in that he dodged all the bullets and wasn't grazed or even injured. Since he had seen and knew Tony Barron, he was able to provide the police with the name of one of the shooters. However, neither of the guns that were used was recovered from the crime scene so there was no way that ballistics could be helpful in the police investigation.

However, on January 2nd Barron was in a car stopped for a traffic violation, and a .22 caliber sawed-off rifle was found inside the vehicle. It was thought that this was one of the weapons used to shoot and kill Yanez. So the police presented the case to the DA's Office for a filing. It was later learned that the sawed-off rifle couldn't be matched to the Yanez shooting. The only evidence connecting Tony Barron to the shooting came from Fuentes, who could identify Barron as one of the shooters. In the eyes of the jury, Fuentes and his buddy Yanez were NOT very sympathetic characters since they were in the process of crossing out Tony's moniker "Knuckles" when they were shot at. A gang expert testified that crossing out a gang member's graffitied name would be grounds to kill that person in the gang world.

CHAPTER 81 FIRST KNUCKLES TRIAL

The DA's Office recognized that the Pomona community was being inundated with gang homicide cases. The DA's Hardcore Gang Division had assigned their top ace to confront the problem. That was when Michael Camacho came on the scene to see if he could stop this tidal wave of homicides. Camacho had a successful track record on gang homicide cases, and he was the perfect prosecutor for the job.

Camacho had a heavy backload and didn't need another case assigned to him. However, law enforcement pitched the argument to the DA's Office that this Tony Barrow case was a double homicide needing special attention. The argument was gangster killing gangster is one thing but when gangsters kill a totally innocent party (here the killing of the woman on her way to go shopping) then the judicial system needs to come after the perpetrator with all the resources that the community can bring to bear.

Camacho agreed to take on the case, but he had to finish up the cases he had already set for trial. Eventually, it was time for Tony Barron's trial. Camacho called Fuentes to the witness stand to identify Tony Barron as one of the shooters. He had Fuentes explain that he and his homie Yanez were in the process of spraying a line through the name "Knuckles" when bullets began flying. Fuentes told the jury that he got a good look at the shooters and was certain that Barron was one of them.

The Defense attacked Fuentes' identification and claimed that any member of the 12th Street Gang could have done it, because the name "Knuckles" had been crossed out at another location earlier.

It was what would be classified as a simple case since it entirely relied on Fuentes' identification. Either you believed him or not. The jury deliberated for a long time, but they were never able to reach a unanimous verdict. The jury could only muster up ten votes for conviction and two for not guilty. So the prosecutor, Mike Camacho, had to try the Barron case a second time. This time he tried to show how the witness Fuentes personally knew the defendant and therefore his identification could be relied on. Again the Defense attorney hammered on the fact that it was a rival gang member that the jury had to rely on.

The jury deliberated for days and came back claiming that they were hopelessly deadlocked. The judge questioned the jurors if they needed more time and they assured the judge that there was no likelihood of a unanimous verdict. The judge declared the jury deadlocked and declared a mistrial. However, this time the prosecution didn't fare as well. The jurors were hung nine for guilty and three for not guilty.

The DA's Office decided not to retry the case for a third time since there wasn't any new evidence the prosecution could present that would be more convincing to another jury. So it was decided that in the interest of justice that the case would be dismissed against the defendant Tony Barron, who was about to turn 17 years old. This was a great day for Tony Barron since he was given a new lease on life. If he had been convicted of multiple murders, he would have spent most of his life behind bars. Now he had gone through a learning experience of two murder trials which had to have a profound impact on this defendant's thinking and approach to life.

CHAPTER 82 CRUSADE AGAINST BLACKS

It wouldn't take long before the police would learn whether Tony had the smarts to turn his life around. We aren't certain what happened immediately when the defendant was released from custody and returned back on the streets. What we do know for certain was that he started on a killing spree on July 5th that ended six days later on July 12$^{th.}$ His actions would change his life and many others lives forever.

When Tony got out of custody, he needed a place to stay. The 'WELCOME' mat was no longer out for him at his grandparents place in South Pomona. He needed to turn to some of his old friends to help him out with a place to stay and some spending money.

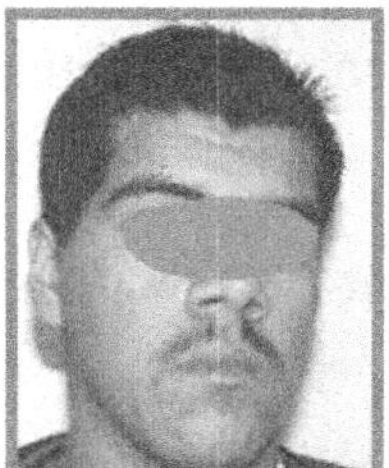

Sal Alonso

It wasn't long before he hooked up with his old buddy Sal Alonso (pseudonym). The advantage of associating with Sal was that he had the use of Sal's mother's car. Tony could get Sal to borrow his mother's older white Nissan Stanza so they could cruise the city of Pomona. Sal lived in San Dimas, the next city to the north of Pomona. Sal missed the excitement that always existed in the 12th Street gang territory in Pomona. Sal knew that Tony was a highly respected 12th Street gang member and whenever he had a chance he hung out with him.

As a result, Sal let Tony keep his belongings at his place since Tony didn't have any place to call home. One of those items was a note written in graffiti by Tony. The note said "Nigger Killers 12 Streets Nuckles Boy Los Sharkies". And another of his notes said, "No warning shots 12 St."

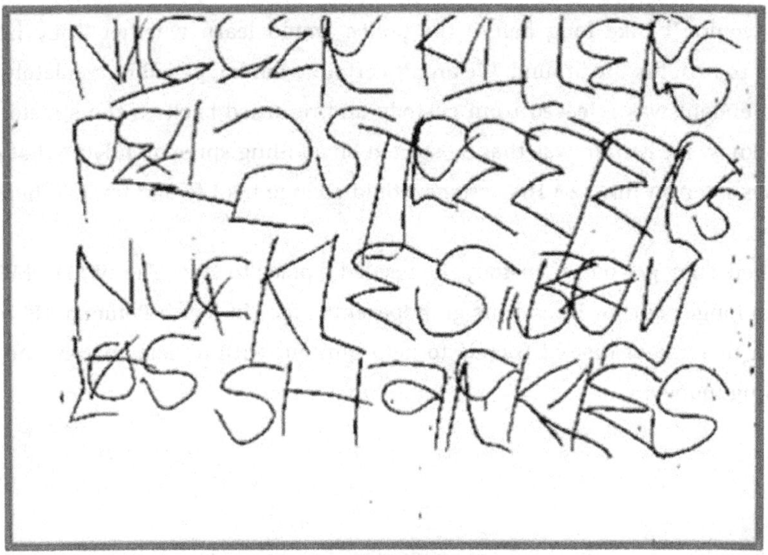

Tony Barron's Handwriting

It wasn't clear whether he wanted to eliminate all Blacks or just make the Blacks in the community scared so they would be more respectful of his 12th Street Gang. The dislike between the 12th Street Hispanic Gang and the Black Ganesha gangs was deep-rooted. Years earlier, the Black gangs had ruled much of Pomona and the Hispanic gangs were forced to be subservient to the Blacks. Tony Barron believed that it was 'payback' time and he was going to impose it one day at a time.

The hatred between the two groups can best be understood by a poem that Tony wrote which was later uncovered stored in Sal's house. It may be hard to read, so it is spelled out more clearly on the right-hand side of the below chart.

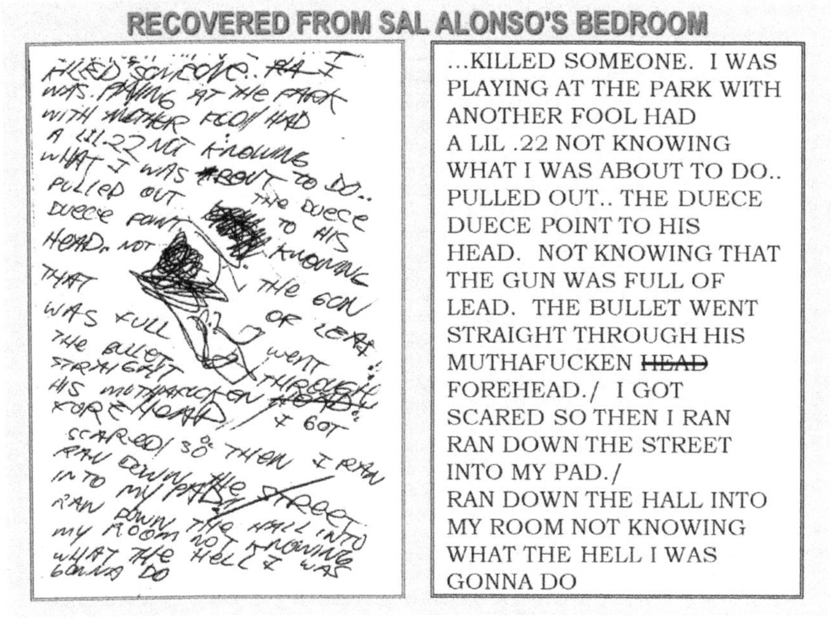

RECOVERED FROM SAL ALONSO'S BEDROOM

...KILLED SOMEONE. I WAS
PLAYING AT THE PARK WITH
ANOTHER FOOL HAD
A LIL .22 NOT KNOWING
WHAT I WAS ABOUT TO DO..
PULLED OUT.. THE DUECE
DUECE POINT TO HIS
HEAD. NOT KNOWING THAT
THE GUN WAS FULL OF
LEAD. THE BULLET WENT
STRAIGHT THROUGH HIS
MUTHAFUCKEN ~~HEAD~~
FOREHEAD./ I GOT
SCARED SO THEN I RAN
RAN DOWN THE STREET
INTO MY PAD./
RAN DOWN THE HALL INTO
MY ROOM NOT KNOWING
WHAT THE HELL I WAS
GONNA DO

This was a description of a homicide he committed on July 5, 2003. For Tony to explain what he had done, he had to set it to rap lyrics. (Strange how rap music is so openly accepted as being harmless.) When he wrote "THE DUECE DUECE POINT TO HIS HEAD" he was referring the fact that he used a .22 caliber handgun to shoot the victim. Tony felt he was a one-man purging machine of Blacks in the city of Pomona.

[illegible] believed that it was [illegible] time and [illegible] one day at a time.

The hatred between the two groups can best be understood by a poem that [illegible] wrote, which was later uncovered [illegible]. It may be hard to read, so it is spelled out more clearly on the right-hand side of the below chart.

[illegible]

CHAPTER 83 SEARCHING FOR BLACKS TO KILL

In order to prove that actions speak louder than words, Tony went into the nicer part of the city looking for Blacks to kill. It was midday in July and the weather could be best described as HOT. Tony and his friends pulled into the parking lot of Ganesha Park, where the city had built an Olympic size pool for local kids to use to cool off and learn to swim. The main job of the city recreation staff was to chase off the 'druggies' and the gangsters from congregating in this beautiful park. The rec center and the manicured grounds made the place look like a safe haven for kids and seniors.

Tony and his homies cruised through the park looking for Black youths but were disappointed when they couldn't find any. They exited the park and drove across the main thoroughfare, White Street, into a well-established middle-class neighborhood. These homes were built 50 years earlier in the Spanish mission style. The houses had white stucco exteriors with classic Spanish tiles decorating the roofs.

The residents of this area were hard workers who were proud of their neighborhood. Tony and his crew weren't thinking that the people who lived here loved this place since it seemed such a safe haven for them and their family members. The only regret Tony was feeling was the fact that he hadn't seen one male Black. Tony abruptly told the driver to go around the block since he thought he saw someone walking alone down the street.

The driver complied, and as they were coming around the block Tony told the driver to slow down. Tony's gloomy expression turned to glee as they slowly drove up from behind what looked like a young male. By now the car was creeping along as Tony glared at his prey. The youth was Desmond Boykins, who was dressed with a black shirt and blue jean shorts. Tony didn't have a clear view of his face. His arms and legs seemed slightly dark. Was this guy just a darker Mexican, or could he be a Black? The guy wasn't dressed like a gangster or doing anything threatening. He looked like a kid walking to a friend's house just down the street.

Tony couldn't be sure until the car was slightly in front of the person. At this point Tony was certain that the person was Black. Without saying a word, Tony reached into his lap and raised his trusty .38 handgun and leveled it against the window's ledge.

Just like a big game hunter in Africa, Tony wanted to make sure he could bag himself a Black. Holding the gun as steady as he could in a moving car, he aimed for the head and squeezed off a round. Tony may have recognized that hitting a person's head wasn't all that easy to do. Then he decided to shoot the victim in the mid-section. He fired his .38 at this young Black a total of four times. Tony's approach was successful, as the young man turned to his right side as his knees went out from under his feet. The victim's body fell like in slow motion into the landscaping of the Red Apple plants next to the sidewalk.

Not a word was spoken by the killer or the victim. The victim's only sin was the fact that he was Black. He hadn't done anything to anyone that would justify his execution. Tony, who had just beaten a double homicide case months earlier, may have felt like the Teflon man. Tony felt good about his KILL and couldn't wait to read about his accomplishment in the newspaper.

Desmond Boykins Shot on Alameda St., Pomona

Because the victim had been shot in the face, his mouth started to ooze blood on the landscaping. By the time the paramedics got to the victim, he was in total cardiac arrest. The only witness to the shooting couldn't identify the people in the car but only remembered that it was a small white car with several occupants. The coroner was able to remove the bullet from the victim, and it was .38 caliber slug. But at that stage there was no gun that had been recovered to compare the slug to. At the time, the police didn't know what to make of this one shooting. The police had no idea that Tony Barron was involved. They thought it was a random shooting and didn't have any reason to believe that this was a "Hate Crime" or, for that matter, a gang homicide.

CHAPTER 84 LOOKING FOR MORE BLACKS

Killing one Black wasn't enough, so the very next day Tony was off to find another one to kill. This time he again was the passenger in a small white car that began traveling across the city streets looking for Blacks. Instead of driving around the residential areas, this time Tony had the driver go through the light industrial area near the railroad tracks. As they were pulling up to a group of warehouses, they spotted four blacks waiting at a local company to see if they would be hiring additional workers.

These Blacks weren't doing anything except trying to find work. Tony was ecstatic that he had four Blacks within his sights. As the car came to a crawl, Tony held up his .38 revolver and this time he held his arm outside the passenger window. He pointed it at two of the men standing near the warehouse door. Tony felt compelled to yell several racial slurs at the Blacks. Two of the Black men, M. Brady and L. Lewis (pseudonyms), could see the gun pointed at them. They spun their heads around looking for a place of cover. Tony continued to try to point the gun at the group, which started to take evasive action.

Tony needed to make a split-second decision whether to get off an accurate shot or merely spray the area of the Blacks. Tony recognized that this wasn't an ideal shooting situation. As disappointed as he was, he told the driver to get out of the area and they would try another day. So this incident ended without a shot being fired, and no one was killed or injured.

The police were called, and they came out and took a crime report. No one saw any type of pattern emerging from the sparse facts. No one was identified as being involved in the assaults, so the police just shook their heads wondering what was going on.

Several days later on July 10, 2003, Tony had hooked up with his buddy Sal Alonso. They were interested in looking at a special smoking pipe for sale at the local tobacco shop. Sal was driving his mother's white Nissan Stanza, license number "2WLZ599." After admiring the pipe in the store, they knew that they couldn't afford it. In their mind they added the pipe to their dream list in hopes that someday they would be wealthy enough to buy it.

Since Sal was driving, they pulled out of the parking lot making a right turn to get on to the main thoroughfare, which was Holt Avenue. As Sal negotiated the turn onto Holt, Tony in an excited voice said, "Pull over here." Tony pointed to the right near the Pep Boys auto store. Sal immediately pulled into the store's parking lot and looked for a place to park. Next to the auto store he spotted a parking space and pulled in and stopped.

As soon as Sal parked the car, Tony jumped out and rapidly walked back up to the main street. Standing near a bus stop on Holt Avenue was a group of Blacks. They seemed to be talking to each other as they continually looked for the bus. None of the Blacks were wearing gang clothing or had any tattoos showing some type of gang affiliation.

Pep Boys Store on Holt Ave.

Tony Barron walked in stealth mode not attracting any attention. He slipped along the backside of the bus stop where the Blacks had congregated. As he walked with his .38 revolver in his hand next to his leg, no one paid any notice to this short 17-year-old Hispanic kid. When he was within earshot, Tony shouted out several racial slurs, which caused several of the Blacks to turn to look as to what was going on.

Tony raised up his gun and held it with both hands and pointed it at the closest Black and pulled the trigger. Unfortunately, that person was Antaun Wheatley, who was hit by one bullet that went through his side and exited on the other side, proving to be fatal. This victim at first didn't seem to know that he had been shot. Initially he started to run toward the tobacco shop. By the time he reached the driveway his body turned like a corkscrew as he slumped to the concrete driveway.

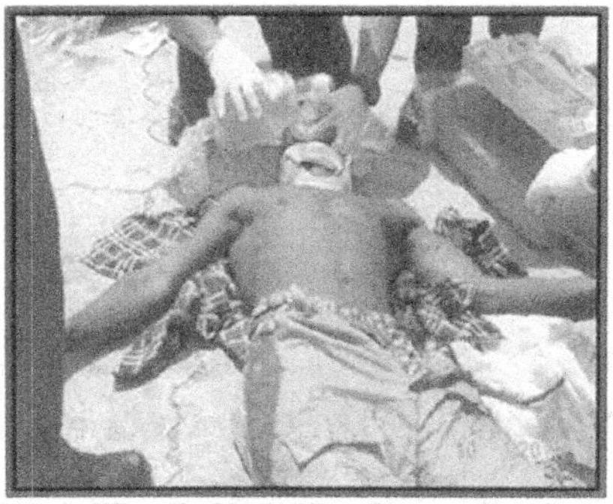

Antaun Wheatly Shot at Bus Stop on Holt Ave.

Tony may have been surprised how easy the shooting had gone until he saw the second young Black, who started to run for his life. Tony spun around and aimed at the fleeing victim and started shooting at him. Even though the guy was running, Tony was able to hit him in the leg. The victim ran to the tobacco shop next door and fell to the floor, surprising the clerk. Luckily this victim, Mark Doyle (pseudonym), wasn't seriously injured.

Across the street, a woman named Mary was waiting for her daughter to withdraw some cash from a nearby ATM machine when she heard the shooting. She looked around and saw a young male Hispanic running who was wearing a red shirt. Later she was more specific that the red shirt had checkers on it. Since she was some distance away, her description of the shooter was that he appeared to be around 17 years old. (Defendant Tony Barron was only one month from being 17)

A mechanic working in the Pep Boys shop heard the shooting and ran out to get a look. What attracted his attention was a white Nissan Stanza that sped off through the parking lot. Not knowing what happened, his first response was to glance at the license number of the car. He could make out what looked like a 'Z559.'

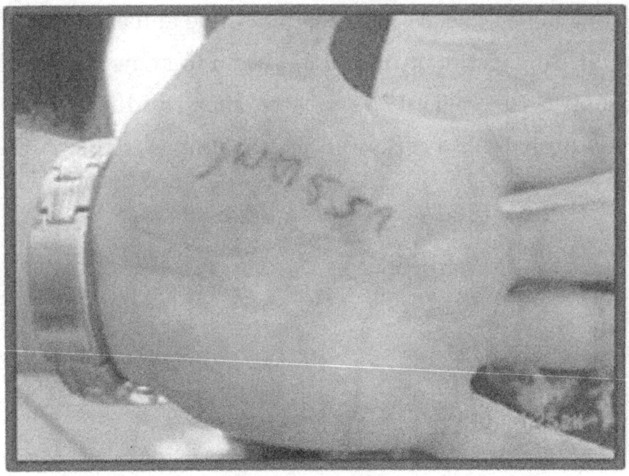

Pep Boy Workers Tried to Get License #
2W7559

As he stood in the parking lot he was met by Ralph Martinez (pseudonym), who was the assistant manager of the store. He likewise glanced at the car and tried to scribble down the license number on the palm of his hand. All he was able to see and write down were the first several letters '2W7.' As he stood there he saw one of his mechanics staring in disbelief at what had just happened. Martinez told the mechanic that he only go a partial license number. The mechanic stated he had gotten a good look at the license and knew the latter numbers were Z 559.

With the added numbers he wrote down on his palm '2W7559.' When the police officers arrived and started asking questions, Martinez walked up to one officer and showed him the palm of his hand.

The fact that the police had a license number seemed to be a great break in the case. However, the detectives knew that the license number couldn't be correct since in California the license numbers start with a number followed by three letters and ends in three numbers. They searched the DMV database and found no such number. They figured that there may be a slight variation of the numbers, so they ran it multiple ways. However, none of the various combinations of the numbers matched up to the type of car described.

As promising as the license number appeared to be, it turned out to be a major disappointment. However, at the police 'roll calls' the duty sergeant told their police officers to be on the look-out for a white car with some type of license similar to '2WVZ559.'

CHAPTER 85 SOMETHING HAS TO BE DONE

Many of the residents of Pomona were at a loss to explain what was happening to their otherwise safe suburban city. Over the years, the city had gone through gang warfare in the south end of town but nothing happened uptown. The next day after the shooting, the Pomona officers were on a heightened alert. They had little to go on except the fact that witnesses had indicated that they had seen a small white four-door car. In the last shooting, witnesses had reported a license number.

One of the patrolling officers had that description etched into his memory. While patrolling, he continually turned his head from side to side. He would glance down the side streets for any type of small light-colored vehicle. Out of the corner of his eye, he spotted a small white vehicle traveling to his side. His eyes focused in on the description of the car and he noticed it was a white four-door Nissan Stanza.

Bingo! Could that be the car they were looking for? The officer had to maneuver the patrol car behind the white car to check out the license plate. The vehicle had a license number of '2WLZ599' which was slightly different from the "2WVZ559" he had been told at roll-call.

License Plate of Sal Alonso's Mother's Car

The officer didn't want to catch the attention of the driver, but he pulled up to be parallel to the vehicle and tried to get a good look at the driver. All he could see was that the sole occupant was a Hispanic who was driving. In both of the prior shootings, the witnesses all said that there were two or more occupants in the shooting vehicle.

Even with these slight discrepancies, the officer thought he had enough to check out the driver and the car. As they drove to the next intersection, the officer pulled his patrol car behind the white Stanza and turned on the red lights. The driver turned his head slightly to look back and apparently recognized he needed to pull over. The driver started to move over and cautiously pulled to the curb.

Car Sal Was Driving When Stopped
Car belonged to his Mother

When the officer approached the car, he thoroughly looked inside to see if there were any other occupants. The officer asked for a driver's license and Sal Alonso handed him his license. The officer started asking some general questions about where the car was the day before. Sal didn't know how to answer since he wasn't even sure why the officer stopped him.

Sal was trying to think what he should say about himself and the car. He continued to give what seemed to be evasive answers. After several inconsistent answers, the officer made the decision to arrest Sal and transport him to the police station. The officer turned Sal over to the detectives at the station.

The first detective didn't know what they had. They had a car that matched the description of the fleeing vehicle, but the license number was a little mixed up. In order to straighten things out, the detective needed Sal to start talking. The detective pulled out his Miranda card and started reading line by line. Sal listened intently and when asked whether he understood his rights Sal nodded and said in a low voice, "Yes." The next question was, "And do you want to waive your rights and talk to me?" Sal looked stunned and at first he didn't know how to answer.

When asked again, Sal uttered something like, "I guess not." The detective accepted Sal's refusal. Since Sal didn't seem too adamant in refusing to talk, the detective stated, "If at any time you change your mind, let me know and we will be more than willing to listen to whatever you have to say."

There is no way of looking into Sal's mind, but undoubtedly he started to weigh his friendship with his pal Tony Barron. Sal must have come to the conclusion that it was better for him to save his own skin than stick his neck out to protect his buddy Tony. As the detective was about to leave, Sal said, "Is it about the gun?" This surprised the detective. He responded that it was about a number of things which included something about a gun.

Sal didn't want to take the blame for the gun, which he must have figured the police would soon find it in his mom's car.

All of a sudden Sal started talking as though he wanted to minimize his involvement in the shootings. He explained that he had a friend by the name of Tony Barron who he would drive around. He said that Tony had hidden a gun in the back portion of the front passenger seat. The officer asked how to locate it, and Sal described how to remove the seat back panel.

Back Door of Sal's Mother's Car

The detectives were eager to locate the gun. So with the information from Sal, they obtained a search warrant to search Sal's mother's car, which had been impounded. When they looked into the back panel of the passenger seat they found the gun, a .38 caliber revolver wrapped in a glove just where Sal said it would be. The gun had one GRL-brand bullet loaded.

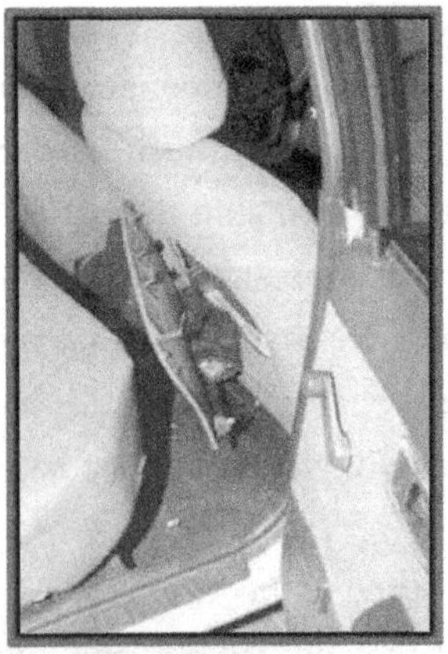

Gun Was Hidden In Back Panel of Passenger Seat

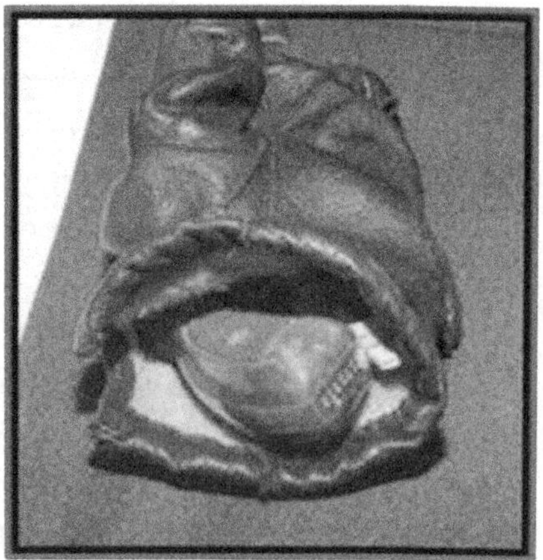

Gun Hidden in Glove Behind Seat

CHAPTER 86 CAN BALLISTICS HELP?

The handgun was a great find, even though it was a revolver and not a semiautomatic. The unfortunate thing about a revolver is that it doesn't automatically eject the fired shells like a semi-automatic does. At the Pep Boy store murder, there weren't any shell casing found at the crime scene that could be compared to this firearm found in Sal's car.

The police continued to question Sal about what he knew about Tony Barron's involvement in the shootings. Sal said that the day before he had parked next to the Pep Boy store and had dropped Tony off to go back to the tobacco shop. Tony had walked around the building and disappeared from Sal's sight. Sal heard shots fired and then Tony ran back to the car and jumped in and said, "They're shooting at us." Sal told the detectives that he drove North up Garey Avenue to the Interstate 10 Freeway. There he turned onto the westbound onramp to the 10 Freeway going toward his house in San Dimas.

Interstate 10 Freeway
Where Barron Threw Out Shell Casings

As they were driving along the freeway, Sal noticed that Tony was removing expended shell casings from the revolver and throwing them out the car window. Sal noticed that when Tony was doing this they were driving along the construction area of the freeway approaching the 57 Freeway interchange.

Once the detectives received that information, they recognized how important the finding of those shell casings could be. If they were recovered, that would corroborate Sal's story. Also, that would connect the handgun and car to the shooting in front of the Pep Boys store. As valuable as these shell casings might be, how could they search the I-10 Freeway at the 57 Interchange? This is one of the most heavily traveled freeway interchanges in Southern California.

In order to search the area, they would have to close down the freeway for a considerable time. In order to close down a freeway they would need the equivalent of a papal decree. Closing down a freeway would take more than an Act of God.

The Interstate 10 Freeway is the southernmost cross-country interstate highway in the USA. It extends from Jacksonville, Florida to end up at the Pacific Ocean in Santa Monica, California. It was one of President Eisenhower's planned interstate highway systems he created in 1956. This 2,460 miles of highway is like an artery that pumps blood into the American economy. It is understandable no one takes lightly the closing down of the I-10.

The detectives drove Sal out to the section of the freeway he had described. Since the events had occurred just three days earlier, Sal was able to point out the section where he remembered Tony tossing the shell casings.

The Pomona detectives had developed a good rapport with the California Highway Patrol. The detectives explained to the CHP that they were conducting a homicide investigation in which the shell casings were crucial to the case. The bottom line was that the CHP contacted CALTRAN and the Okay was given. By the next day, the CSI team was marching along the closed freeways looking for shell casings.

A search for a needle in a haystack would be easier than looking for small .38 caliber shell casings along the I-10 Freeway. The CSI team showed unbelievable perseverance, and the end result was they recovered three shell casings, two of which were in good shape while the third one had been run over. Sal's description turned out to be extremely accurate.

Recovered Shell Casings from 10 Freeway

Unfortunately, there were a number of travelers on the westbound 10 Freeway who were delayed. Undoubtedly some were late for appointments or maybe missed their appointments. Others were frustrated for having to wait in their car, especially if they were headed for a restroom. Every day, law enforcement has to make decisions that impact all of us. The big question was whether the closing down of the I-10 was worth the inconvenience to the freeway travelers.

For the first time, the evidence seemed to be coming together. They sent the gun from Sal's car, the bullet recovered from D. Boykin's body, and the shell casings found along the freeway to the Sheriff's Crime Lab. After several days the word came back that the Firearms Identification experts had been able to form an opinion that the gun found in Sal's car was the one used to fire the expended shell casings and the bullet recovered by the coroner from the body of D. Boykins.

The ballistics evidence was going to be crucial to the prosecution of the homicides. Now the Boykins murder was connected to the Pep Boys murder and these two crimes could be charged in the same case.

CHAPTER 87 WHAT ABOUT DNA?

As good as the ballistics evidence was, it didn't directly incriminate Tony Barron. The detectives had the word of Sal that it was Tony who did the shooting at the bus stop in front of Pep Boys. Now the question was, what evidence was there to prove Tony was the actual shooter? Several of the witnesses claimed that the shooter was wearing a RED shirt. The witnesses' description of the shirt was that it had a checker design. One witness thought it had a floral pattern.

Since the detectives knew of Sal's involvement, they had no problem obtaining a search warrant for his residence. Sal lived with his mother in the city of San Dimas. He mainly occupied one of the bedrooms. The police did a thorough search of the house, and in Sal's bedroom they found a RED checkered shirt. Sal explained that was the shirt that Tony Barron was wearing at the time of the shooting of A. Wheatley on the sidewalk in front of the Pep Boys store.

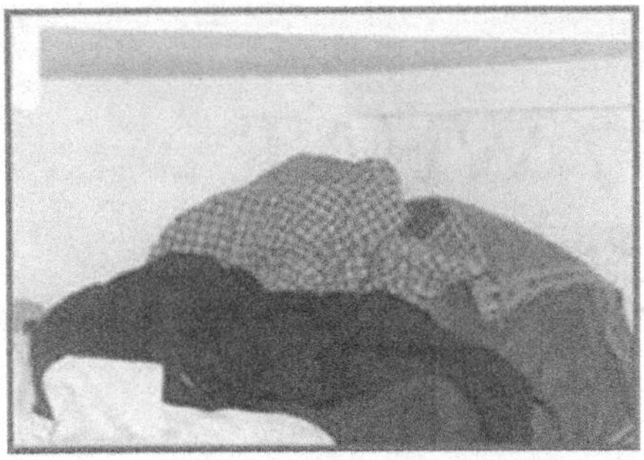

Red Shirt Found in Sal's Bedroom

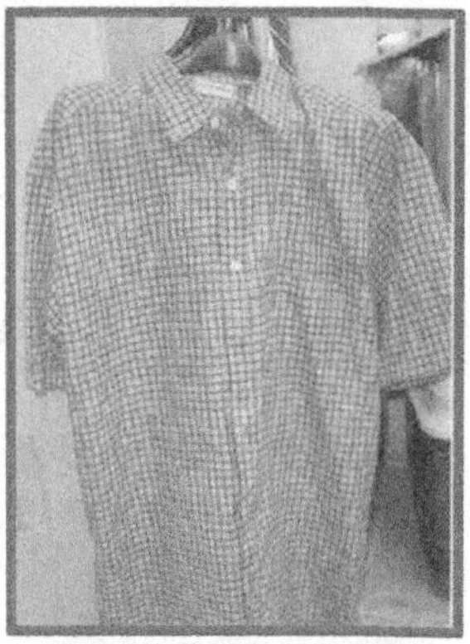

Barron's DNA on this Shirt

The detectives decided to pick up the red shirt and keep it for evidence. The witnesses at the Pep Boys store said that the shooter definitely was wearing a red shirt. When the police showed the shirt to the witnesses, they indicated that it appeared to be the shirt they saw the shooter wearing.

The red shirt certainly was becoming more significant. Sal claimed that it belonged to Tony since Tony didn't have a permanent place to live and had asked Sal if he could leave his personal belongings in Sal's room. Sal had agreed that Tony could leave his personal items at his home. However, Sal's mother disliked Tony so much that she would not permit him to spend the night at the Alonso house.

The police decided to attempt to find DNA on the shirt to determine if the person who had worn it was Sal or Tony. Sal claimed that Tony had been wearing the red shirt and when he ran back and got into his car, Sal noticed that Tony was perspiring. Sal said that he had perspiration circles under his arms.

The police on occasion have been able to obtain perspiration DNA results. Since it was a longshot, the police thought it was worth a try. They sent the shirt to the Crime Lab to be analyzed. Several months later the police received back a report that the DNA found on the red checkered shirt matched Tony Barron only and totally eliminated Sal Alonso. This was the type of corroboration that the police needed to support Sal's testimony that it was Tony Barron who was seen running back to the car after the shooting in front of the Pep Boys store.

As stated earlier, Tony Barron had no place to permanently reside since his grandparents didn't want him at their place. As a result, Sal's bedroom sort of became Tony's storage locker. When the detectives conducted their search warrant for Sal's house, they came upon certain gang-type items which they seized. One of those items found in Sal's bedroom was a bat with the name "Knuckles" written on it. There were also some notebook pages with a shark on them. The detectives were well aware that the shark was the symbol of the 12th Street gang. Even though these were Tony's items, why would Sal still hang on to them? The reason was that Sal was a wannabe gang member. For a long time Sal looked upon Tony Barron as his mentor, and he hoped someday he could be like him and even possibly be a part of the 12th Street gang.

CHAPTER 88 WHAT ABOUT FINGERPRINTS AND HANDWRITING?

The detectives dug deep into their Forensic Evidence bag to see what else might help connect Tony to this series of murders in Pomona. When they seized Sal's mother's car they were ecstatic when they found the gun that turned out to be the murder weapon in two of the homicides. The detectives weren't finished with the car. They knew they had no difficulty proving that Sal was using the car.

What about trying to show that Tony had been in that car? They had the CSI team dust the car for latent prints. Needleless to say, many people had been in and out of the little white Stanza. The technicians were inundated with an endless number of latent prints that mainly came back to Sal and his mother as well as dozens of friends that Sal drove around town.

The technician lifted a latent print on the outside top of the passenger door window. When they ran it through the fingerprint database, it came back as a match to Tony Barron's fingerprints. Again this was an additional piece of evidence corroborating Sal's story that Tony was in the vehicle the day of the shooting.

In spite of the latent print, some of the best evidence against Tony Barron came from his own words in his own handwriting. As stated earlier, there was a note found in Sal's bedroom which perfectly described how some of the killings were carried out.

While Tony Barron was awaiting trial, he wrote several incriminating letters. In one he said how much he enjoys the excitement of shooting people, it makes him laugh. All of these writings were reviewed by a handwriting expert who formed the opinion that they were written by Tony Barron. This form of Forensic evidence was highly probative of Tony Barron's aka Knuckles state of mind and intent.

The detectives decided to show a photo lineup to the Black men who were attempting to obtain warehouse jobs when some people in a white car came by and pointed a gun at them. The photo lineup included a photo of Tony Barron with five other men. These Black men were able to identify Tony Barron as the one who pointed the gun at them. One of these men got such a good look at the suspect that he was able to identify the weapon to be a .38 caliber revolver that was pointed at them.

CHAPTER 89 NEED FOR EXCEPTIONAL PROSECUTOR

There was no question who would be given this new case involving Tony Barron. Prosecutor Michael Camacho was the Ace Prosecutor in the Hardcore Gang Division. However, The DA's administrators were desperately trying to transfer Camacho to the Major Crimes Division. The problem facing the DA's Office was that several of the Major Crimes prosecutors had been appointed to be judges. This had left Major Crimes short-staffed, and there were a number of publicity cases that had not been assigned to a permanent prosecutor.

This created tension among the supervisors in the DA's Office. There was a tug-of-war over Deputy DA Michael Camacho. It was more like the sports teams negotiating a trade of a champion player. Somehow Hardcore Gang Division won to keep Camacho for the Barron case, but upon completion of the case he was to report to downtown Major Crimes Division where he already had a caseload waiting for him.

It was never revealed that the Hardcore Gang Division had to give up two rookie prosecutors in order to keep Camacho on the Barron cases. One would think that Mike Camacho must have felt great to have the two prestigious parts of the DA's Office fighting over him. The answer was that Camacho didn't gain anything like a bonus or even longer vacations. All he got was a giant headache of having to deal with two bosses in each Division.

After the decision was made to assign Camacho to the Barron case, he directed his attention to building a strong case against this defendant. He recognized that his first challenge was how to get witnesses to come to court to testify. Camacho knew how scared some of the witnesses were. They have to live in the area where the defendant's gang members still live and control the neighborhood. There was legitimate fear of retaliation.

Camacho wasn't naïve. He had prosecuted dozens of cases against members of the 12th Street gang. With the help of the Sherriff's gang detail plus the Pomona Police Department, Camacho had been able to convict many of the gang leaders. However, it seemed like an endless task. The wannabes came into the gang and took the place of the older shot-callers who had been sentenced to state prison.

Camacho knew the only way to convict Barron was to make some type of deal with Sal Alonso. If Camacho could get Sal to testify against his buddy Barron, then Camacho needed to figure out how to corroborate Sal's testimony. (Remember what you had learned from the Gallegos case, in which Eva Avila had to be corroborated.) Camacho went to work trying to find various acts that could be used to show corroboration.

The answer was that Forensics could provide the necessary corroboration. Camacho went through all the ballistics evidence and realized that the gun in Sal's car could prove that it was used to kill Desmond Boykin as well as Antaun Wheatley. Camacho arranged meetings with the Ballistics expert to find ways to make the ballistics evidence understandable for the jury. Next Camacho had to determine how to use the latent prints on Sal's car that came back to Barron as part of the corroboration.

Then it was on to DNA evidence from the red shirt to connect it to Barron as the one who wore it. Of course, there was some handwriting that could be used to corroborate Sal's testimony. Camacho realized that the handwriting was more than corroboration evidence since it could be used to prove that Barron originally wrote the graffiti that was on the garage doors in the original case against him.

Camacho had to make a pivotal decision whether to refile the Graffiti double homicide case that had ended in two hung juries. With all the new charges, could Barron be prosecuted for killing Yanez and Leautland-Garcia? Undoubtedly the new evidence of the shootings certainly painted a more vivid picture of the fact that Barron was capable of shooting people.

If they included the Graffiti killings incident, the Defense would claim that the DA's Office was being vindictive. The DA's Office had tried to convict Barron in two prior trials, now they were combining other cases together hoping to find a jury that would convict him of the Graffiti killings.

Some people might blame the DA's Office for not doing a better job of presenting the case to the jurors. If Barron had been convicted originally then Desmond Boykins and Antaun Wheatley would still be alive today. Camacho had to ignore all the criticism and only consider what would be best to get a jury to convict this defendant. Camacho didn't want to get involved in the 'Blame Game.' As far as he was concerned, the consolidation of the charges had been made and now it was on to building a solid case in which 12 jurors would be willing to find Barron GUILTY of all the charges.

CHAPTER 90 PREPARED FOR TRIAL

After reviewing all the reports and interviewing the civilian witnesses, Mike Camacho started to compartmentalize the evidence into groupings. Just like in the other cases that we have discussed, you the reader are familiar that Camacho liked to create and use visuals such as Charges Against Defendant and Locations Map. This case was no different; however, this time he had to decide what would be the most effective way to lay out the 13 different charges against defendant Barron.

Camacho started out listing the charges in the order they appeared in the charging document. The first count was the murder charge involving the shooting of Antaun Wheatley at the bus stop in front of the Pep Boys store. However, the Boykins murder was count seven, and the Graffiti double murders were counts ten and eleven. It wasn't long before Camacho realized it was too confusing to discuss the charges in the order they were listed on the charging document.

Camacho wanted to think like a juror. Then he found that it was easier to explain the case to the jurors by breaking the case down into chronological order as to when they occurred. He wanted them to think of it as four separate incidents or crimes all being tried in one trial.

CHARGES AGAINST DEFENDANT

INCIDENT	DATE	COUNT	VICTIM	CHARGE	CODE	SPEC. ALLG Street Gang All Cts
2443 Angela St. Pomona	12/15/01	10	Jose Yanez	Murder	PC 187	Firearm Discharge Death; Multi-Murd
		11	Leautaud-Garcia	Murder	PC 187	Firearm Discharge Death; Multi-Murd
		12	Henry Fuentes	Attempt Murder	PC 664/187	
	1/2/02	13		Carrying Load Gun by Gangster	PC 12031	
1674 Alameda St. Pomona	7/5/03	7	Desmond Boykins	Murder	PC 187	Firearm Discharge Death; Multi-Murd
		8		Carrying Load Gun by Gangster	PC 12031	
252 S. Buena Vista. Pomona; Photo of M Brady; Photo L. Lewis	7/6/03	3	M. Brady	Assault w/Firearm	PC 245(a)	Pers.Use Firearm
		4	L. Lewis	Assault w/Firearm	PC 245(a)	Pers.Use Firearm
		5		Carrying Load Gun by Gangster	PC 12031	
304 E. Holt Ave. Pomona	7/10/03	1	A. Wheatley	Murder	PC 187	Firearm Discharge Death; Multi-Murd
		2	M. Doyle	Attempt Murder	PC 664/187	Firearm Discharge Death
		6		Carrying Load Gun by Gangster	PC 12031	Firearm Discharge Death

At the top of the chart was the previous Graffiti case in which one of the taggers was killed as well as a lady who had was merely walking to her car. Also included was an attempted murder charge which involved the other tagger who ran away.

Camacho believed that with the additional shootings this third jury would be willing to find the defendant guilty of the Graffiti double homicide. His next group of charges involved the shooting of Desmond Boykins. Camacho explained that ballistics would prove that the recovered gun was the one used to shoot that victim.

That was followed by the two Assault with a Firearm charges against two of the four Blacks who were standing near the warehouse. The main piece of evidence was the positive identification of the defendant by the victims.

Finally, Camacho finished off the chart by discussing the shooting that occurred in the front of the Pep Boys store. He outlined his evidence proving Tony's involvement. That was based on Sal's testimony that Tony got out of the car and shortly thereafter he heard shots fired. Tony ran back and got in the car with a gun and told Sal to drive. Minutes later Tony was seen throwing the shell casings out of the car window on the I-10 Freeway. Witnesses would describe the shooter as wearing a checkered red shirt. Camacho went on to say that such a shirt was found in Sal's bedroom and the DNA on the shirt matched Tony Barron.

The jury trial commenced. When it came time for the Opening Statement Camacho pulled out the above Charges Agst. Def. chart and walked the jurors through all four incidents. When Camacho felt that the jurors understood the charges and the various incidents, he went on to orient the jurors as to where the various events occurred. He used a Map of Locations chart which made it clearer where everything that the jurors needed to know was located. Camacho pointed out on the map where every one of the eight incidents occurred. He could see some of the jurors nod and smiled when he pointed to certain locations as though they recognized those sites.

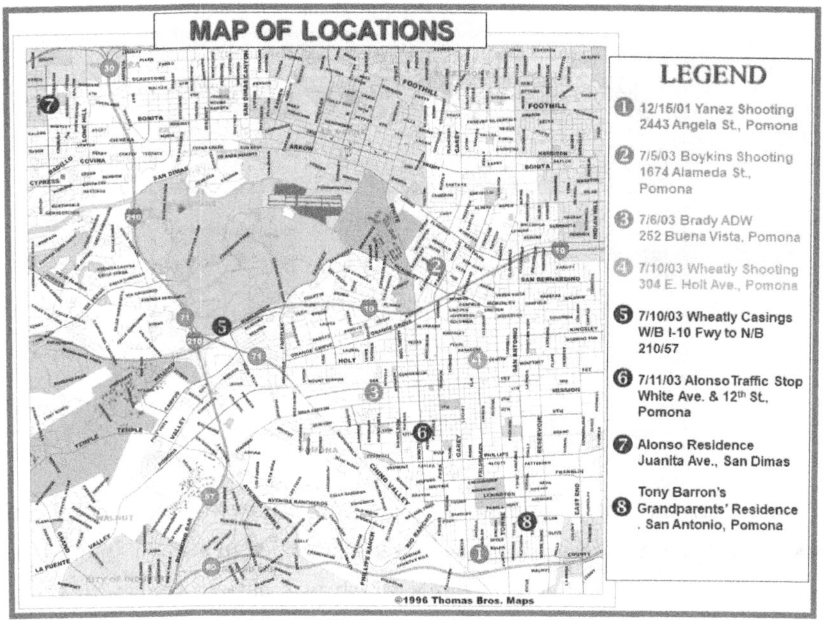

Camacho knew that the jurors would have difficulty understanding the officer's testimony regarding finding the gun in the back of the passenger seat. He knew that words alone couldn't adequately describe where the gun was hidden. As a result, Camacho had prepared a graphic which he showed the jurors. This visual consisted of a series of photos of the hiding place for the gun. Camacho didn't want there to be any misunderstanding about the basic facts of the case.

This visual showed Sal's photo to the left and showed various photos of his mother's car. It was important to convey to the jurors the exact location of the gun in the car. When a person says that the gun was in the back of the seat, one thinks of the pocket area where magazines and small items could be placed. What Camacho did was to show a photo of the rear portion of the back of the passenger seat.

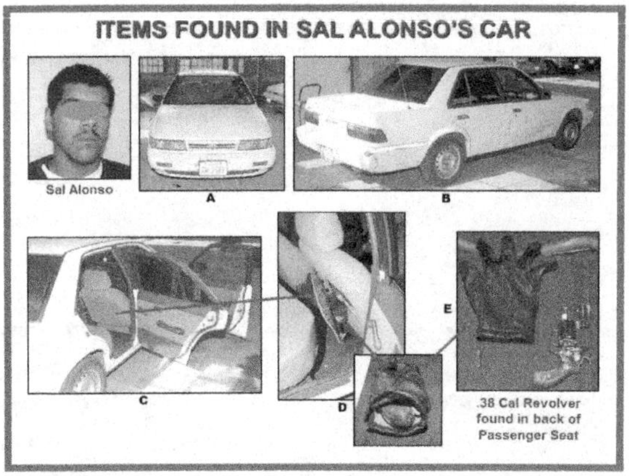

Then Camacho put in a photo showing how the back panel could be peeled back. Next Camacho showed how the gun was wrapped in a glove. In other words, this visual consisted of several photos which was able to convey to the jurors exactly where the gun was secreted.

Camacho took a look at the jurors to see if they were still following him. Seeing that all jurors looked like wide-eyed sponges anxious for more, he moved on to the next part of his Opening Statement. After that, he started on the actual facts of the murders. Starting with the shooting of Desmond Boykins, Sal claimed that he had not been with Barron when the defendant did that shooting, Camacho was going to have to rely on using Sal to testify that Barron had told him that he had shot someone and he could read about it in the newspaper. That referred to a newspaper article that was found in Sal's bedroom.

What Camacho did was create a visual that he could show to Sal with the newspaper article which talked about the shooting of Desmond Boykins on Alameda Street. What was included on that visual was a map showing where Alameda Street was located. Also contained on that map was a green area showing the location of Ganesha Park.

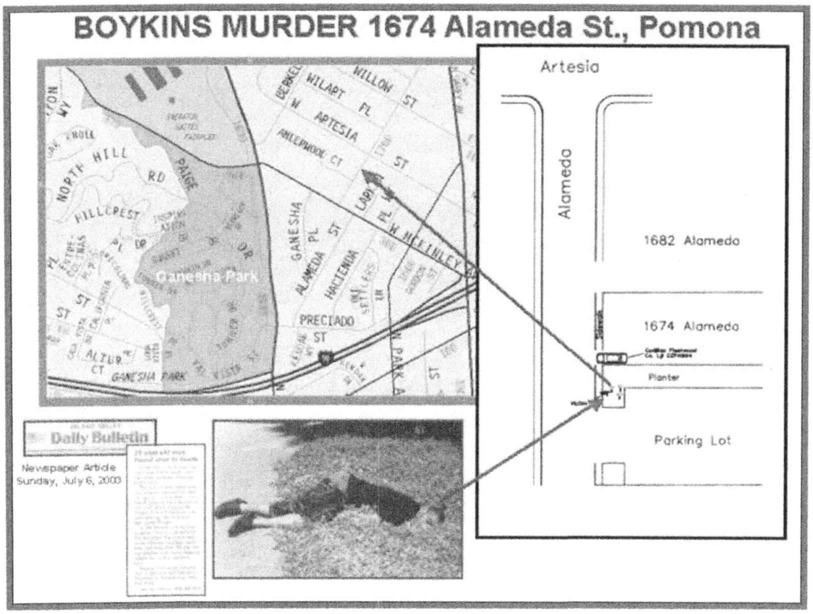

That green area on the map, Ganesha Park, was going to become important in corroborating Sal's testimony. Sal's car had received a citation next to Ganesha Park on several occasions before the shooting of victim Boykins.

Although this wasn't a critical piece of evidence, at least it confirmed that Sal's vehicle had been there several days before the Boykins shooting. In the below visual Camacho had placed a photo of Sal's mother's car with the registration papers. Under that he listed the citations proving that the car was at Ganesha Park shortly before the Boykins shooting.

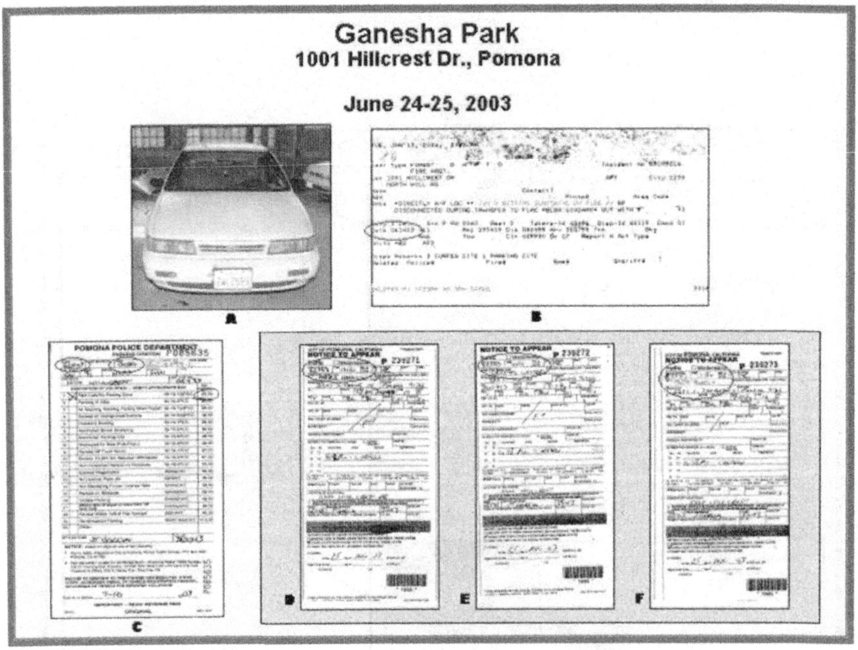

CHAPTER 91 READY FOR THE EVIDENCE

After both sides had made their Opening Statements to the jury, the judge instructed the jury as to how the trial would proceed. The prosecution would present their evidence first, which would be followed by the Defense having an opportunity to present evidence if they wished to. Both sides were pleased to be trying the case before a judge who was pleasant and flexible.

The trial was set before Judge Charles Horan in the Pomona courthouse. This judge can be best described as an authentic personality. What made him so well liked by attorneys from both sides was his low-key approach to courtroom proceedings. Jurors appreciated his comfortable approach and his not taking himself too seriously.

One might think the judge would be a pushover since he was so well liked. However, what some attorneys didn't recognize was that the judge always knew exactly what he was doing. He was one of those unique persons who knew the difference between the small stuff that wasn't terribly important and the big stuff that was non-negotiable.

I, the author, knew the judge when he was Chuck Horan and worked for the DA's Office in downtown L.A. I admired his insightful mind in which he could remember the complex case law better than any attorney or judge. We all thought that Chuck had a 'photographic memory' since he made it look easy to recall cases for every situation. When it came to the Law of Homicide, he could rattle off all the various degrees and rules on self-defense.

I remember many Friday afternoons years earlier after the courtrooms had closed for the day, you could hear the sound of someone strumming a guitar. When you followed the musical sounds, it always led to Chuck Horan's DA's office, which was filled with admiring law clerks and staff joining him in musical verses. As a maverick prosecutor, when it came to trying the worst of the worst, he had an astonishing record of obtaining convictions. It was a great loss for the DA's Office when he moved on to become a judge.

Prosecutor Camacho was pleased to be able to try the Tony Barron case in Judge Horan's court. Besides it being a pleasant place to try a case, the best part was that Judge Horan knew the law better than any other judge in the Pomona Courthouse. Prosecutor Camacho knew he needed a judge who understood the finer points of law, especially in this case. It was imperative for the prosecution to get before the jury certain incriminating statements by the defendant. The Defense was going to claim that certain parts of the defendant's statements were too highly prejudicial and should not come before the jury.

It would be easy for the judge to make a finding that the statements were too prejudicial. However, the prosecutor asked the judge to delete the prejudicial and allow the remaining probative portion to come in. Judge Horan was willing to take the time to personally take out the prejudicial parts. Some judges wouldn't want to take the time to make a clean copy. For Judge Horan, he just considered it as part of his job.

Camacho was very pleased to have a judge who was extremely knowledgeable on the law, especially in this Barron case. Camacho didn't want to take a chance that Barron would beat the case or end up with another hung jury with the defendant back on the street to kill more Blacks. Some may say that if Barron were released he certainly had learned his lesson. Well, that was what some thought when Barron was released after the Graffiti murders hung juries. Of course, now we know that Barron was just emboldened to kill more people.

CHAPTER 92 TIME TO CALL THE WITNESSES

F or prosecutor Camacho, it began like deja vu as he put on the parade of witnesses as to the Graffiti shooting that occurred on December 15, 2001. Since the witnesses had testified twice before, they anticipated the questions and gave the same answers as before. Prosecutor Camacho had more evidence of Tony Barron's involvement in the 12thStreet gang activities as well as his propensity for shooting others.

The prosecution had given immunity to Sal in order to have him to testify for the prosecution. When Sal was called to the witness stand, he was less than happy to be there. He didn't like being considered a snitch, but the prosecution had him locked into the story he told the police. Since his statements to the detectives were recorded, he couldn't stray too far from what he had told the detectives.

Camacho recognized the pressure that Sal was feeling and took this witness slowly through the various incidents. As to the Boykins shooting, Sal wanted to distance himself from it and denied any involvement. He testified that Barron had called him the morning after the Boykins shooting and told him that he had shot "some nigger" the day before, and if he died it would be in the newspaper. Sal went on to indicate he bought a newspaper which did report the murder. As a matter of fact, he still had that newspaper in his bedroom, which the detectives later found.

After Sal's testimony on the Boykins shooting, Camacho switched his question to the Pep Boys shooting. Sal related to the jury that he had picked Barron up from a motel in Chino and drove him directly to the tobacco shop in Pomona. Sal said Barron went into the shop to look at a special meth pipe he wanted to purchase. After a short time, Barron came out of the store and told Sal to leave. That was when he pulled out of the parking lot and turned on Holt Avenue. Almost immediately Barron instructed Sal to return to the shop. At that point Sal pulled into the Pep Boys parking lot and parked on the side of the building. Barron jumped out and walked back in the area of the shop. Shortly thereafter Sal heard several gunshots and within minutes Barron jumped back into the passenger seat and laid low in the seat.

Barron told Sal to get out of there, and that was when Sal gunned the car to leave the Pep Boys parking lot. As they were driving away Barron in an elated voice bragged that he had shot "some nigger." Sal didn't know where to drive, so he headed up Garey Street in the direction of his home. They had to take the I-10 Freeway, which he drove toward the 57 Freeway. As they were driving on the I-10, Barron started removing the expended shell casings from a revolver he had in his lap. Sal continued to drive and Barron rolled down the passenger side window and began throwing the shell cases to the shoulder of the roadway.

They pulled into Sal's driveway in San Dimas and the two of them exited the car and dashed into Sal's bedroom. All this time Barron was carrying his gun and now he began to wipe it with a towel. Barron asked Sal if he could hide the gun for him. Sal shook his head explaining that his mother wouldn't permit it.

The two of them hung out in Sal's room for a short time. Barron wanted to change his clothes and removed his red checker shirt that was full of perspiration. Then he threw it in Sal's closet. After changing clothes, Barron stated he wanted to return to Pomona. Then Sal drove him downtown and dropped him off.

Sal went on to testify that later in the day he noticed that Barron had left his .38 handgun on the floorboard of the car. It was at that point that Sal on his own placed the gun in the back panel of the passenger seat.

Prosecutor Camacho would have preferred a more plausible answer to how the gun somehow ended up in this special hiding place in Sal's car. However, the prosecutor understood that often witnesses want to minimize their involvement. Camacho accepted Sal's testimony and directed his questions to the next day when

Sal was detained by the Pomona officer. Sal explained how he was stopped and that he did ask the detective if this was about the gun in his mother's car.

There was only one other area that Camacho wanted Sal to testify to. Camacho asked about conversations that Sal had with Barron after their arrests and while they were both in custody. Sal related that Barron told him to say that it was a guy by the name of Oscar who did the shootings. Later during that conversation, Barron bragged to Sal that he had made the front page for another murder.

CHAPTER 93 MORE WITNESSES

After Sal's testimony, the next group of witnesses pertained to the Boykins shooting. The main witness was one of the residents who couldn't identify the shooter inside the car. His memory was that there were three occupants in the car and that he believed it was a small white car. After the shooting, he ran to a nearby residence and called the police to respond to the location.

The the next witnesses pertaining to the Boykins shooting were the coroner who removed to bullets from the victim's body. Later the ballistic expert would conclude that they had been fired by the gun that had been found in Sal's car.

Next was the evidence regarding the Pep Boys shooting. The other Black person who was shot at was a Mr. Doyle who was standing at the bus stop with victim Wheatley. Mr. Doyle said after he was shot he ran to the tobacco shop, but he did see Wheatley fall to the ground. Then prosecutor Camacho asked if he could identify the shooter, to which he claimed that he hadn't gotten a good enough look at him. Immediately after he testified, he contacted the prosecutor and said that he could identify the defendant as the shooter after seeing him in the courtroom.

Prosecutor Camacho had a tough decision to make as to whether he should recall Mr. Doyle to the witness stand to tell the jury this new revelation. Prosecutor Camacho knew that this was extremely relevant evidence, but was it reliable evidence? After some reflection, the prosecutor thought that he would be best to leave it up to the jury to decide if Mr. Doyle truly could identify the defendant as the shooter.

Doyle was recalled and he told the jury that it was Tony Barron who was the shooter. On cross-examination he admitted that he only saw the shooter for a second and from 36 feet away. Doyle admitted that he had a prior strike conviction. He testified that the prosecutor had made no promises relating to a pending charge against him. Prosecutor Camacho agreed to a stipulation which was read to the jury in which Doyle had said, "You got to do something about my case."

Undoubtedly prosecutor Camacho had to wonder why all of his witnesses weren't choir boys who had been brought up by Mother Teresa. However, that isn't the real world for prosecutors. As the old saying goes, you take your witnesses where you find them. When you are in Hell you can't expect saints for witnesses.

The next set of witnesses didn't have unsavory backgrounds. Maria Sandoval testified that she was waiting for her daughter to make a withdrawal from an ATM. She told the jury that she saw a person come up to a group of Black men and started shooting them with a grey handgun. She saw the one Black man fall to the ground and the shooter ran off. Her description was that the shooter was a young male Hispanic, five foot six and 150 pounds wearing a red checked shirt with a Raider's baseball cap.

Then Camacho had the two workers at the Pep Boys store provide the license plate number of the fleeing white car. Each man got only part of the license number, which they thought was 2W7559. The one man was able to identify a photo of the white Nissan used by Sal which had a license plate number of 2WLZ599. He was also able identify the red checker shirt which the shooter was wearing.

When the Coroner testified he stated that the victim Wheatley was shot twice, with one bullet entering through his back and exiting his chest and then striking his arm. He was followed by a witness who was involved in finding the three spent shell casings on the freeway shoulder. The testimony of the ballistics expert was that those shell casings were fired from the gun recovered in Sal's car.

To complete the ballistics evidence, the officer who originally stopped Sal in his white Nissan was called to describe why he decided to detain Sal and have him and the vehicle transported to the police station, where eventually the handgun was found in the back panel of the passenger seat.

CHAPTER 94 TIME FOR THE EXPERT WITNESSES

The rest of the witnesses were law enforcement personnel dealing with the DNA found on the red checker shirt which came back to the defendant. Another forensic expert testified to the latent print of the defendant found on the window area of Sal's car. The handwriting expert testified that certain graffiti writings were written by the defendant.

The prosecutor called a gang expert to explain to the jury the activity of gangs and what is considered doing something for the gang's benefit. This expert explained that the 12th Street Hispanic gang had long had a reputation for an animus against African-Americans, especially those living within its territory, and the that killings enhanced the gang's reputation and intimidated Blacks from wanting to reside in their territory.

The gang expert opined that the defendant continued to be an active 12th Street member and the notebook found in his jail cell reflected that he personally held an animosity against Blacks. The expert's findings were that the shootings on July 5th and 10th had been for the benefit of the 12th Street gang by making a racial statement as well as enhancing the defendant's own reputation in the gang.

Prosecutor Camacho had a lot of loose ends that he needed to pull together with the testimony of the detectives in the case. The detectives testified that the defendant did talk to them and a videotape of the interview was played for the jury. Although Barron totally denied that he had been involved in any of the shootings, he was willing to admit that he had been to the tobacco shop to buy a meth pipe and did hear some shots when he was walking away.

The main use of the videotape was to show his gang involvement. He willingly admitted that he was a member of the 12th Street gang and he went by the moniker of "Knuckles." Then some audio recordings were played for the jury of his jailhouse visit from his 12th Street gang members. At one point in the tape, Barron said that the "Black fools" on the street near the tobacco shop were stupid, because the victim had told the police he had seen the assailant but could not identify him. Then Barron said, "My crime partner (Sal) said it was me." Although this wasn't the greatest admission for the prosecution, it was something tying him to the Pep Boys shooting.

Then the prosecutor started asking questions about the searching of Sal's bedroom. The detectives explained how they seized the red checker shirt, some graffiti with the name "Knuckles" on it, and a drawing of a shark (which was the symbol for the 12th Street gang), as well as the newspaper that contained the story about the Boykin shooting.

The trial was long and the prosecution brought in so many witnesses who didn't want to be testifying in court. The Defense had utilized their right of cross-examination to raise questions about their credibility. Throughout the trial, the Defense had zeroed in on the weaknesses that the prosecution had in the first shooting involving the crossing out of the graffiti. The one witness to that shooting was a rival gang member, and his attitude was that the matter could be better handled on the streets.

It was now up to the Defense to decide what witnesses they would be calling. Again the Defense concentrated on the graffiti shooting, but no affirmative Defense was presented as to the other incidents. Undoubtedly, the jurors and even the prosecutor were hoping to hear from the defendant. The defendant, Barron, might not be considered the sharpest knife in the drawer. However, he was smart enough to know that if he took the witness stand he would have convicted himself on every charge.

If he testified, he could deny his involvement in all the shootings; however, he would never be able to conceal his immense pride he had for his 12th Street gang in their fight to exterminate the Blacks from their barrios.

CHAPTER 95 TIME FOR ARGUMENT

Attorneys love when it is time to argue their case. Deep down inside, every attorney has an ego that feels that they possess the oratorical skills of William Jennings Bryan. They believe that they can convince the juror to their side. Mike Camacho had tried many gang cases to jurors and has learned that certain approaches work better than others. Camacho recognizes that merely using words alone won't be convincing to most juries. It isn't the loudest or the longest orator that has the biggest impact on the jurors.

When Camacho argues to a jury, he speaks in measured statements using a strong, confident voice exuding sincerity. He projects a seriousness that the jurors can feel and are eager to listen to. Camacho knows that jurors' interest spans are relatively short, like an elastic band that needs to be lengthened. That is why Camacho takes his message and packages it with visuals to keep the jurors' minds engaged.

When Camacho started to argue about the Graffiti shooting, he used the visual to show how the defendant was connected to the graffiti by his moniker "Knuckles" (sometimes shortened to "Nuckles").

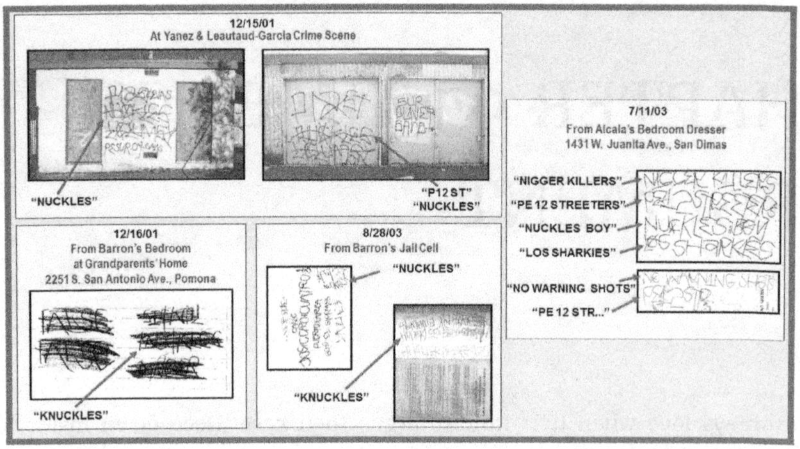

Then Camacho used photos to demonstrate how the rival Olive gang had crossed out the defendant's moniker. That was followed by the graffiti writing Barron had left in Sal's bedroom. This one graphic explained all that the jurors needed to know about the defendant's use of graffiti. Although this chart may seem too busy with information, it told the jury what they needed to know. Camacho gave the jurors time to digest every detail on the visual.

Along the same lines, Camacho wanted the jurors to understand what items were found in Sal's bedroom that were really the defendant's. Part of the below visual shows the other gang items, such as baseball bat and numerous photos of sharks, which symbolized the 12th Street Gang. To the left, Camacho showed the red checker shirt that had the defendant's DNA on it.

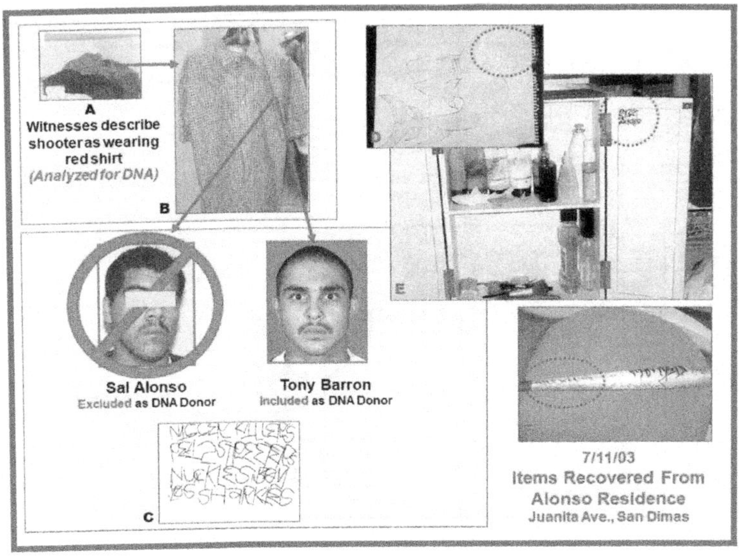

Camacho reused many of his charts from his Opening Statement in order to show that he had proved everything up by live testimony from live witnesses. He used the next graphic to illustrate how close the witnesses were in writing down the correct license plate number. The other photos in the visual are of the freeway where the spent shell casings were thrown out by the defendant.

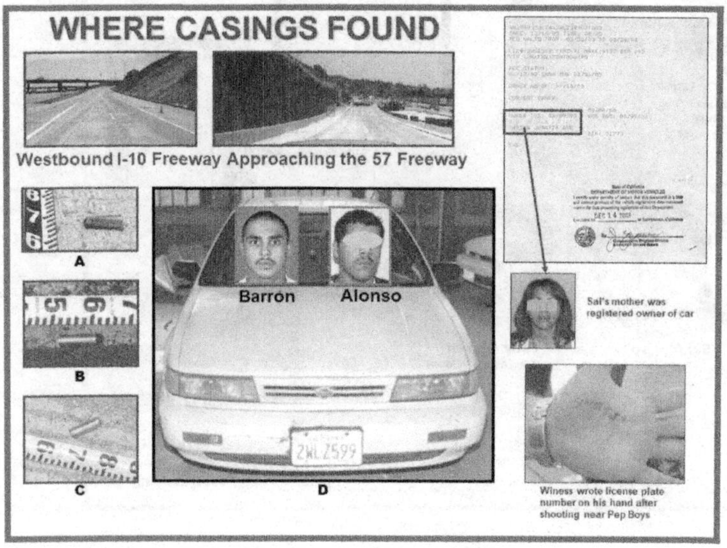

Again, some people would say that the chart is too congested with too much information. However, Camacho understood that jurors will "zone out" if an Argument is too long. To be an effective litigator, an attorney has to learn that "less is more." Camacho had mastered the technique of combining several issues in one and thereby saving precious time in his Argument.

CHAPTER 96 DEALING WITH THE DEFENSE

Camacho used his Argument to cover all the legal and factual questions. Camacho had twice tried and received hung juries on the Graffiti shooting that occurred on December 15th. He knew this was his last chance to get justice for the victims' families. He used the below graphic, which spelled out the entire case in a nutshell. Would the combining of all the shootings strengthen the Graffiti case?

Camacho didn't want to insult the jurors' intelligence by continuing to go over the evidence. But he felt he couldn't afford to have one juror get lost in all the lengthy testimony. He went through every incident by date and hammered away with the evidence that supported that fact.

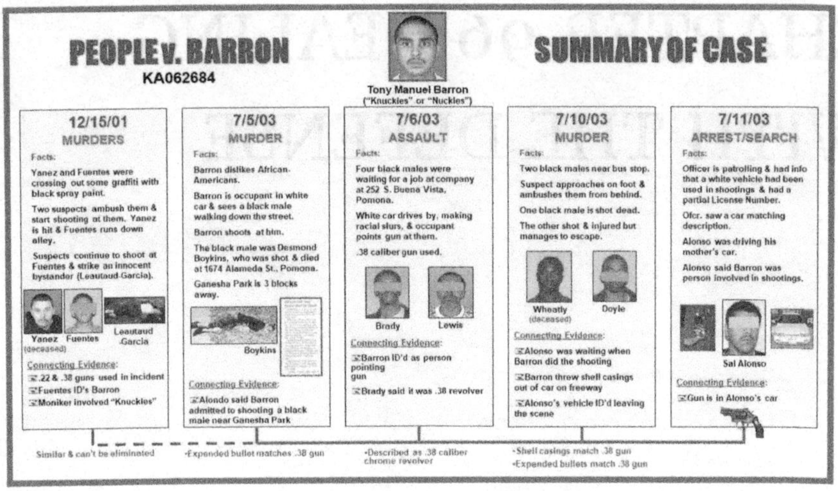

Both sides argued. The Defense attorney attacked the prosecution witnesses. The Defense touched upon all the weaknesses of the prosecution's evidence, especially attacking Sal. The Defense made Sal look like the worst type of Judas who turned on his good friend Tony Barron.

CHAPTER 97
CONCLUSION

The jurors withdrew to the jury deliberation room and commenced their deliberation. At the end of the first day of deliberation, the jurors were excused to return the next morning. The jurors continued their deliberation for one and a half more days. They seemed to have reached a deadlock, so the judge made inquiry as to how they were doing. The foreperson indicated that they had reached verdicts on every charge except for the Graffiti shooting. The judge told them not to reveal how they were split but only as to the numbers. The foreperson said that the division was nine to three.

The judge ordered them to continue their deliberation, which they did. Eventually, they told the judge that they were hopelessly deadlocked, at which time he agreed to take the verdicts on the charges they had agreed on.

Camacho in his charcoal black suit sat stoically in the DA's chair at counsel table while the jurors and court staff were rounded up. When everyone was ready, the judge ordered the foreperson to provide him with the verdicts that had been agreed to.

At that point Camacho had a sinking feeling that the Graffiti shooting was at a hung-jury stage, but he didn't know whether the nine-to-three split was for guilty or not guilty. Then the clerk started reading the verdict forms. She stated that the jury convicted the defendant of two counts of first-degree murder with findings that the victims were intentionally killed because of race. This was good news for the prosecution in that the jury found that the offenses were committed for the benefit of a criminal street gang with specific intent to promote, further, and assist in criminal conduct by gang members.

What was interesting was that the jury acquitted the defendant of the crime of assault with a firearm against the group of Black men who were waiting for a warehouse job.

Camacho turned his head slightly to the right to gain a view of the defendant. He could see his attorney talking to Barron. The defendant's expression was devoid of any emotion. Camacho thought that this was a bittersweet moment. His mind focused on the third hung jury; this time it was hung nine to three for conviction of the defendant for the Graffiti shooting of victims Yanez and Leautaud- Garcia.

Camacho was especially sad for Ms. Leautaud-Garcia's family. Here was a lady who was a law-abiding citizen doing nothing wrong and had no gang affliction however she was gunned down by Tony Barron and his homie. What went through Camacho's mind was whether the outcome would have been any different if he could have gotten in the tagger's Dying Declaration stating that it was "Knuckles" who did the shooting.

The obstacle was the coroner who testified at each trial that the victim Yanez was shot through the larynx, making it impossible for him to speak. Therefore, the Defense argued that the witness was making up the fact that the victim, his fellow gang member, was trying to identify the person who had shot at him. Camacho shook his head in disbelief.

As much as Camacho wanted Tony Barron to be convicted of Ms. Leauland-Garcia's killing, he had to face reality and recommended that case not be retried for the fourth time. The defendant, who was 17 years old, was sentenced on the other murders to Life Without the Possibility of Parole. Because of his age, the defendant couldn't have been eligible for the Death Penalty. At least now Tony Barron will never be able to victimize Blacks on the streets of our communities ever again. However, there isn't any such guarantee for Blacks who work for the prison or even those who are housed in state prison where Tony Barron is serving his time.

Needless to say, Tony Barron appealed his case on the basis that Sal Alonso was an accomplice and wasn't sufficiently corroborated as required by law. The appellate court carefully reviewed the record and found that Sal's testimony was sufficiently corroborated.

His other objection was as to the introduction of the defendant's interview to the detectives. The Defense's position was that the interview was too prejudicial and therefore should not have been admitted for the jury to hear. As to that point the appellate court noted that the trial judge had made the prosecution edit out several sentences in which the defendant was demeaning women.

The appellate court held that the defendant did receive a fair trial and that Judge Charles Horan had been more than fair in protecting the defendant's rights. It seemed the judicial system had done its job of getting a BAD DUDE OFF THE STREETS.

We all can stand back and wonder what caused a 16-year-old male to possess such utter contempt for another race to meticulously go out and hunt them down. We can say he had a poor family relationship. Which is true, but what explains the cold, calculating manner in which he carried out the killings?

We may not be able to explain the malignant heart of the defendant. However, what is most amazing is what drives a prosecutor like Michael Camacho to be willing to try the Graffiti killings three times. I considered myself a conscientious prosecutor; however, I doubt that I would have had the tenacity to try the case three times. Camacho had to tolerate the problems of the reluctant witnesses and listening to Defense attorney and others complaining about how such a third trial was a waste of the courts' precious time.

In my book, Michael Camacho will forever be a SUPERSTAR PROSECUTOR.

What I, the author, find interesting is that the Manson Family Helter Skelter case generated worldwide publicity. Charles Manson was trying to create a racial war. However, in the Barron case, he was trying to kill blacks for the benefit of his 12th Street Gang. The news media gave almost zero coverage of the Barron racial war. Most experts claim the difference is in who the victims were. In the Tate-LaBianca murders, the victims were celebrities and wealthy people. In the Barron case, the dead were only a woman going Christmas shopping, a guy waiting for a bus in front of Pep Boys, and a kid walking to a friend's house.

The Manson killings were a little more sordid, and the body count was seven to a mere four in Barron's case. But my point is that the news media can't and don't cover all homicides in the same manner. The news media purposely discounts gang-related killings. The media may feel that gang killing isn't 'NEWS,' it is merely a fact of life that we as a free society want to ignore.

One of the reasons I wrote this book was to show you the reading public that a lot of what goes on on the streets is never reported or at least under-reported. I know as a fact that book publishers shy away from anything dealing with gangs and especially racial killings. However, I think the Barron cases of the world need to be talked about. There are people in our midst who have such racial hatred that they will kill innocent people for no other reason than for the color of their skin.

Hopefully you the reader weren't turned off by discussing such a contentious subject. Hearing about gang violence is depressing, but how do you solve the problem if you won't talk about it? Maybe the only answer is that KNOWLEDGE CAN BE ENLIGHTENING.

CONCLUSION

DA Delta Force Series

I wanted this DA Delta Force Series to provide you insight as to how one bureaucratic agency, the DA Major Crimes Division, was doing an exceptional job for the public. It has proved to be exceedingly effective in taking on the toughest criminal cases and handling them successfully. The DA's administrations would like to claim that Major Crimes Division was their creation. Granted, the Division would not have come into existence without their direction.

Without a doubt the Major Crimes Division has had excellent leadership under the direction of its two head deputies, Curt Hazel and Pat Dixon, who molded it into what it became. Their idea was to select the finest attorneys in the DA's Office and not to micro-manage such talented and highly motivated individuals. Their approach was to provide their attorneys all the resources they needed. Occasionally their boss would ask them to conduct a briefing on the status of their cases.

On occasion, the Major Crimes' prosecutors were asked to show a draft PowerPoint presentation of their Opening Statement. In that way, the prosecutor was pleased to show off what he or she had done. This was a brilliant approach, since the attorney never felt that he or she was being told what to do but instead being given an opportunity to show his or her unique approach for presenting the case to a jury

The undisputed success of the Major Crimes Division has to be attributed to the stellar attorneys who did an excellent job in preparing and presenting their cases in the courtroom. I have highlighted in my DA Delta Force series only a limited number of the extraordinary prosecutors who served in the Division.

The first DA Delta Force book in the series was titled the ***Prosecutrix Fight for Justice***, in which I discussed Eleanor Hunter, who demonstrated a No Fear attitude in taking on the toughest cases. She demonstrated an uncanny resolve to see that the old Symbionese Liberation Army terrorists were brought to justice for a bank robbery-murder that had been overlooked for years. It took a lot of courage on her part to stand up for what was right.

The second book of the series was ***The Top Gun DA*** starring John Monahan, who was a phenomenal prosecutor. He had the talent to work with detectives and to construct solid cases that could stand up in court. Elite units like the Delta Force have learned that it takes a team effort to win the battle. Prosecutor Monahan had the foresight to know what evidence was needed and how to use that evidence to be persuasive to the jury. He never wavered, even when some of the deadliest killers would give him the 'evil eye.'

The ***Best of the Best DA*** discussed two incredible prosecutors, Tony Manzella as well as Hoon Chun, who never gave up when everything seemed to be going wrong with their cases. Prosecutor Manzella stood up to the Mexican Mafia and recognized that the Achilles' heel of this band of gangsters was their self-imposed Green Light. Tony was 'one of a kind.' When he walked into the courtroom, he exuded the confidence of a Philadelphia Lawyer (the lawyer who knows the most detailed and minute points of law) while at the same time he possessed 'Street Smarts.'

As to Prosecutor Hoon Chun, he demonstrated unlimited resolve as he had to deal with crisis after crisis in the Timothy McGhee (Big Bad Dude) case. Hoon had the mindset to see that the 'glass was always half full' when it was practically empty. I told him to his face that there was no way he would be able to convict a paraplegic for committing robbery/murder. Well, he quickly proved me wrong in the Cruz case and got the killer sentenced to state prison.

Finally, this book, ***The Superstar Prosecutor***, has highlighted three remarkable prosecutors, Darrell Mavis and Jeff Ramseyer as well as Michael Camacho. Each was highly talented, but at the same time they were acutely sensitive to the needs of their witnesses. Prosecutor Mavis was a legal genius who was like a chess player thinking three moves ahead. Putting aside his intellect, he had a practical side of knowing how to get things done.

Prosecutor Ramseyer was a remarkable prosecutor who would have left a long legal legacy if it hadn't been for his untimely death. The DA's Office was lucky to have him the short time that he was a part of the DA's Office.

However, Prosecutor Camacho could best be described as an unassuming workaholic. He tried and convicted more gangbangers than any other prosecutor. He truly has made many communities safer places to live by reducing the gang violence. Camacho is the type of prosecutor I wish we could clone since he embodies all the marvelous qualities an attorney should have.

Several of my books from my Los Angeles True Crime series highlight other Major Crime Division deputies. Pat Dixon and Alan Jackson did the ***Killing of a Legend*** and ***Killing in the Castle***. Deputy Bobbie Grace was highlighted in ***The Old Lady Killers*** and my other book ***Date with the Devil***. Also, Karla Kerlin did a great job in the ***Killers on the Road to Vegas***.

Other books I have been involved in were ***Meet Me For Murder***, highlighting Dave Walgren, and ***You'll Never Find My Body***, highlighting Beth Silverman. And one of the original members of the Major Crimes Division was Craig Hume, who was highlighted in ***Honeymoon with a Killer***.

Certain critics may say that elite units aren't perfect and occasionally make mistakes. Sometimes they aren't always victorious in court. However, the decade between approximately 2000 and 2010 without a reasonable doubt was the Golden Age for the Major Crimes Division. During those years the members of the team were extraordinary.

It was as if there was a perfect alignment between the sun, the planets, and all the moons. During those years there was an esprit de corps created that magnified the accomplishments of the entire Division. It was like the little train that slowly approached the hill saying, "I think I can . . . I think I can" and slowly made it to the top.

My DA Delta Force series has focused on the cases handled by the Major Crimes Division, Without a doubt, Major Crimes Division is a truly an elite group and we all can be proud of their accomplishments. It is certainly worthy of being called the DA DELTA FORCE.

Made in the USA
Monee, IL
04 November 2026

67379296R00236